D1761401

NILE PERCH

THE ULTIMATE GUIDE
FOR ANGLERS

NILE PERCH

THE ULTIMATE GUIDE
FOR ANGLERS

Barrie Rickards and Tim Baily

With a Foreword by John Wilson

THE CROWOOD PRESS

First published in 2008 by
The Crowood Press Ltd
Ramsbury, Marlborough
Wiltshire SN8 2HR

www.crowood.com

© Barrie Rickards and Tim Baily 2008

All rights reserved. No part of this publication may be reproduced or
transmitted in any form or by any means, electronic or mechanical, including
photocopy, recording, or any information storage and retrieval system, without
permission in writing from the publishers.

British Library Cataloguing-in-Publication Data
A catalogue record for this book is available from the British Library.

ISBN 978 1 84797 000 8

Dedication
We dedicate this book to the Nubian people; the Nubians on safari; and the
whole African Angler team.

Acknowledgements
Our first thanks go to John Wilson for his generous support, not only with this
book and for doing the foreword, but also for his help on the lake with
numerous safaris, and for his films. Bob Kimber, with John Wilson, features in
our pioneers' stories of Chapter 2, and we thank them kindly for that.

   A great many people have supported this venture and the safaris; we cannot
thank everyone, but must list the following with considerable gratitude: African
Angler team, past and present both Nubian and Egyptian; Antoine Riad, who
helped Tim get the exploration started; Peter Baily, who puts up with Tim, his
brother; Mohamed el Shabrawy and American Express (Egypt); The Basma
Hotel, Aswan; Geoff Currier; Vince Davies; Paul Goldering; Alf Hogan of the
Queensland Government Primary Industries; Lorraine Kimber; Rebecca and
Fern Lyne; Jennifer and John Mondora; Olivier Portrat, many of whose beautiful
pictures grace this book; Chris Parr; Rapala; Salah Musbah, who was Governor
of Aswan in Tim's early days; Shakespeare (UK) Ltd; Christine Taylor; Will
Wragg; Youseff Mohammed. And finally and especially, Tim's business partner
and our friend Nabil Abed El Moete; Wendy Green, who sorted out the chaos;
and Tom Corder and Mandy Lyne who did things with computers when others
couldn't. And to all the above, our thanks for their tolerance and friendship.

Typeface used: M Plantin.

Typeset and designed by D & N Publishing, Lambourn Woodlands,
Hungerford, Berkshire.

Printed and bound in Singapore by Craft Print International.

CONTENTS

FOREWORD

Having known authors Tim and Barrie for more years than I care to remember, I can think of no others more qualified to pen this extraordinarily comprehensive work dedicated to a single species of freshwater fish. Barrie for his structured, methodical approach to everything he tackles, including his geology background with regard to understanding the make-up of massive Lake Nasser, one of the planet's longest man-made lakes. And Tim, simply due to his 'hands-on' approach of organizing Nile perch angling safaris for over fifteen years (no other Westerner has spent more hours in pursuit of this enigmatic species), in the course of which he has accrued a phenomenal amount of experience. Moreover, I can think of no other angling location on this earth so well documented as is Lake Nasser in this lengthy volume, and I felt truly delighted, if not just a little proud, to be asked by my two friends if I would write this foreword.

As always, dialogue between Tim, Barrie and me often reaches points where we agree to disagree, and nothing is perhaps more controversial than deciding what and which type of line and breaking strain to use when targeting Nile perch. For instance, it would not be beyond the bounds of possibility to hook a 20lb perch on your first cast of the day, and one of 200lb on the second. This has in fact happened. So how do you choose a line to match? That's the predicament – especially when taking the lake's rocky shoreline, islands and promontories into account, which can all too easily shred your line

in seconds. It is, after all, a flooded desert, around whose rocky, honeycombed mountain tops Nile perch love to wait in ambush for their next meal of baby croc, monitor lizard, Egyptian goose gosling or any one of several fishes, including their own kind, to pass by.

As Barrie mentions, in the past when fish were perhaps a little more prolific than they are today, I have indeed caught some wonderful perch on the lake whilst filming for television (and I have much to thank Tim Baily for), on what would be deemed decidedly light and 'sporting' tackle with lines down to 20lb test. And whilst there are 'safe' areas where light tackle can still be used in experienced hands, nowadays I tend to play safe by using 30lb mono or 40lb braid for shore fishing, and for the rigours of trolling 35/40lb mono or 50lb braid. I even go to the lengths of having two identical trolling outfits made up and ready to go, one with 35lb mono, and the other with 50lb braid – simply because being a much finer diameter, the latter works any lure a good 2 to 3ft deeper than the equivalent mono outfit. Sometimes this can be critical when working around pinnacles and sunken islands, and may mean the difference between getting hits and not getting hits on a particular lure. Incidentally, I much prefer the extra durability of 'fused' braids, as opposed to 'soft' types – and those with a tough outer casing are particularly recommended.

As for leaders and so on when trolling (with both braid and mono reel lines), I use 4ft of

100lb test clear mono connected by a small but strong 'black' swivel to the reel line (I hate tiger-fish bite-offs, too), with a large, strong snap swivel on the business end for quick lure-changing. For shore fishing when using a 30lb test mono reel line, I step down to an 80lb test, 4ft clear mono rubbing leader. But if using braid, I add a 20ft rubbing/shock leader of 80lb mono, jointed to the braid using the reliable 'Albright knot', which passes smoothly back and forth through the rod rings to alleviate the abrasive actions not only of the rocks, but of the Nile perch itself: chafing around its gill plate, and especially its jaws, is what all too easily wrecks lighter strain leaders. So my motto is always to be safe rather than sorry. These, of course, are my own personal preferences, which at times conflict with how both Tim and Barrie fish. But this is a healthy difference, in that there can never be 'one', 'best' tactic in fishing. We each develop our own styles along the way, and it is for the reader to decide which tactics will best suit his own requirements.

I guess that, at the end of the day, it's all down to what works for you. For instance, I personally would not use a fixed spool reel to catch Nile perch. With big, powerful fish especially that run and run, using a fixed spool reel will inevitably result in line twist and the deterioration of a monofilament line, through constantly passing back and forth at right angles across a bale arm roller under severe torque. I would therefore use multipliers only for Nile perch,

unless fly fishing. My preferences are the ABU 7500 Big Game fast retrieve, and the 10,000 because it has a larger line capacity, for shore fishing and trolling respectively. But history reveals that even some whopping great Nile perch have in fact been landed using fixed spool reels.

And there is the beauty of this comprehensive volume. You the reader get to know how numerous big fish specialists have landed their PB Nile perch, and on what tackle. You get to marvel at an unbelievable number of inspirational, evocative photos of monstrous perch being played and displayed for the camera – some of the most exciting action photos ever captured within the big fish freshwater scene. You get to read anxious accounts of how world records have been landed. You will even become privy to the most sumptuous ways of cooking Nile perch, gleaned from the chefs of the African Angler safari tem. And after all this, I would be quite astounded if you don't want to get out there on to the wild, wilderness expanse of Lake Nasser to experience at first hand the tail-walking, gill-flaring, dogged, arm-wrenching fight of a head-shaking gladiator called the Nile perch.

Good hunting.

John Wilson, Norfolk
July 2007

INTRODUCTION

In Chapter 1 we shall describe how Tim discovered Lake Nasser as a Nile perch venue par excellence, and Chapter 2 is the account of other pioneers, Bob Kimber and John Wilson – but here we shall describe how Barrie himself got involved, and then outline our approach to this book.

In 1993 Barrie attended a major angling fair as a consultant for Shakespeare. In one of his spare moments he was wandering along the other stalls to see what was on offer. Passing a small stall that had photographs pinned on display boards he hesitated, momentarily, because some of the photographs were of large Nile perch, and this was a fish he had always had a (theoretical) interest in. His hesitation was fatal, because a fist came out of the exhibit and, literally, took him by the scruff of the neck and hauled him in. The fist was attached to the strong arm of Vince Davies of Davies Angling, one of the original trio who discovered the fishing potential on Lake Nasser with Tim Baily. Their adventures are outlined in Chapter 1. As Vince hauled Barrie in, he said, 'You look like a likely m... customer!' (He caught his breath before he fully uttered the word 'mug'!)

He went on to say that he'd noticed Barrie's interest in the Nile perch pictures and that he had no intention of letting him go without a fight. Barrie was then given the 'big sell' as to how marvellous a safari with Tim Baily would be; that Nile perch were guaranteed; and that the cost, including air fares, would be £350. The sneer of disbelief on Barrie's face betrayed him immediately, so Vince gave a detailed cost breakdown and more details of the safaris themselves. More importantly, perhaps, was that Vince gave Barrie a couple of phone numbers of others who had been on the earliest pioneering trips with Tim – at a time, incidentally, when permission to fish the lake was by no means certain because it is mostly in army territory. In fact, everything Vince claimed was true, and there really were no hidden extras, and it really was dawn-to-dawn fishing, if that is what was wanted.

You will learn more about these early safaris in chapters 1 and 2, and will see how they have grown into rather more luxurious trips in recent

Tim Baily and Nabil, partners in the Lake Nasser safaris (The African Angler).

John Wilson with his personal best Nile perch of 141lb, caught on a Reef Digger lure. (John Wilson)

times. We shall try to convey something of the essential atmosphere of being in a wilderness environment of great beauty, with a small group of people, including Nubian guides, each of whose ancestral home is now covered by the waters of Lake Nasser itself. These men are now guides up to 200ft above their spiritual homes, amongst small hills that were once rather bigger hills separated by khors.

Although we shall concentrate on Lake Nasser, because this is where most of the modern techniques have been worked out, we will also

mention in various places (for example in the Foreword, Chapter 5, and Appendix II) where Nile perch occur in other waters, and where they might be fished for, such as Lake Victoria, and Murchison (Kabalega) Falls on the Nile in Uganda. For the moment we shall just try to bring home the scale of the lake for UK anglers. Lake Nasser was formed in the 1960s as a result of the construction of the Aswan High Dam, a major hydroelectric power and irrigation project. Its width is about 22 miles (34km) at its widest point, and its length around 245 miles

(395km), and it extends from Egypt into the Sudan, though fishing is only in Egypt at present. If you laid Lake Nasser out along the length of the UK it would stretch from central London to northernmost North Yorkshire, and it can be a few miles wide, too! At first sight it can be daunting, yet at the same time exciting and quite breathtakingly beautiful when you have left behind any signs of human activity – as at Aswan, or Garf Hussein further south, both likely safari starting points.

Obviously, because the lake is so huge, it needs to be divided up into manageable proportions, and in effect, the guide teams are there for that very purpose. The safari team always explains where you are and why you are there, and you may try previously known areas, or explore totally new regions.

For all these reasons we have structured the book in a particular way. Thus in Chapter 1 Tim explains how he gained access to Lake Nasser, recognized and realized its potential, and then opened it up to 'ordinary' anglers, and at a much lower price than the existing big game safaris. To learn how one man and a few friends 'cracked' such a challenging water and environment will help you appreciate what is going on when you make the trip yourself – and if you don't, reading of a pioneer in action is always captivating for the angler.

In Chapter 2 Bob Kimber, like Barrie one of the converts, tells us how he became involved, and how it interested and excited him; and John Wilson, one of angling's greatest pioneers, tells of his staggering experiences at Murchison Falls. Then in Chapter 3 we describe the nature of the safaris, how they are run, and how enjoyable they are. The origins of Lake Nasser and its eco-development are discussed in Chapter 4, along with the role of Nile perch in history – there is, for example, a sacred necropolis of Nile perch near Luxor, and there is a Nile perch featured in the paintings on the ceiling of the Sistine Chapel in the Vatican.

After this we go on to the fishing itself, in chapters 5 to 14 – we hope everything you need to know, but giving examples of how things have worked in terms of catches. One of the staggering things about the lake is not only does it hold the world records for boat- and bank-caught fish, but the number of 200lb fish, at the time of writing this, is ten. No other water, anywhere, has produced results of this magnitude. The capture of the very first 200lb fish, a world record taken by Wilma Macdairmid, the Scottish pike angler, was recorded from start to finish on a thirty-six frame film by Barrie, and a full account of this momentous event is covered in Chapter 12.

The final chapter discusses future challenges, both on Lake Nasser and elsewhere. Then follows a series of appendices covering the biology of Nile perch, their global distribution and where to fish and how to get there, and how to cook them! Finally there is a bibliography of videos (no other books!), and a bibliography of mostly scientific literature. For future editions we welcome ideas and suggestions, so please feel free to write to us via the publishers.

Sketches by the artist Rebecca Lyne of Tim Baily (head) and Barrie Rickards (back view!).

1 THE BIG ADVENTURE BEGINS

Throughout the Pharaonic era, fishing featured highly in ancient writings, tomb paintings and even religion, although a recent inspection of quite a number of tombs revealed surprisingly few fish as compared with other animals. The Nile perch was associated with the goddess Neith, and at that time it was believed that she turned herself into a Nile perch to navigate the deep waters of the primeval ocean Nun. In her honour, Nile perch in mummified form were enshrined as a token of worship, particularly at Esna where her cult was the strongest. We have not found any information about Nile perch sport fishing during the more recent history of Egypt throughout the last hundred years or so, but there must have been quite a lot going on. Historically Egypt was important to the British and the French, and we can imagine colonial officials taking out a rod and line to catch the fabled Nile perch.

This was the position until 1993 when Tim Baily managed to persuade the authorities that there was potential for sport-fishing tourism on Lake Nasser. The seed of the original idea about setting up a Nile perch-fishing safari operation on Lake Nasser was put into Tim's mind from watching one of John Wilson's early *Go Fishing* films about angling for Nile perch at Rusinga Island, located off the Kenya shoreline of Lake Victoria.

Initial Enquiries

In 1992, Tim started to make enquiries with the authorities in Aswan about starting up a fishing safari operation on Lake Nasser – and almost scrapped the idea because he came up against an impregnable wall of officialdom. Tim was told that Lake Nasser was a closed area under the control of the army, and that no foreigners were allowed anywhere near it except at Abu Simbel to view the temples of Rameses and perhaps get a glimpse of the lake from the walls of the High Dam.

Tim's luck changed while he was in Cairo wondering what to do next when a friend of his, Antoine Riad, whom he had had the pleasure of working with during his earlier tourism days in Egypt, phoned to suggest they meet for dinner and a chat.

That dinner changed Tim's life. They met up at the outdoor restaurant at the El Salaam, a great venue full of Eastern character and excellent food, and caught up with what was going on in Cairo. They eventually got round to discussing Lake Nasser as a likely tourist destination and the brick wall that Tim had come up against in Aswan, and Antoine said that he might be able to help by arranging a meeting with the Governor of Aswan who had a far-thinking attitude towards tourism.

Antoine is one Egypt's most innovative businessmen; from managing a small tour operation in Cairo he has built up the very successful tourism empire, the South Sinai Travel Group, which now owns several hotels in Egypt. Antoine was one step ahead of Tim when it came to ideas of tourism on Lake Nasser because his company had already conducted a preliminary on-site survey of the lake. One of Antoine's managers had rented a boat, spent a week on the lake, and had written a report about his findings. Antoine's team were Egyptians who did not have the same travel restrictions as foreigners, so the military allowed them onto

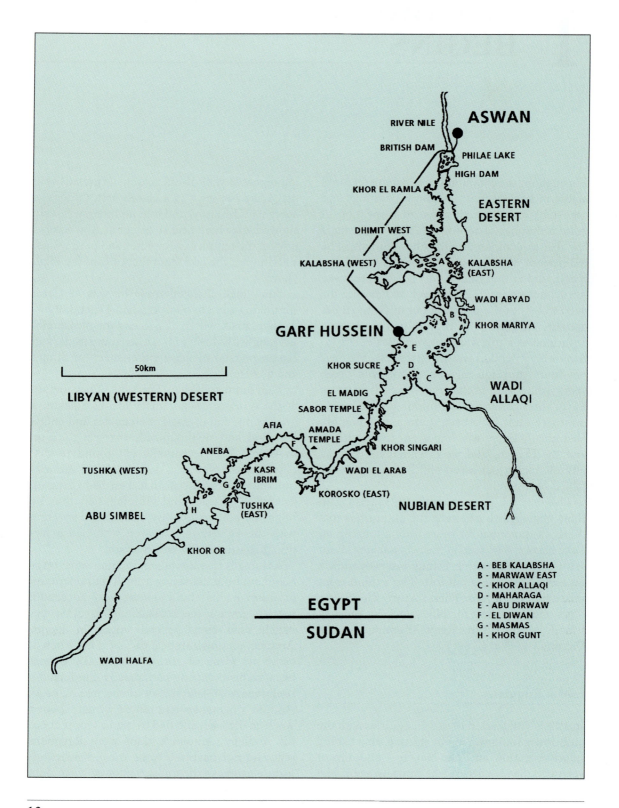

ASWAN

RIVER NILE

BRITISH DAM

PHILAE LAKE

HIGH DAM

KHOR EL RAMLA

EASTERN DESERT

DHIMIT WEST

KALABSHA (WEST)

A KALABSHA (EAST)

WADI ABYAD

B KHOR MARIYA

GARF HUSSEIN

E

KHOR SUCRE

D

C WADI ALLAQI

EL MADIG

SABOR TEMPLE

50km

LIBYAN (WESTERN) DESERT

AFIA

AMADA TEMPLE

KHOR SINGARI

ANEBA

F

TUSHKA (WEST)

KASR IBRIM

WADI EL ARAB

G

ABU SIMBEL

H

TUSHKA (EAST)

KOROSKO (EAST)

NUBIAN DESERT

KHOR OR

A - BEB KALABSHA
B - MARWAW EAST
C - KHOR ALLAQI
D - MAHARAGA
E - ABU DIRWAW
F - EL DIWAN
G - MASMAS
H - KHOR GUNT

EGYPT

SUDAN

WADI HALFA

Barrie Rickards with a 100lb-plus Nile perch.

the lake. Tim remarked, 'Antoine, if the military allow Egyptians on to the lake, why can't we persuade them to let foreigners on the lake as well – you can see the potential?' Antoine agreed, and promised to arrange a meeting with the Governor of Aswan to discuss the possibilities.

OPPOSITE: Lake Nasser, together with key locations mentioned in the text.

The meeting was a success, and while Tim and Antoine were sitting in the Aswan governor's office, the governor made a phone call to a friend who was a high-ranking general who commanded the Egyptian Army in Upper Egypt. The governor was speaking Arabic, but the gist of what he said must have been along the lines of 'Well, why don't we give these foreigners a chance? You never know, it might be good for tourism and Aswan's economy – that is, if your security will allow it?' It seems the security was satisfactory because they were allowed to go ahead, and Tim was given permission to explore Lake Nasser.

Exploring Lake Nasser's Potential

After the meeting with the governor Tim stayed in Aswan and started to gather information, and one of the first things he did was to go down to the fish collection wharf in Aswan. He knew there was a freshwater fishing industry on Lake Nasser, but did not know very much about it. Visiting the fishing wharf in Aswan, previously off limits to foreigners, was a first-time experience for him. Later he took Barrie with him. It was a bustling wharf with eight or ten shabby, blue wooden boats that looked like small old-style North Sea trawlers tied up to it. Lots of good-natured noisy workers and fishermen in galabiyyas (national dress, a loose robe) were unloading fish into equally scruffy trucks full of blocks of ice. Most of the fish they were loading seemed to be tilapia (*Tilapia niloticus*), but as Tim wandered through the slush on the wharf, trying to keep his feet dry, he came across a truck that was loading Nile perch. When he looked into the back of this truck he could see that it was almost full, and was amazed at the size of many of the Nile perch – they were huge. This sight immediately stimulated his somewhat dormant enthusiasm for fishing, and got him thinking about what it would be like to have some of those monsters on the end of a rod and line.

The next step was to organize an expedition to Lake Nasser to explore the potential of freshwater sport fishing on the lake, which had to be properly conducted and equipped. So after finding out as much as he could in Aswan, he flew to London and made contact with a friend, Peter Moss, an 'old African hand' and a consultant ecologist for the United Nations Environmental Agency. Peter's job with the UN was to establish and provide advice on wildlife conservation parks throughout the world, and luckily he was available and was keen to join the expedition. Tim also met up with Vince Davies of Davies Angling in Staines, Middlesex. Vince had been Nile perch fishing on the 'Jade Sea' – Lake Turkana in Kenya – and was keen to discover a new area for Nile perch fishing. He

offered to provide the angling expertise and the correct fishing tackle that the expedition would need to land monster Nile perch.

The first fishing trip on Lake Nasser was not a safari because the team was based at one of Antoine's hotels in Aswan, The Basma, from where they set out each day to go fishing on the lake in hired boats. When they were not fishing, they conducted research interviews with various authorities connected to the fishing industry.

The first day they went fishing on Lake Nasser was Sunday 17 January 1993. The day was a complete blank, which was rather discouraging. Their guide was an old crocodile hunter called Mourad Mohamed Goma, who owned a more or less suitable boat. Mourad knew the lake intimately and was no doubt an expert at hunting crocodiles, but he had never done any fishing and as a result was not much help with the expedition's main objective. The day was spent trolling blind (they had forgotten to bring a fish finder) along a weedy shoreline up to about 6 miles (10km) from the High Dam.

That evening over dinner at The Basma hotel they decided to spend the next day conducting some research to see if they could find out where they were going wrong. The most rewarding interview was with Dr Mohamed El-Shahat, the Director General of the Fishery Management Centre, where they met some experienced fish biologists. Information was obtained about the distribution of Nile perch *Lates niloticus* ('Samos' in Arabic), their relative abundance in 'fish landed' returns, water depths and temperatures, breeding habits and seasons, fishery management problems, and also some advice on locating the large Nile perch.

On day three it was decided to attempt a long trip with Mourad, leaving early in the morning and aiming to omit heavily fished waters near Aswan; they planned to carry on upstream towards Khor Kalabsha, the intention being to start fishing on the northernmost point of this khor (flooded desert valley). All went well until fishing was about to start, at which point the outboard engine developed an incurable fault and broke down. Two planks were uprooted from the decking, and the boat was gradually paddled to a net mooring buoy to wait for a fish-collecting boat to tow the research team back to Aswan. This was achieved, and they finally arrived back at The Basma hotel. They decided that the rest of the day should be spent driving to Garf Hussein (80 miles/120km away) to see if arrangements could be made to hire a traditional fishing boat to carry out one more attempt to fish in what seemed likely to be a better area. Another day of fishing had been lost, but much valuable experience was gained, and arrangements were made to hire a boat at Garf Hussein for a full day of fishing.

On day four, which was the last full day they had available on the lake, they began fishing at a place called Abu Dirwaw, close to Garf Hussein, at about 10.15am, and the first Nile perch was caught at 10.35am. Subsequently seven Nile perch and nine tigerfish were caught up to 5.15pm in the afternoon, after which no contact was made with any fish at all. The two largest Nile perch measured 48in and 46½in and weighed about 65–70lb, and the largest tigerfish measured 27½in and weighed 5½lb. One very large Nile perch was brought up next to the boat but managed to unhook itself, and at least another half dozen good fish were hooked and lost.

As a result of this amazing day's fishing, which was obviously in virgin waters because none of these fish had ever seen a lure before, the practicality of a sport-fishing project on Lake Nasser was well and truly confirmed.

Tim Baily, afloat in the earliest days on Lake Nasser.

A typical catch on Lake Nasser in the very early days.

Finding a Boat

Tim couldn't wait to get back on the lake to do some more fishing, so a few days after Peter and Vince had flown back to the UK, he decided to head back to Garf Hussein and see if he could find a local fisherman who had a boat for hire on a more permanent basis. He didn't have much luck because most of the professional fishermen asked for too much money for their boats; but as they explained, 'We make good money from fishing, and if we hire our boat we need to make about the same money – if not a bit more.' Eventually Tim was introduced to an old man wearing the traditional galabiyya and headdress, which might have been white at some stage, but was now somewhat soiled. But the old man looked a pleasant fellow, with a broad, toothless smile. He told Tim that he owned a fantastic boat, so they set off together to inspect it – but it turned out to be an old wooden hull with hardly a lick of paint remaining. It had been pulled up on the shore, high and dry, and on closer inspection Tim was not at all impressed: it had been out of the water for so long that all the woodwork had dried out to such an extent that he could see chinks of light showing through between some of the deck planks. When questioned as to whether the boat would even float, the old man replied, rather indignantly, 'Oh yes it will, all we have to do is to put it back in the water and then sink it for two or three days to let the wood absorb the water and swell out again, and then it will float!'

Tim was desperate, so agreed to this plan, and with some help from onlookers they pulled the boat into the lake and filled it with large stones so that it sank in shallow water. Sure enough, as soon as the boat was submerged, they could see the wood starting to absorb the water, tiny air bubbles making their way out of the dry wood. Tim was encouraged and told the old man he would be back in two days with an outboard motor and that they would then go fishing for Nile perch together.

On the appointed day Tim returned to Garf Hussein to find the old man's boat still sunk in the lake and the old man nowhere to be seen. Eventually he was located having a leisurely traditional sweet tea with a friend, and he was not at all taken aback when asked why the boat was not ready for the planned fishing trip: 'Why hurry? And who knows, maybe you weren't going to come back?'

Again with the help of some onlookers (there are always plenty of onlookers in this part of the world) they managed to pull the boat closer to the shore until there were a couple of inches of freeboard showing above the water, enough to start bailing with a couple of old buckets. As they bailed, the boat gradually came to the surface and started to float – in a fashion. There was a steady trickle of water still leaking into the bottom, and this trickle gradually increased as they loaded it and fitted the Yamaha 35HP outboard motor and fuel tanks. Tim was concerned about the amount of water seeping in, but he had come a long way and didn't want to pass up the chance of a day's fishing, so threw caution to the wind and thought to himself, 'To hell with the crocks, let's do it!' They headed north to a group of barren-looking islands that were clearly visible from Garf Hussein – and they were close enough to the mainland just in case there was any trouble with the boat.

The First Fishing Expedition

The islands they had decided to fish must have had a local name, but as Tim's team got to know the lake, they gave their own names to areas that were important to them. The islands where they were fishing were later christened 'Shaban Rabbi' islands. There was always a story behind the names they gave to key places on the lake. In this case, Shaban was lost at night in his fishing boat and could not find were we were camping, so Rabbi, carrying a can of petrol, ran to the top of a hill and lit a huge bonfire; this was seen by Shaban and saved the day – or should we say night?

As Tim and the old man 'putted' along up the coast in their leaking boat everything seemed to be working reasonably well, just as long as the old man, with Tim helping, kept bailing water out of the boat. They started by trolling a likely looking area and were soon into a nice 40lb Nile perch, which they kept. After several hours, four good Nile perch up to about 60lb were landed and kept, filling up the boat and gradually increasing the trickle and the amount of bailing that was required to keep the boat afloat. As the afternoon wore on the old man became more and more excited about the fish Tim was catching, and kept asking if he could have a go as well. Eventually Tim let him have a rod, and he managed to land a small perch of about 20lb. It was a heavy rod so he didn't have much of a problem cranking the fish in – he was delighted.

Soon it was almost time to go back to Garf Hussein; by this time the old man was trolling as well and really enjoying the experience – when suddenly they got a double hook-up with two very lively fish of about 60lb. Chaos reigned while the two of them tried to keep a foothold in the very rickety boat and fight strong fish at the same time. The old man could not believe the strength of the fish he had caught, and just stood there shouting in Arabic (which Tim did not understand) while holding on to the rod and letting the fish have its own way. Eventually the old man's fish managed to snag up in a bush, and it required some clever boatwork to untangle, with one hand holding a rod with a struggling fish on the end. All this took some time, and neither was paying any attention to bailing so the boat was gradually filling up with water. It got to the stage where there were three choices before the boat sank: jettison all the Nile perch they had caught, cut the line of the fish they were fighting, or beach the boat. They chose to beach the boat. They were lucky there was a sandy beach nearby where they could safely run the boat aground and eventually land the fish. Tim insisted they release the two fish, much to the dismay of the old man who saw only the money side of the argument – 'crazy foreigners'!

No more proof was needed that the Nile perch fishing on Lake Nasser was something quite special, so Tim settled down to concentrate on setting up a company to take anglers on Nile perch safaris into this desert lake.

The Business Develops

How the business developed from this point onwards is a rather long-winded story, so we will skip most of it; after all, this is a book about Nile perch and not an autobiography. Bob Kimber, one of the pioneer anglers on Lake Nasser, gives a good account of his impressions of the first safaris exploring the lake and its amazing Nile perch fishing, in Chapter 2.

To start with, Tim hired boats and worked with several local people who could not understand, or were not interested in, the importance of good service. It was hard to find key people because, sadly, many of the locals in Aswan applied the short-term attitude, which was to get as much money out of tourists as they could, as quickly as possible. It was an uphill struggle, having to use unreliable boats that were not fitted out properly, and local guides who had no experience of how to catch Nile perch.

On the other hand, each safari was a wonderful adventure, despite the problems. Anyone who came on a safari during those first few years was a pioneer and had to understand this before signing up. What made it very special was the chance to catch a fish that quite literally was beyond the wildest dreams of most anglers. In addition, especially for Tim who has a passion for wild places, was the fact many of the areas they were visiting had never been seen by a white man before.

The turning point came when Tim met Nabil Abed El Moete: Nabil was to become his partner in safaris, and one of his best friends. Nabil is an exceptionally good-natured man who is well liked and respected throughout the Aswan business community. To start a successful business in a country with a different culture and language to your own it is essential to find a good partner who can understand what your objectives are, and then help you to translate them into the local system. Nabil and Tim got on very well in this respect, and the new company started to take shape.

Building the Boats

The boats had to be built using materials and expertise that was available locally. The choice was limited to either wood or steel, because glassfibre did not exist in Upper Egypt. They built the hulls from solid steel using a design that was similar to a dory and was already quite common on the Nile. The new boats were built for tough work in remote areas, and big enough to live in as well as act as a fishing platform. Each was fitted with long-range fuel tanks and plenty of storage area for equipment. The bow deck was flat and provided a forward casting area, and there was an all-round deck in case a quick manoeuvre were needed when that big fish took a dive under the boat. The stern was a spacious trolling or casting area, and each boat was fitted with a fish finder, and weighing scales up to 220lb. There were reasonably comfortable on-board sleeping facilities, with two bunks, each with a full-size single mattress; this area also provided daytime seating.

For the first three years, everything was transported in the fishing boat: camping equipment, provisions, fuel, guide, cook, plus visiting anglers and all their equipment. This was a lot of people and equipment in one boat, which meant that camps had to be set up on the shore before the angler could start to fish properly. But as time passed and more were built, some of the extra fishing boats came to be used as small 'supply' boats, to carry the camping equipment and safari staff; and in 1997 it became normal procedure to use one of the fishing boats as a 'mother' ship. This move made it possible to give anglers the option of three of them sharing one fishing boat, which brought the cost of the safari down. By 1999 the company had built the first of their proper mother ships, of which they now have four. There is plenty of space to relax on these vessels, and to have sit-down meals.

This style of safari, with the fishing boats supported by a mother ship, remains to this day, although all the time improvements are being made to the efficiency and comfort of all the boats.

The Safari Team

The people who are responsible for making everything run smoothly are the Nubians on the lake and the Egyptians who run administration and logistics – and there is a bigger team behind the running of a boat safari operation than most people realize. In the front line there is the office staff who make sure that all visitors' travel arrangements are correct, and that their arrival and departure from Egypt will be trouble free. Then there is the safari itself, with the logistics staff who make sure that each trip is correctly

provisioned with all its needs, from tons of petrol and diesel fuel down to the simple napkin to be laid out on the dining table.

Then there is the workshop that has to keep dozens of engines running smoothly for trouble-free fishing. The safaris are exploring remote areas, and it is essential that everything is correct and operating efficiently and that nothing is forgotten. The workshops and stores are in large steel barges in Aswan.

The safari staff and guides are the most important requirement for a successful expedition, and a great deal of attention must go into selecting and training safari staff, especially the fishing guides. To become a qualified guide requires a minimum of eighteen months' training before he is given command of his own fishing boat. A good guide should have a 'hunting instinct' and a genuine feel for fishing. Fishing is almost a vocation, and to be successful you have to enjoy doing it. A good guide will experience a genuine thrill watching his guest angler catching that Nile perch of his dreams. The personality of the guide is also important, as is his ability to communicate. All the safari staff and guides on the lake are Nubians.

In Summary

Let someone else sum up, in a few words, their impression about going on a safari into a desert lake:

> Tim Baily organises the safaris, and it is through his enterprise that sport fishing anglers find themselves in the desert of southern Egypt. It must be emphasised from the very outset that the term 'safari' is precisely what a fishing trip to Lake Nasser is. The environment is rugged, though incredibly beautiful, remote, demanding and hostile. Yet despite this Tim has evolved an adventure which is remarkably civilised in several aspects, primarily centred about the social and culinary side of the trip.
>
> Martin Gay article
> 'More Than Meets the Eye'.

2 PIONEERS' STORIES

Bob Kimber and John Wilson

Lake Nasser

by Bob Kimber

Thanks a million for the recent safari; it was great to be on the lake again, despite the windy weather conditions. In retrospect I think I like the challenge, as a fish earned gives far more pleasure than just sitting back in the boat trolling over a known hotspot. J.B. and company were in good spirits – though some of their theories on the fishing made me smile: if they are not catching, they believe fish are either not there, or not feeding, and nobody came up with the fact that the fish *were* there and *would* feed, but they just couldn't catch them. I think people's expectations of Nasser are now so high that they expect the fish to just come to them regardless of conditions. I wonder how many people on safari without you present would have raised that big boy at our last stop. Not many. I suspect most would have quickly concluded there were no fish present or they were not feeding. What you were saying about concentrating on one area, rather than moving, is probably more relevant when the fishing is hard. After all, if the fishing is easy you can get bored hauling fish out of the same area, so a change is sometimes needed. If the fishing is hard, however, moving might seem the easy answer – but often you just move from one hard area to another. You should probably pick an area where you know there are fish, and try to devise a way of catching them. Anyhow, I'm rambling on – which just shows that Nasser is as interesting as ever. Let me take you back in time now.

It is March 2000, and I have just completed my tenth Lake Nasser safari, so obviously I am something of an addict. I was lucky enough to be on one of the original 'Reconnaissance Safaris' put together by Tim Baily, and from that point on I have developed a passion for the lake unsurpassed by any of the other 'exotic' locations I have been fortunate to fish. In fact it would be true to say that Nasser has formed a major part of my life for the past seven years. I have countless wonderful memories of life on safari, and have forged some great friendships – I even met my wife on the return flight after one trip. Tim Baily really has a lot to answer for.

So how has it changed over the years? Well, the lake itself has changed little, of course, although the level has risen steadily over that time. Even at its seasonal low it is now well above areas where you could once stand and fish. Yes, this huge lake is actually getting even bigger. But other things never change: the magic of just being in such a wilderness, the magnificent sunsets, sleeping under the awesome desert sky, and of course Tim's jokes. (Hands up all those who have heard him tell the one about the ships of the desert.)

The First Safari

The start of my first safari found me and four friends at a slipway close to the High Dam. We had made the journey from Luxor by road, an interesting experience, but not one I was eager to repeat on a regular basis. Waiting for us were two boats, and the most polite way to describe them would be 'functional'. These were to serve not only for fishing purposes but also as our mobile camp. Everything had to be crammed on board, so as you can imagine space was at a premium. We duly set off: two boats stuffed to the gunnels with equipment, food, fuel, three

Nubians, Tim Baily – plus five anglers and all their gear.

The fishing turned out to be very hard. I believe it would have been a difficult week regardless of our knowledge at the time, but our tactics and lure selection certainly did not help the situation. The trolling was done exclusively hard against the shoreline, and we were very unselective in the areas we tried, the only criteria being that they appeared rocky and deep – and that's a lot of shoreline on Nasser. Sometimes we would troll endless stretches for what seemed like hours, with little or nothing to show for our efforts. During all this, the guides were enthusiastic and excellent at handling the boats, but had not at that stage developed the feel for finding fish. Tim, too, was very frustrated by the poor results, but did not then have the resources to improve things. This is not meant as criticism: Nasser is a vast area with major seasonal changes in water temperature and level, and getting to grips with it was going to be a huge undertaking.

Meanwhile our shore fishing was attempted in much the same areas as the trolling, and we did catch greater numbers of fish – but the average size was very small. We also had limited success from the shore with small tigers – in fact, it was while using a small spoon intended for tiger that my friend Terry hooked and lost a perch of around 45lb, easily the biggest we hooked from the shore all week. The biggest actually caught on the trip was 57lb, and luckily enough fell to my rod. It was taken on a trolled Yo-Zuri Formurat, a deep diver about the same shape and size as a Big S. (Depth Raiders were still to be discovered, and we made little use of Rapalas or Russelures.) Although our methods now seem a little crude, they did represent progress over an even earlier safari, where the members had apparently spent several days trolling in open shallow weedy areas. It seems funny now, but at the time who knew any better?

We did quickly discover the difficulties presented by the fact that our fishing boats doubled as supply boats: moving camp, which we did regularly, entailed a great deal of loading and

Bob Kimber with a 100lb-plus Nile perch.

unloading during valuable fishing time, and needless to say, this was more than a little frustrating. But life in camp was great fun, dinner being one of the undoubted highlights of every day. The food was prepared by our Nubian chef in a small field kitchen set up on the shore, basically a couple of gas rings and a grill. Using these limited facilities and working alone he prepared dinner for everyone – all things considered, quite a feat. Dinner was served with us seated on a tarpaulin on the ground (the luxury of chairs had not yet arrived), with lighting provided by the traditional safari hurricane lamp purring in the background.

John Wilson and Mohammed Elephantine with a big fish. (John Wilson)

Sleeping options were boat or shore. For the shore, a mattress was taken from the boat and laid directly on the ground, which obviously left you at the mercy of the scorpions. Not surprisingly, we mostly opted for the boat, although I think we all tried the shore at some stage. So with five anglers and three Nubians, the boats did get a little crowded. Tim always slept on the shore, and it was wonderful drifting off to sleep with the desert sounds broken only by Tim's unbelievable snoring....

Safari in the Year 2000

Now it is March 2000, and I have been ferried to the lake from Aswan's smart new airport in air-conditioned comfort, my transfers in Luxor having been smoothly handled by Abercrombie and Kent. There to greet me is Tim, who has decided to take time out and join me for the week.

At the edge of the lake we step aboard an enormous barge that Tim has recently purchased. He plans to convert it into a floating lodge, but currently it is being used as a pontoon to moor the boats that are not already out on safari. Tim has a fleet consisting of a dozen fishing boats and four supply boats. He proudly shows me the new boat that we are to use for the week. Like all the boats, it has been specifically designed and built for the job. The accommodation is excellent: it is fitted with comfortable twin beds with plenty of space to manoeuvre between them, and room for all your kit underneath. The deck is spacious and clear of any obstructions, with a rail round the outside so you can walk right around the boat – so no more gymnastics required whilst playing fish. A permanent rod rack is standard, and the latest versions have forward steering complete with integral fish-finders. Long-range fuel tanks mean an end to all those stops to siphon fuel (in the past often practised with a cigarette dangling from the lips).

And in the evenings you can sort your gear using electric lights, the battery being charged during the day by the outboard. We are to be accompanied by one of the large supply boats, which not only transports all the food, fuel and equipment, but also has a fully fitted kitchen and dining area.

Out on the lake, owing to some high winds, the fishing was not at its best. If this sounds familiar, it has to be said that it is not typical of my trips – on occasions during the intervening years I've experienced some truly spectacular fishing. Sometimes, though, it's fun to have to work at it – it's a good test of just how much has been learned over the years.

We hardly trolled the shoreline at all, but instead concentrated on offshore marks that often appeared to be in the middle of nowhere. Beneath the surface, however, they had all the features likely to appeal to big fish. (The fish-finder is now of paramount importance.) Often we would troll extremely intricate lines, searching for the right spot. On occasions we would try a more stealthy approach, cutting the engine and anchoring or drifting, casting lures from the boat. This strategy has proved very successful.

The shore fishing was very selective. There are, of course, now plenty of known hotspots, but Tim and his guides have also developed a sixth sense for new areas that are likely to produce. It would be true to say that at some of the heavily fished areas the fish have become wise to conventional techniques. However, using a stealthy approach and something they have not seen before still brought us some success. We did particularly well with wobbled dead tiger-fish, which we had previously caught using a fly rod and small trout patterns. (Catching the bait was fun in itself.) Overall we certainly did not hammer the fish, but with the knowledge of Tim and the guides, and by working at it, we caught our share. Better hook-holds would have given us a couple of 'biggies'. We also found some prolific areas for tigers, taking fish close to double figures on lures, and others up to 6–7lb on an eight-weight fly rod – great sport.

The crew were superb, great company and taking a real pride in their work. I have noticed lately that a real sense of team spirit has developed within everyone associated with the safaris. At the end of a full day's fishing we would be treated to a splendid three-course dinner served at the dining table on the supply boat, usually accompanied by one or two ice-cold beers. Then, after a comfortable night's sleep (only disturbed by Baily's snoring, no change there I'm afraid) we would wake to a cup of tea or coffee freshly prepared. (On some of my earlier trips I can recall making the coffee myself just to try and coax the crew out of bed in the morning!) Finally, heading back to Aswan on the last day, I had the same thought that I've had at this point on all nine previous occasions: when can I do it again?

Reflecting now on my ten safaris, it's clear that the progress made by Tim and his team is remarkable, particularly if you know something of the red tape and the major obstacles that have been encountered along the way. For me, all the refinements that have been made so far are for the better – but the safaris still maintain the charm and magic of the early days. I hope this never changes. It is a serious wilderness and all real anglers love it for that.

The Nile Perch of Murchison Falls

by John Wilson

Though the Indian mahseer and Africa's Nile perch are from separate continents, they are of course both, first and foremost, huge, predatory 'river species' designed by nature to feed upon other fishes, including their own kind; and more importantly, they are purpose built to live happily in the fastest of currents. This is something that many Nile perch enthusiasts, who have only ever caught them from lakes such as Victoria or Nasser, have probably never considered. One look, for instance, at the identical, bony, steeply angled, 'wedge-shaped' forehead of each fish proves immediately that, like the mahseer, Nile perch are indeed purpose built for holding station in fierce currents close to the bottom amongst giant boulders and the black bedrock of their mother river, the Nile.

In order to hold station behind large rocks where currents converge, perch sometimes literally stand on their heads (held down by water pressure), and their large, rounded black tail can actually be seen just below the surface – great pointers for the opportunist lure enthusiast. Indeed, were those anglers who have only ever caught perch in stillwater to hook a sizeable specimen of, say, 50–70lb amongst the turbulent waters of the Nile itself, an entirely different and surprising, vastly more powerful battle would be experienced and enjoyed.

Yes, at various times throughout the ensuing battle, these fish will catapult themselves up through the surface film, in that glorious, gill-flaring, headshaking routine that we have come to love of the species. There are few more awe-inspiring sights in fresh water than a 100lb-plus 'buffalo' of a perch attempting to throw the lure whilst tail-walking. But between the jumps of sizeable river perch there is an exceptionally powerful and dogged fight, when the angler is at times totally helpless, especially when these fish turn those deep flanks across the flow and hurtle off downstream. There have been times at Murchison Falls when, precariously perched on the rock, I felt my arms were literally going to be wrenched from their sockets, or that I might even be pulled in, such is the ferocity of the fish.

And with Nile perch very much in mind, were I to choose the most awesome, the most dangerous, yet most beautiful, game-packed and photogenic angling location from all the sixty-plus countries I have fished during the past forty years, then spectacular Murchison Falls in Uganda would win easily. It even surpasses the legendary River Kaveri in southern India, where for some fifteen years during the 1980s and 1990s my love affair in search of those massive mahseer became insatiable, resulting in dozens of memorable hour-long battles with whoppers over 70lb, including three over 90lb, and ultimately their capture.

Yet quite simply there is, to my mind, nowhere to match the inspirational spectacle of Mother 'Nile', the world's longest river, as she winds her way through Murchison National Park, suddenly to be forced through a fissure in the rocks mere yards wide at the top of a steep gorge, then to drop 150ft into a huge foam-topped pool and a maelstrom of 'rocking' whitewater. Here, Nile perch of truly world-record proportions live – the largest ever landed here during the 1990s weighed 237lb, to the rod of Marco Magyar – plus sementendu catfish and vundu catfish, both capable of reaching weights in excess of that magical 100lb mark. They share this hostile environment in a permanent 'dog-eat-dog' situation, with a myriad of lesser weird and wonderfully colourful species, from electric catfish and giant eels, to snapping turtles weighing anywhere from 30 to 50lb, which at times just won't leave your ledgered deadbait alone.

OPPOSITE: Marco Magyar's 237lb fish from Murchison Falls.

Fishing the Falls

I was first captivated by the splendour of Murchison Falls whilst still a boy living in London during the 1950s, when I saw them in that famous and original motion picture *King Solomon's Mines* starring Stewart Granger and Deborah Kerr, in which the location was featured as a backdrop. They are even more breathtaking in real life, with one small and one monumental cataract. In the dense equatorial canopy of hardwood trees overhanging the main pool – aptly called the 'Devil's Cauldron', where rocking water hurtles downstream through a long gorge between banks over 300 yards apart – there also live some of the most brilliantly coloured birds I've ever seen, from carmine bee eaters and weaver birds, to the majestic African fish eagle, with kites, vultures and storks working the thermals overhead.

After half a mile of seemingly unfishable water (to the uninitiated), these are, in fact, the most productive spots of all, which I find by far the most exciting, comprising fierce currents and swirling eddies, some an acre or more in area and over 30ft deep. The Nile then slowly starts to widen, and reduces in speed to around walking pace.

Now it is half a mile wide between tall sedge- and reed-lined banks, where Cape buffalo and elephants are likely to venture out from the jungle to drink. So boat fishing here, whether on the drift between pods of noisy (and potentially dangerous) hippos or at anchor tied up alongside the marginal canopy, is actually far safer than bank fishing. Whereas up at the falls, taking your life into your own hands by casting from steep-sided, dangerously rocky promontories into the swirling pools below, is order of the

At Murchison Falls, you have to fight both the fish and the water.

hearted, believe me. Tsetses are similar to our European horse fly in that you can't feel them land, only the bite when they fly off – and some people's legs and arms puff up to enormous proportions. Then at the end of the day's fishing, the reality is that before wild animals start to patrol as darkness looms over the gorge, you must start the long, unbelievably steep and strength-sapping climb back up to where the 4×4 is parked.

To boat fish below the falls in the slower water, suitable craft are hired at Paraa Ferry, some 4 miles downstream from Murchison, where long, fibreglass canoes and a 25ft (7.5m) Parks boat are available via the Parks Office.

Of all the lost whopper perch I've had on the end of my line during the several trips I've made to Murchison, the one I would most have liked to see inhaled an 8lb catfish I was slowly reeling in, instantly ripping over 100 yards of 35lb test line from my 10,000 multiplier against a firmly set clutch, despite our eventually following in its pursuit. We were tied up to the bank whilst boat fishing the wide neck of the gorge, half a mile below the 'Falls' at the time. Unfortunately the second, and 'flying' 8/0 hook of a two-hook pennel rig on a 100lb-test 3ft mono trace, presenting an awaka deadbait (a silver shoal fish), had reversed itself into the catfish (the first 8/0 had actually hooked the catfish), and once we came up close to the perch with neither of the two hooks finding purchase, it simply spat the catfish out. I was, in fact, filming an episode of a twelve-part *Fishing Safari* series for Discovery Television at the time, so I was doubly fed up, because without an end result we had to dump the hook-up footage.

How big? Well, I've lost count of the huge perch that I've taken from Lake Nasser weighing between 100–150lb. All I can say is, this felt larger by far, even taking flowing water into account, and I would have loved to have seen it at least jump once to evaluate its size before coughing the bait up. But it wasn't to be.

For those wishing to target the perch of Murchison, allow me to offer a little advice: use a powerful 9½ to 11ft 'up-tide'-style rod and

A just reward – an Indian mahseer. (John Wilson)

day. Though should you fall in? Well! It's a case of 'goodnight nurse'. The currents here are far too strong to swim against (up to 20 knots), and along the sandbanks at the end of the gorge are the longest, meanest, fattest crocodiles in Africa, presumably waiting for their next meal – it is certainly no coincidence that they are there.

I shall be forever grateful to my guide and fishing friend Paul Goldring of 'Wild Frontiers' in Entebbe for his organized, safari-style approach to fishing for perch at Murchison. For this, a long and extremely steep walk downriver is necessary in order to reach a fishable level: in the most intense heat (it is best to walk during the cool of dawn) and with the added problem of tsetse fly bites, this is not fishing for the faint-

Two smiling men at the Falls (John Wilson and Paul Goldering)…

multiplier combo with nothing less than 35–40lb test mono. And take a couple of spare bulk spools along, because some days those rocks just eat up your line. But for heaven's sake, do not, on any account, fish with braid because the rocks are horrendous and will quickly shred braid to bits. (*See also* Tim's and Barrie's comments elsewhere in the book.)

Lures such as Rapala's floating/diving 'Super Shad Rap' work unbelievably well, as does their CD (countdown) 18, in either orange or blue mackerel. But also take along some large rubber shads, because in the deep holes, especially where 'jigging' is possible, these could prove invaluable. A 'cast' net is handy for procuring fresh live- and deadbaits in the form of alestes and awakas, the two most common silver shoal fish in this part of the Nile.

Or you can light-ledger close in to the bank (I take along a small telescopic rod and fixed-spool reel loaded with 8lb test, for this very reason) with either sweetcorn or plain old bread paste to catch the same, plus several, barbel-like fishes, which make great baits. Spinning using tiny size 00 Mepps lures will also produce some nice bait in the form of alestes and awakes, plus baby tigerfish, which Nile perch adore.

Now here is the most important part of all: do *not* hook your livebait through its lips, because every time you tighten up to control it, it will swim upwards, and you want your bait to swim *down* into deep water close to the rocks where the largest Nile perch lie. Obviously you cannot afford to put any lead on the line because of the rocks, so hook once only behind the fish's dorsal fin with a 6/0 or 8/0 hook, and allow it some free line to swim down into the depths, which it will do with surprising ease despite the treacherous currents. Something you will notice here is that after 10–20ft or so, there is often a layer of water going in completely the opposite direction, and maybe deeper down still, it could be going the other way again; such is the awesome force of subsurface currents at Murchison. So watch the line carefully where it enters the water in order to work out the flow patterns so you can encourage your bait into a 'taking' zone: it may literally take a completely different route each time you lower it into the swirling water.

Incidentally, for working a livebait around the slower, more even-depthed eddies further downstream, I use a simple sliding pike float rig (with a bullet above the 100lb test hook trace swivel to keep the bait down), stopped several feet above bottom by a bead and power gum stop knot. And if drifting by boat, an exceptionally effective yet little practised method is to simply freeline the bait (live or dead) around 30–40 yards behind the slowly drifting boat; fish it any shorter, and it may not get down close to the river bed.

Whatever the bait presentation, don't be tempted to put the rod down even for a second. Keep your reel in free spool the whole time under gentle thumb pressure, and when the unmistakable surge of a Nile perch engulfing your bait is transmitted up the line (of this you will be in no doubt whatsoever, despite constant pressure against the line, because it is as if your line has been suddenly connected to a lorry hurtling around the M25) – lower the rod tip, click the reel back into gear, and wind steadily, waiting for the line to become 'bowstring' tight, before whacking the rod back and literally holding on, power-pumping furiously whenever you can in order to heave that perch up, and away from those deadly rocks. And do you know what? I wish I was there with you. (*See* Appendix III for more information about Lake Victoria and Murchison Falls.)

…and one smiling croc. (John Wilson)

3 SAFARIS IN THE NUBIAN DESERT WILDERNESS

A typical quiet bay for a camp. Barrie found an excellently preserved jackal skull at this camp.

When we first started to think about how we would set up a sport-fishing programme on Lake Nasser we were faced with what one might describe as adventurous problems in that we had a lake more than the size of an English county to explore. In addition, the area was wild and remote, with no facilities at all, and no help would be at hand if a problem presented itself. Lake Nasser has a surface area of 2,026 square miles (5,250km²) and a shoreline length of 4,865 miles (7,844km). We were allowed to explore the larger segment of the lake that is in Egyptian territory, 83 per cent of the total, but politics and so-called security are the main stumbling blocks when it comes to getting permission to enter the Sudan from Lake Nasser: to this day, Lake Nubia remains virgin territory when it comes to fishing the area with a rod and line.

From the start we realized that we could not fish the lake properly by arranging one-day fishing trips out of Aswan, which would confine us to a very small area of the lake in the north: it was obvious we had to mount a safari-type operation to take anglers into this remote desert lake. Fortunately Tim already had a considerable amount of experience with this type of safari expedition, having already spent ten years of his life (in the 1970s and 1980s) working in the 'overland' business; during this time he owned his own company, which had pioneered Trans-Africa expeditions involving safari-type journeys in 4×4 vehicles, which took anything up to three months to cross the African continent. These Trans-Africa expeditions were similar to the safari operation that Tim was setting up on Lake Nasser, except that instead of using 4×4 land vehicles, this new venture would be using boats. Everything had to be very well organized, because where the boat safaris were operating there were absolutely no facilities other than those that they would take with them.

The boats had to be tough for the type of work they would have to do. In particular, trolling in relatively shallow rocky areas presents the ever-present danger of ramming submerged rocks (which happens frequently), so this quickly ruled out the use of glassfibre as a building material for the boats. The tough steel hulls worked well, and the only real disadvantage was the weight of the boats, causing them to be slower than we would have liked – but this lack of speed was a disadvantage we soon learned to live with.

The fishing boats are supported now by mother ships that have become an essential component of a well organized safari unit. The mother ships are between 50 and 65ft long, and carry the safari equipment, provisions, fuel,

A patient John Wilson, relaxing on the mother ship as lunch is served.

cook, helpers and so on, leaving the fishing boats free to get on with the job they are designed for, namely catching fish. On the mother ships there is plenty of space to relax and have sit-down meals; all are fitted with a toilet and shower, a built-in kitchen, and large ice-boxes to keep drinks cool. Each mother ship also has a 240v generator that can be used to charge camera batteries.

This style of camping is comfortable, but still maintains the adventurous atmosphere of being out in the wilds, and is as close to the real meaning of the Swahili word 'safari' as you are likely to find anywhere. Most people are pleasantly surprised at the standard of food on safari. The style of cooking is a blend of Western taste merged with Nubian cuisine, which is superb. With approximately one member of staff per angler, there is little to do except relax and fish to your heart's content. One of the things that make the safaris a real pleasure to be on is the safari staff: without exception these are all Nubians, a particularly friendly and hospitable people. We decided from the very start that the people we would explore the lake with would be Nubians, because, after all, it was the Nubians who used to live in this section of the Nile Valley before it was flooded by Lake Nasser.

The Story of the Bedouin Girls

Although it is a very rare occurrence, should anglers complain about the facilities they are provided with, Tim likes to tell them the story of the Bedouin girls. Tim was helping to guide a fishing boat on a particularly slow day, when very few fish were being caught and his anglers were growing restless. Then along the shoreline they noticed a large flock of sheep with camels and donkeys scattered among them. Tim thought this would make an interesting diversion, so he suggested they go and meet the Bedouin who were looking after the herds. As he said: 'They are a really interesting people who normally live in the open desert but have come

to Lake Nasser to water their livestock – these particular Bedouins are closely related to the Nubians, though they speak a slightly different language.'

So they pulled the boat into the shore and got out close to the herd of animals. Almost immediately they were surrounded by four or five important-looking dogs that were taking seriously their responsibility as guardians of the herd, and had come to check out who the intruders were. These dogs left Tim and his companions in no doubt as to who was in charge of the area. Then about half a mile away they spotted three figures leading some pack donkeys with skin containers strapped to their backs. Slowly this little group made their way towards

Looking from the Khor out to the main part of the lake: an idyllic campsite. Note the small stealth boat.

the visiting anglers and their Nubian guide, who shouted a welcome to them in Arabic.

As they got closer, the visitors realized that the three figures were in fact young women, who at first were extremely shy about coming anywhere too close to them. However, they must have been reassured by the friendly Arabic greetings from the guide, and they had the back-up of their small pack of important-looking dogs, still keeping a very distrustful eye on the visitors. From what Tim could make out from behind the colourful red and black veils the women had pulled across their faces, two of the girls were very young – probably in their late teens – and the third woman could well have been their young mother. They were lovely, healthy-looking women, and once they had become used to the visitors, they displayed a great sense of humour and fun, laughing and chatting to each other about these strange-looking visitors – who could well have been the first white people they had ever seen.

The fishing guide was speaking to them in Arabic, and translated something of what the women were saying. Apparently they had been on their own for the past month or two, left to look after the herds while their menfolk were on an expedition to Aswan; the latter had taken in some of their stock to sell, and were also buying provisions before they returned to their women in the wilderness.

To Tim, at least, it was a sobering experience to meet these desert people, and he found himself wondering about the common belief that females are the weaker sex. Here were three women who could survive alone in the desert, with never a roof over their heads: so surely this was in contradiction to the common belief that women were the weaker sex – though he supposed it would depend on which society they were a part of.

Soon it was time to return to the mother ship for lunch, so they bid farewell to the three women and went on their way. At lunch they described to the other anglers on the same safari their experience of meeting the Bedouin women, and while doing so, Tim overheard one

Boatman extraordinaire, *the guide Ramadan.*

angler remark 'B—y h—l, the beer isn't cold enough!' And Tim found himself wondering if those Bedouin girls have *ever* had a cold drink in their lives, let alone three cooked meals a day and a comfortable bed to sleep on – and he thought to himself, 'Where is the real meaning of life disappearing to?' (Mind you, a lack of cold beer on safari is a serious problem, and one that we try to avoid at all costs!)

Stealth Boats and Houseboats

More recently we have introduced what we call 'stealth boats': these provide anglers with an alternative fishing platform if they wish to fish areas more quietly and efficiently. The main fishing boats have to be big enough to live in, and whilst they are also excellent fishing platforms, a stealth boat has the advantage that it can be quietly drifted or rowed over underwater promontories or past rocky drop-offs, allowing anglers to cast lures or wobble deadbait without the commotion caused by a bigger boat. The stealth boats we use are light aluminium skiffs known as 'sea arks', powered with 10hp or 15hp engines. The sea ark is also light enough to be towed easily by the larger boats between fishing grounds. It is a hugely exciting experience to catch a big fish in one of these smaller boats.

The latest project – ready for safari operations in January 2008 – is safari houseboats that the African Angler is building in Aswan: these boats are designed for an even more comfortable side of safari life. Barrie and his family used one of these in 2007, and he can highly recommend them. Safari houseboats are 40ft long and powered by two 85hp outboard engines with long-range fuel tanks. They sleep four people comfortably in two separate cabins, each with two comfortable beds. These boats can accommodate up to a maximum of six persons if two sleep on the spacious sun deck and enjoy the unique and peaceful experience of sleeping under the desert stars.

Safari houseboats are comfortable and spacious, and when teamed up with a mother ship, provide almost all the amenities you would expect to find in a hotel. There is a toilet and shower, and a small galley with a washing basin, an icebox with cold drinks and amenities for making tea or coffee. The electricity supply comes from an on-board generator, and both 12v and 240v electric systems are installed. The sun deck has a shaded seating area, ideal for relaxing and watching the lake go by, and there is plenty of space for sunbathing or just lazing around.

From a fishing point of view, the idea behind these boats is that the anglers using them will go fishing each day in the smaller 'stealth' boats. The more anglers who can share the same accommodation space, the more competitive will be the price for a safari fishing holiday. Alternatively, two people could be really comfortable with a cabin and their own living room with en suite facilities: these houseboats will be ideal for families.

If you decide to come fishing for Nile perch on Lake Nasser there are two sorts of safari to choose from. A few safaris are run by local Nubians based in Aswan, but here we describe the safaris organized by Tim because these are the most common, and the ones we know all about. The most common is called a Lake Nasser safari, and is designed for anglers who would like to come on their own or with a friend, and then join in the atmosphere of a sociable camp with other anglers. These safaris have fixed start days every Tuesday of the year, and they end on a Sunday. Anglers who would like to book a single place on a safari are also welcome. The safari unit is made up of two or three fishing boats, supported by a mother ship.

Then there are the Nubian safaris, which start and end on any day of the year and can last for as long as is required; this is ideal for anglers who would like to have the flexibility of deciding how long they want to stay on a fishing safari. This safari offers a degree of independence that many anglers prefer, and is ideal for two anglers or a small group of friends who would like to set out and explore the lake, at their own pace, on a fishing adventure that has few equals anywhere.

If you have never been on a boat safari to Lake Nasser, you might well ask the question 'What is so special about a boat safari into a desert lake?' First of all, you have to be the right type of person to enjoy this sort of outdoor experience – but if you have a sense of adventure and love nature and the outdoors, you will be sure to enjoy the desert lake boat safari experience. In a way, fish are a bonus. Aside from terrific angling, the lake is a lovely place to visit, where

The mother ships give an air of luxury, with drinks on the afterdeck and a dining room on the upper foredeck.

the weather is nearly always sunny and bright. The shoreline is a variety of desert landscapes – hilly and rugged, or flat and sandy with clean freshwater beaches. It is a magical wilderness of stunning desert scenery, bordered by the clean water of the lake, which is dotted with rocky islands. There is an atmosphere of tranquillity, vastness and adventure, and it is a wilderness where anglers literally have hundreds of square miles to themselves.

There is a striking variety of birds, mammals and reptiles. More than 100 species of birds have been recorded: wild duck, Egyptian geese, pelicans, herons, egrets and various species of hawk, kite, falcon and eagle will be among the birds seen. In most areas there are crocodiles and monitor lizards; other types of wildlife include Dorcas gazelle, jackals, desert fox and various smaller desert mammals.

The night sky is one to behold. Being in such a remote location, and many miles from any form of town, there is no residual glow from streetlights, power plants or any other forms of man's development. This results in absolute darkness, which provides the stargazer with a fantastic night sky, and probably the very best view of the Milky Way you will ever see. At night the desert silence is absolute except for the sounds of nocturnal creatures, and the feeling of isolation, freedom and peacefulness can be overwhelming.

4 LAKE NASSER AND ITS ORIGINS, BASIC FISHING, AND PEOPLE

Local fishermen greet the iceboat with their catch. The iceboats also supplement our ice rations in camp.

For about half its length the Nile is really two massive rivers. The Blue Nile, with its source in the Ethiopian Highlands, joins the White Nile at Omdurman, close to Khartoum, the capital of the Sudan. The White Nile is the longest river in the world. From Lake Victoria in east central Africa it flows generally north through Uganda, Sudan and Egypt to the Mediterranean Sea, for a distance of 3,470 miles (5,584km). From its remotest headstream, the Luvironza river in Burundi, it is 4,160 miles (6,695km) long.

At the turn of the 19th century, agricultural production was being outstripped by the growth of the population in Egypt and the Sudan, and the Nile had to be controlled if there was to be agricultural stability along its banks. Harnessing the power of the Nile would also yield the hydroelectric power necessary to develop industry. To the increasingly industrial societies of the region the choice was clear, and in 1899 construction of the first Aswan Dam was begun by the English, and completed in 1902. Its height was raised in subsequent building campaigns of 1907–12 and 1929–34.

Even with these big projects to elevate the wall level of the first dam, there was still an inadequate reservoir area behind the dam, and in the event of extreme flooding it was necessary to open the sluices to relieve the water pressure against it, flooding farming areas in the Nile Valley that were supposed to be protected. A second dam was necessary at Aswan, and in the early 1950s, designs were drawn up for what was to become the High Dam. Completion of the High Dam in the 1960s by the then USSR created Lake Nasser, the second largest man-made lake in the world. The High Dam construction stretches nearly 2¾ miles (4km) across the river's path, and rises to over 330ft (100m) from a base almost ¾ mile (1km) wide. Many people find it hard to grasp just how big Lake Nasser is; one can quote figures, but they don't mean very much until you are actually on the lake – and even then it is still hard to appreciate the vast area involved.

An example of what these statistics really mean was brought to Tim's attention while he was sitting in an Egypt Air flight waiting to take off from Luxor to London Heathrow, when it was announced on the aircraft TV monitor that the flying distance between Luxor and London Heathrow was 2,500 miles (4,000km) and the flying time 5½ hours. One does not have to be a brilliant mathematician to work out that this is about half the shoreline distance around Lake Nasser, and that it would take a commercial passenger airliner more than ten hours to fly the distance of Lake Nasser's shoreline.

To put it more accurately, the larger portion of the lake is in Egyptian territory: where we fish is 83 per cent of the total. The Sudanese call their smaller body of water (17 per cent) Lake Nubia. The border between Egypt and Sudan lies 30 miles (40km) south of Abu Simbel,

Sheep and other animals are herded along the shores of Lake Nasser, often by Bedouin tribesmen.

which is one of the starting points for Lake Nasser angling safaris, and home of the relocated spectacular tombs. The following is a summary of the lake's parameters:

Coordinates:	22° 25′N–31° 45′E
Max. length:	550km (341 miles)
Max. width:	35km (22 miles)
Surface area:	5,250km²
	(2,027sq miles)
Average depth:	25.2m (82.7ft)
Max. depth:	130m (426ft)
Shore length*	7,844km (4,864 miles)
Elevation:	183m (600ft)

*Approximate due to annual flooding

The safari team calculates distances in the number of hours that it takes a fishing boat to cruise between two given points, not in mileages that don't mean as much to a fishing safari on the move. Thus the main starting points are linked as follows, in terms of cruise timing: Aswan to Garf Hussein, 9 hours; Aswan to Abu Simbel 23 hours; Garf Hussein to Abu Simbel 14 hours.

As we have mentioned, the purpose behind building the High Dam was to provide Egypt's rapidly expanding population with cheap electric power, and a constant supply of water that would allow farmers to irrigate their land even during the region's persistent droughts. These were the positives behind constructing this dam – but what about the negatives?

The most serious criticisms, especially when it comes to the long-term consequences, concern silt and salt. Each year the Nile brings down approximately 130 million tons of silt in its muddy flood. Before the dam was built, about 90 per cent of this silt was simply washed into the Mediterranean Sea, but that still left between 10 and 15 million tons of it to be deposited on the Nile flood plain. However, since 1964 practically no silt has passed the dam, and instead it is accumulating in the southern, upstream half of Lake Nasser. Although it may take more than a hundred years before silt seriously reduces the capacity of this huge reservoir, critics claim that the loss of rich soil has already caused irreparable damage to the fertility of the Nile valley and the delta area. A pair of coffer dams in the Sudan could have been used to prevent this silting, and also to relocate the trapped silt for agricultural purposes as the coffer dams filled up alternately.

A simple fisherman's camp, often mostly made of reeds. With no rain, waterproofing is less important than coolness.

Camels occur on some of the Lake's islands.

The Nile may no longer bring silt to its fields, but it does bring salts, dissolved in the water. Modern irrigation systems leave the salt behind – about 250 tons per square mile every year. If the accumulation of salt is allowed to continue, fields will become toxic to plants, and the salt will eventually form a crust that would turn them back to desert. Furthermore, the amount of water that is taken from the River Nile by the countries along its banks is starting to significantly reduce the river's flow, and this, together with declining rainfall in Ethiopia and central Africa due to global warming, may well cause serious problems in the future. Just one example of this massive loss of water is that about 14 per cent of the water contained in Lake Nasser evaporates, reducing the amount of Nile water downstream.

Environmental disaster or not, the discovery of Lake Nasser as a sport-fishing venue was probably one of the most exceptional events in the annals of freshwater sport-fishing history during the past fifty years.

The Fishing Environment and Seasons

Lake Nasser has a large head of smaller fish that provide good sport throughout the year, with frequent captures of fish in the 20–30lb bracket. Most newcomers are surprised when we refer to a twenty- or thirty-pounder as a 'smaller' fish, because the vast majority of freshwater anglers are normally delighted if they catch a fish of even 10lb. But as old hands know well, Nasser is hardly your average lake, and what this means is that you must get Lake Nasser into perspective and decide what it is you really want out of your safari. If you are preoccupied with size of fish, then winter is probably the time to come – but keep in mind that this season has its down sides, such as wind and (relative) cold. Thus there is more chance that you might be holed up for one or two days, losing valuable fishing time, with a strong wind making it impossible to reach the best areas where the perch can be caught.

Also, the shore fishing is not as good as it is during the summer months. In winter, generally speaking, Nile perch lie much deeper in the water than they do in summer, which makes it more difficult to reach them from the shore, and there are fewer of those 'smaller fish' in evidence.

From what we can gather, the reason for this predominance of bigger fish during the winter months is the fact that the large females are on a big feed, building up their energy and eggs prior to spawning in late January and February, in much the same way as the European perch.

If you are looking for exceptional all-round sport with plenty of fish from 15–20lb upwards, then the time to come is between March and July – though that's not to say there are no big fish moving at this time: Darren Lord caught his 202lb 40lb line class world record in June.

The summer months are a good time of the year for both shore fishing and fly fishing, because the Nile perch are in shallower water chasing tilapia, which spawn at this time of year. Then after spawning, the huge population of tilapia fry are growing up and dispersing – all this taking place in water 10 to 20ft deep. May to July are good months because although the weather is hot, the young tilapia fingerlings have put on some weight and provide an additional food source close to the shoreline.

At this time trolling can be very rewarding, working the shallower water and then from time to time looking for big fish in deeper water. (In summer the big fish tend to be more spread out, feeding over a larger area, which makes them a bit more difficult to locate; hence covering ground can pay off.)

The moon phase seems to affect in a small way the quality of fishing. From our own observations, daytime fishing tends to be better during periods of dark nights rather than when there is a moon, and especially a full moon. This is probably because Nile perch also hunt at night – so when there is a full moon their 'sight' sense is more effective, and as a result they probably feed more effectively, leaving them less hungry during daylight hours.

We are often asked, 'What can I expect to catch on a safari?' Fishing being fishing, who knows for sure? Most anglers can expect to capture at least one Nile perch of 50lb plus. Beyond that, anything's possible – perhaps even another world record? We do not like to promise Nile perch of 100lb plus – they are there, and they are often caught: we have broken the last three (IGFA ratified) Nile perch all-tackle world records with fish of over 200lb.

It is also almost impossible to answer the question 'How many fish can I expect to catch in a day?' or 'How big will they be?' Some days you might catch nothing at all, and the next day you might have eight to ten fish, some may be up to 100lb or even more. Barrie's average daily catch is between two and seven fish.

John Wilson of the television *Go Fishing* programme series said:

> Another interesting experience is shore fishing... Where else, for instance, can you work artificial lures from the shore either in fresh or salt water, and encounter fish in the 20–100lb-plus category. Nasser is quite unique in this kind of experience, believe me.

Barrie Rickards, in *'Kings of the Nile' Coarse Fishing* wrote:

> What happened next will stay with me to the end of my life. One second the lure was wobbling quietly towards me, perhaps 25 yards away. The next it was hit with unbelievable power...

Wildlife on Lake Nasser

At night, whilst sitting in camp under the desert stars, one hears all sorts of sounds: frogs, crickets, the call of an owl, howling jackals, nightbird calls and the tantalizing splash of big fish feeding near the camp. When it's quiet and the lights have been turned off, the camp comes alive. Little gerbils have a good scout around for bits of food, and a desert fox or golden jackal is likely to be checking out the rubbish hole. We

TOP LEFT: Stone-curlew are common and nest on tiny islets. (Olivier Portrat)

TOP RIGHT: Awe-inspiring dawns and sunsets are common.

RIGHT: Egrets criss-cross all sections of the lake … (Olivier Portrat)

BELOW: …and are a constant source of pleasure to the angler. (Olivier Portrat)

encourage these remarkably tame animals by feeding them: at several of our camps on the lake, foxes and golden jackals – lovely creatures, about the size of a small Alsatian dog – have become remarkably tame because we feed them.

No matter what time of day the supply boat arrives, one or two of them will come trotting over the hill to welcome us. They will sit quietly for most of the day waiting for night, and as soon as it's dark they seem to lose most of their fear of us and will come as close as 10ft away

ABOVE: A grebe. (Olivier Portrat)

RIGHT: A heron's nest – herons often nest on the ground, trees being rather rare. (Olivier Portrat)

from where we are sitting to pick up the food we put out for them.

We do not feel that by feeding them, on the odd occasion when we happen to be camping where they are, that they will grow reliant on our hand-outs and as a result lose the ability to fend for themselves in the wild.

We are lucky to be able to offer our anglers the experience of seeing these animals so tame and close at hand.

Geology

If there is one thing more conspicuous than the fish and the wildlife on Lake Nasser, it is the rocks. The Nubian Desert is one of the driest on earth, and once away from the shoreline it's rocks, rocks and more rocks (and sand derived from rocks!). Many anglers ask about the rocks and the structures they see in them, so here are a few answers.

Almost all the rocks you see are sandstones, and they are of Jurassic/Cretaceous age (the same age as dinosaurs: roughly 60–200 million years old). Nearer Cairo the Nubian sandstones

RIGHT: Kites and their nests are a frequent sight. (Olivier Portrat)

BELOW: Pelicans. (Olivier Portrat)

ABOVE: Foxes visit almost every camp at night. (Olivier Portrat)

BELOW: Monitor lizards, up to 7ft (2m) long, are often seen in the early morning. (Olivier Portrat)

include some marine beds, but on Lake Nasser most of the sandstones are non-marine, and they include fossil sand dunes (seen in section, on the cliffs, when you are trolling) and parts of fossil river courses and deltas, and probably lake deposits, too.

The sandstones contain fossil plants in places, such as ferns, and larger branches, and in one or two places (as at Maharaga) there are trails in the sandstone of fossil mussels. Another feature of the sandstones is layers rich in iron (the red iron oxide, haematite) and circular, cannonball-like structures of an iron mineral called marcasite (not of jewel quality, sadly!); this last mineral may rot away, leaving a spherical hole in the rock. The sandstones are said to be friable, which doesn't mean that they'll make a welcome addition to the evening meal, but that the sand grains of the sandstone are only poorly cemented together (by

Lizards abound from May onwards. (Olivier Portrat)

the mineral silica – as in silicon chips). And this is the reason you have to be careful when bank fishing, because friable sandstone can collapse beneath your feet! But for the same reason, the sandstone weathers into hollows and caves – and the question is: would the Nile perch fishing be quite so good if the sandstone wasn't friable? The answers to the important things in life are to be found in the rocks.

Other rocks are granites, especially in the northern part of the lake nearer Aswan. These provide islands of giant, rounded, boulder-like outcrops, and the crystals of quartz (silica) and feldspar are large and easily studied.

The Nubian People

We feel it is important to give the reader some background about the Nubian people who are probably, as a race of people, the best Nile perch sport-fishing guides in the world.

When the Aswan High Dam was built in the 1960s the resulting reservoir flooded a 340 mile length (550km) of the Nile of the Nubians' original homeland; they had to abandon all their farms and villages, and were relocated in Egypt and the Sudan. Tim got to know the Nubians

and respected them, so he decided that because the Nile perch were now living in Nubian territory, it would be fitting to crew his safaris exclusively with Nubians. What a good decision that turned out to be.

Throughout the history of Nile perch fishing on Lake Nasser all the safari staff and guides have been Nubians. They are a naturally friendly people with a very relaxed way of life as compared to the 'fast' life we lead in the Western world; perhaps we can learn something from them. You can't beat the Nubians for spontaneous and genuine friendship, and for fun.

The Nubians have a long history, and traditions that can be traced back to the dawn of civilization. Their territory is called Nubia, and it stretched along the banks of the Nile from Aswan to the sixth cataract just south of Khartoum. The Nile river is the main artery for Egypt and Nubia, and is a determining factor of the geography of the region in that the whole area is relatively rainless, and it is only because of the river's annual flood that these areas became habitable.

Along this great river the Nubians developed one of the oldest and greatest civilizations in Africa. Until they lost their last kingdom (Christian Nubia) only five centuries ago, the Nubians and their ancient kingdom of Kush were the main rivals to the other great civilizations of Egypt. As the Ottoman Empire encroached upon the Nubia region in the 1800s, many Nubians migrated to remote areas along the Nile. Distinct groups evolved and were named according to their locations; for example, those who settled near the Wadi Kenuz became known as the Kenuzi, and those in Dongola as the Dongolawi.

Sudan has been the main homeland of Nubians throughout their long history, but now many of their descendants also live in Egypt; with a population of slightly above 350,000, they are a minority in both countries. Being of African descent they resemble other Sudanese people more than they do the Egyptians.

The Nubians were converted to Christianity during the sixth century, and remained of Christian persuasion until they were influenced by the gradual process of Islamization that took place from the fourteenth until the seventeenth centuries. This influx of Arabs into Egypt and Sudan has contributed to the suppression of the Nubian identity. A major part of the Nubian population was totally 'arabized': they were converted to Islam, and the Arabic language became their main media of communication, although they retained two of their old, indigenous Nubian languages – the Kenuzi speak Kenuzi-Dongolawi, while the Fedidja speak Fedidja-Mahas. Most of the men today are bilingual, speaking their Nubian language and Arabic. Women are less likely to speak Arabic, however, especially at home, which means that almost all Nubian children grow up speaking two languages.

Nubians have dark skin and are visibly distinct from their Egyptian neighbours. Despite the strong influence of Arab culture, the majority of Nubians still maintain their own unique characteristics, in their culture (dress, dances, traditions and music) as well as in their indigenous languages, which are still, to this day, the main form of communication among the Nubians themselves.

In old Nubia, men migrated to the big cities to find work, while the women farmed the land, cared for the animals and did household chores. Today, since their newly allocated land is located far from their dwellings, men do most of the field work while the women work at home. Some women have also found employment as schoolteachers, public service workers and seamstresses.

The typical Nubian house is very spacious, with several large rooms able to accommodate the extended family members and guests. In the centre of each home is an open courtyard. The front of the house is colourfully painted with geometric patterns, most of which have religious connotations. The colourful designs are a distinctive and admired feature of Nubian culture.

The distinguishing soft rhythms of Nubian music and songs are borrowed by other ethnic groups in Sudan. In Egypt, these rhythms are commonly used by some Egyptian-Nubians who sing in Arabic. With its very distinctive chanting and intonation, Nubian songs and music are acclaimed and accepted among non-Nubian Sudanese and Egyptians. Nubian singing is one of the memorable features of safaris on Lake Nasser.

Local Fishermen on Lake Nasser

Egypt is very densely populated (65.8 million), and all these millions of people need to be fed. One of the most convenient and accessible forms of food is fish – while the stocks last. In Egypt this need for food has created a vigorous commercial fishing industry. But despite heavy fishing in the Red Sea, the Mediterranean Sea and Lake Nasser and the River Nile itself, Egypt still has to import fish from Russia.

There is no 'modern' commercial fishing on Lake Nasser – by which we mean modern equipment capable of hauling the fish out in huge quantities. The Egyptian government has been wise not to encourage modern commercial fishing because one of Egypt's problems is to find a livelihood for its population, and the policy on Lake Nasser is to give the people work, rather than making only a few very rich.

ABOVE: *Egyptian goose and goslings. These birds seem quite unafraid of Nile perch and crocodiles.*

LEFT: *Crocodiles have been persecuted in the past and are very wary of boats and humans.*

The local fishermen on Lake Nasser are almost all Saidi (people from Upper Egypt) or 'fellaheen' (farmers or peasants), who come to Lake Nasser from villages located in the fertile Nile valley to spend up to three months on the lake living in small, simple camps, mostly on islands close to productive fishing areas. The Nubians themselves are not fishermen, as a general rule.

The Saidi fish Lake Nasser using methods that have changed little over the centuries; an exception is the use of nylon, introduced to make their nets. Their small wooden fishing boats are built on the Nile using the same building methods that have been employed since the days of the Pharaohs. These wooden boats are powered by strange-looking oars with oversize counter-weights on the rowing handle – sometimes just a big chunk of rock strapped on tight. You have to be strong and fit to row one of these boats around a lake all day – or for that matter half the night as well, because most of the serious fishing takes place at night, especially when there is a full moon.

The local fishing boats are manned by two and often three or more fishermen, depending how big the boat is; they use gill nets which they make themselves, to catch tilapia, smaller Nile perch, tigerfish and a species of *Alestes*, a large sardine look-alike. These old methods of fishing are not as efficient as modern scientific methods, but they have helped to maintain viable sport-fishing ventures alongside the need to provide food for the population. Although the old style of com-mercial fishing is the norm on Lake Nasser, it still has some impact on the fish stocks – but the damage is nothing like as great as it would be if modern scientific methods were used.

Long-Term Problems on Lake Nasser

Unfortunately there are some serious problems that will have devastating long-term effects if they are not addressed in the near future. These problems can be summarized as fisheries man-agement, education, destructive fishing meth-ods, nylon pollution, and policing this vast lake.

Sport fishermen go to a great deal of trouble to preserve the fish they capture because they are aware that unless they make a positive effort to try and preserve fish stocks for future genera-tions, there will be no future. But what about the local fishermen, who were there first? Now the sportsman wants to come and share these fish-eries with the locals who kill all the fish they can catch to make a living and feed their families.

On most fisheries in developing countries where sport fishing is still a viable commercial proposition for those who organize fishing trips, the local fishermen are not really very interested in what is going on, and in some cases even find sport fishermen an irritation, especially when their nets are damaged. Because in most cases they do not benefit from any of the money sport fishermen spend, these local fishermen find it hard to understand the reason behind it all. On Lake Nasser, however, we are lucky because the local Egyptian fishermen are good natured, and a naturally hospitable people with an easy-going attitude to life, despite the fact they have so lit-tle in the way of wealth: 'God will provide and look after us,' is their firm belief.

The peasant fishermen on Lake Nasser regard the foreign anglers with a sense of astonished bewilderment. First of all they find it hard to comprehend our wealth and life-style in com-parison with their own. They see our fishing boats and the mother ships, with more servants than there are anglers, and they wonder. And then they see that, after great effort and at huge cost, when a big Nile perch is eventually caught, these strange foreigners put the fish back into the lake, or if the fish is in difficulties they go to great effort and trouble to revive it before returning it. It would be very interesting to read their minds and find out what they really think about us.

There have been many times when Tim, through an interpreter, has been asked the ques-tion 'Why do you return the Nile perch to the lake, especially the big ones?' Tim's reply used to be, 'Well, these fish belong to the people of Egypt, and we come only to catch them for sport.' They don't quite understand the sport side, so we tell them it is rather like football, which they all know about – but how can foot-ball be compared to catching fish? The next question is, 'You say that these Nile perch belong to Egypt and its people, then why don't you catch them and then give them to us?' This leaves Tim in a quandary as to what to say next. Nowadays his standard reply, which seems to be generally understood by the fishermen, is that we have an agreement with the authorities not to disrupt the fishing on Lake Nasser, and that we should return all the fish we catch. Also, foreign tourists bring money into Egypt and provide employment for Egyptians. This they can understand better.

Tilapia is the main food fish caught in Lake Nasser; it breeds naturally here, but there are also three large fish hatcheries that restock the lake with millions of tilapia fry each year. Tiger-fish and *Alestes* are also an important source of food: these two species of fish migrate upstream and are caught in gill nets; after being gutted and cleaned they are soaked in brine, and are eaten rather like soused herring. The cured tigerfish has a very strong taste, and even a small portion will liven up the plain rice that is one of the staple foods of Egypt.

The Potentially Devastating Effects of Longlining

In addition to the traditional net fishermen who target the smaller species of fish in Lake Nasser, there is another group of fishermen who specialize in catching Nile perch. These Nile perch fishermen use three methods with varying degrees of success. The least successful, and one that has not really become established on the lake, is netting – a Nile perch net is rarely found, so we can safely assume that this method is not very useful. This sort of net is very different from the smaller nets you will see the fishermen using for tilapia and tigerfish, in that the overall net is much heavier and the mesh diameter a lot bigger by comparison.

The second method, and one that foreign anglers seem to have helped influence, is casting from the bank using hand-lines. When we first started fishing on Lake Nasser some sixteen years ago, there was very little evidence that the locals were using this method of casting from the shore. In the early days it seemed that a few younger men with little else to do would catch a small tigerfish or an *Alestes*, and then attach it to a length of heavy duty monofilament and cast it from the bank. The time-consuming part of this method was finding and catching the livebait, and then in use it wouldn't last very long on the hook before expiring – the financial reward was therefore never worth the amount of effort involved.

Then foreign anglers came into the picture and introduced lures, and in particular rubber or plastic fish that were much more effective and longer lasting than dead fish. Enterprising merchant suppliers in Aswan soon began importing rubber fish, and hand-lining experienced a surge of popularity from about 1999 onwards. But the method was still hard work, and over the past two or three years the hand-lining method of catching Nile perch seems to be in steady decline.

Dragonflies abound and love the rod rings (but there are no mosquitoes on Lake Nasser). (Olivier Portrat)

Longlining has always been the preferred method of catching Nile perch. As we have mentioned earlier in this chapter, there is no 'modern' commercial fishing on Lake Nasser, and this also applies to the lake's longliners, who still use quite basic methods.

Most longliners are opportunist fishermen who for the most part make their living by catching tilapia, the staple diet fish, which is easier to catch and just as commercially viable as Nile perch. However, there is now a growing number of 'professional' longliners who are becoming better organized, and who are targeting Nile perch full time. Over the past few years the market price of Nile perch has increased and this has encouraged more longliners, with the result that more pressure is being brought to bear on the stocks of Nile perch. Anglers will often be dismayed by the number of longlines in fishing hotspots, and when the fishing is slow the culprit is always considered to be the longliner. However, it is a good idea to get the longliner problem into perspective.

Aside from the 'hotspots', there are literally thousands of other areas on this huge lake where it is not as commercially viable to fish for tilapia or, for that matter, Nile perch, and these smaller pockets will sustain the Nile perch population for many years to come; these smaller areas are harder to find, and are perhaps sometimes not as productive.

Local fishermen have been longlining the Nile dams (and the rest of the Nile system in Egyptian territory) for at least the last hundred years. Over the past fifteen years during which the safaris have been operating on Lake Nasser, the pressure from longlining has remained more or less consistent; however, an increase in the number of longlines has been noticed over the past three years (from 2004) because of a sharp increase in the market price of Nile perch, hence making longlining more commercially viable for the local fishermen.

Longlining is to a certain extent a seasonal effort: it is especially noticeable during the summer months, from approximately mid-March through to the end of August, when Nile perch are more often found in shallower water than during the winter months. It is also hard work, and not as successful as one might at first imagine. There are several difficulties the longliner has to overcome, the least of which is that Nile perch learn the dangers and become wary. Another of his problems is knowing where the best places are for him to lay down his longline. Lake Nasser is a massive body of water, and the local fishermen do not have fish finders to locate the underwater promontories where most of the Nile perch are to be found.

Unfortunately, the visiting angler is now helping the longliners to locate better places to lay their lines. Our fishing guides are inclined to frequent areas where they have caught fish in the past (hotspots), and frequently these places are now also targeted by local fishermen; so the next time we visit the same area we find it strewn with longlines.

Most of the longliners use tilapia fingerlings as bait, but they are not very hardy and die quickly, and will not attract Nile perch if dead. This has resulted in many of the professional longline boats doing their best to catch small squeakers (a species of catfish) and freshwater puffer fish to use as bait, because they are much tougher than tilapia. The problem is that in their efforts to catch squeakers and puffers in the shallow margins, they are also catching tilapia fry, and thousands arc being destroyed. According to the law of the lake, although longlining is permissible, it is not permitted to destroy undersize tilapia fingerlings: they must be allowed to reach a commercial size – but this is obviously not being respected.

And what about the number of longliners operating on Lake Nasser? We have no idea how many longliner fishing boats there are – a lot will depend on the overall number of fishermen populating the lake, which again is an unknown number. Each fishing boat working on the lake is meant to have a licence, but there are a great many illegal fishing boats, and the most popular form of illegal fishing is longlining.

From what we have been told, longlining is also a major problem for sport fishing on Lake Victoria because of the huge number of longlines around the shore of this lake. It is interesting to draw a comparison between the populations living on the edge of Lake Nasser as compared to Lake Victoria. The once fertile land around the edge of Lake Victoria is amongst the most densely populated in East Africa, and this puts a huge fishing pressure on the lake, with so many millions of people to be fed. By contrast, because Lake Nasser is a desert lake, the population living

Golden Jackals are frequently seen around the campsites.

on the shoreline is very small and will remain so for many years to come.

However, yet another problem is caused by the annual flooding of the Nile. This massive inundation makes farming and irrigation difficult simply because the lake rises and falls some 15 to 20ft (4.5–6m) a year. In flat areas that are most suitable for irrigation, vast tracts of the shore are either completely submerged or high and dry for six months of the year.

The destruction of tilapia fry by the longliners is phenomenal, and far outweighs the monetary value achieved by commercially targeting Nile perch using livebait and the longline system. Professional longliners will have three or fours lines in use for each fishing boat; each of these longlines will have between 150 to 200 hooks, making a total of some 700 hooks for each longline fishing boat.

At a conservative average, the longlining season lasts from March into September, which is seven months. As an estimate, we will say that a longline fishing boat will work about 70 per cent of the time, meaning that each longline fishing boat will spend approximately 150 days laying longlines. Baiting 700 hooks for 150 days represents 105,000 tilapia fry killed each year before they can reach a commercial size. To put this waste into perspective, if these 105,000 tilapia fry were allowed to grow into commercial fish of, say, 1lb each, it means that each

longline fishing boat is destroying approximately potentially 105,000lb of commercial tilapia in a year – that is, about 50 tons – and that is the figure for just one longline fishing boat!

We have no real idea as to how many longline boats there are on Lake Nasser. At a conservative estimate let us say there are 150, which means that at least 7,500 tons of commercial tilapia are lost to longliners every year. Unfortunately we must add yet more to this dismal total, because local fisherman, as opposed to professionals, also set out longlines, and there are some 6,000 of them on the lake. Although they get less money per pound, tilapia are a lot easier to catch and they get plenty of them by using gill nets.

These figures are horrifying – but even so, we must still consider the realities, namely that fish reproduce and grow quickly, and Lake Nasser is huge. The lake is the size of a small country, and under normal circumstances produces some 60,000 tons of fish per year.

Thus we might say in conclusion that although longlining is having a gradual effect on the Nile perch population in Lake Nasser, because of the sheer size of the lake and the huge head of fish, this effect *is* only gradual, and it may take many years before the longliners manage to wipe out the Nile perch population. Nevertheless, without proper fisheries management, the situation will only get worse.

5 ANGLING TECHNIQUES IN THE EARLY DAYS

The Nile perch of Africa has always attracted the attentions of anglers. It is, after all, a big fish, and one that fights spectacularly at times, and its upper weight limit on rod and line may not have been achieved, even today.

In Appendix II we give some idea of the wide distribution of Nile perch in Africa. But until organized sport fishing started to take off on

LEFT: Tim Baily in the early days on Lake Nasser, with a big Nile perch.

BELOW: Picture of an early camp. At that time most people slept on canvas on the sand – crocodiles or not!

Lake Victoria in the 1950s and 1960s, rod and line catches were mostly restricted to a few anglers fishing in remote places. These anglers were usually government officials, diplomats or businessmen who happened to be on secondment to one of the African states, and had taken the trouble to sort out some fishing for themselves. For example, if you scan the pages of the *Fishing Gazette* in the 1930s and 1940s you will find occasional pictures, and fewer articles, by Colonel X or businessman Y, with Nile perch in the 30–80lb category. It is what one might broadly term the 'colonial era'. These early catches did cause excitement, however, not only because the fish were big, but also because the locations were exotic and remote, and the stories of the captures were often sagas in themselves, the anglers overcoming many obstacles to do with travel, the physical environment, and the acquisition and use of tackle and bait.

Some of the fish reported in those days were caught on lures cast either from the bank or boat (often a native canoe). Trolling from boats was by far the most common method used – boats were a lot more comfortable than having to battle one's way along an extremely bushy shoreline heavily populated with big game as well as hungry crocodiles and snakes. However, the lures were very rarely what we would call a 'plug' today – rather they were spoons, quite often home-made, or deriving from the House of Hardy salmon-fishing stable.

Now this is interesting, because on Lake Nasser, spoons as such have not as a rule produced fish. Barrie has only had a few Nile perch on spoons, despite a vast amount of effort in his early trips. So it is possible that those pioneer perchers actually caught their fish *in spite of* their lure, rather than because of it – the fish may have been so little fished for, that there was always a chance of something. And it is true that not many of the catches we have seen were of more than one or two fish at a time. A general pattern of 'How to do it' did not, therefore, emerge at that time.

Some Nile perch were caught on live- and deadbaits, the latter sometimes being spun

Another early discovery – that Nile perch destroy lures, hooks and link swivels!

deadbaits, though more unusually a large, dead fish hung beneath a large, cobbled-together float. Some of the bait-caught fish were taken from the bank, but more commonly they were from craft of some kind. Again, no pattern or consistency can be recognized, and they were really one-off adventure-style captures, the angler unusually being involved for most of his time in something that had nothing to do with angling. It was an exciting diversion for him.

When the Nile perch fishers of Lake Victoria came along, the situation started to change. Although originally set up as a commercial fishery for the colonies bordering the lake (Kenya, Uganda and Tanganyika), a sport fishery soon followed. The Nile perch of Lake Victoria came in part from Lake Turkana, but mostly from Lake Albert, and some crossbreeding with *Lates macrophthalmus* means that the Lake Victoria fish are not pure Nile perch.

Nile perch started to gain a reputation as an exotic freshwater fish that could grow to incredible sizes. Many, many catches were made, and

John Wilson in typical smiling mode, with a mega Nile perch of 150lb, his personal best. (John Wilson)

This Rapala SSR has a through-the-body wire, so the fish was still landed.

Small crocodiles are seen frequently, but large ones like this one (dead) are rare.

as well as successful sport fishing on Lake Victoria, other waters were also producing well, such as Lake Turkana and Murchison Falls. However, access to these latter two venues has always been difficult, and they were less of a sport fishery than Lake Victoria.

The techniques used on the East African venues were not dissimilar, although we understand that the use of natural bait was more common on Lake Turkana. Russelures became popular and were very successful, especially on Lake Victoria. These lures look like plugs but are made in various colours of aluminium; they are shiny, and they dig deep with a very strongly vibrating action – and the Nile perch loved them.

Anyone who has seen John Wilson's film about fishing on Lake Victoria will have seen modern lure fishing start to come into play (though it must be said that this kind of fishing had been going on for several years before John made his film). The success on Lake Victoria and at the Murchison Falls probably immediately preceded the discovery of Lake Nasser as a Nile perch sport fishery by Tim. This early pattern of development is also very typical of the early days on Lake Nasser, before the Nile perch started to learn how to avoid the new super-predator, man, and his array of tasty-looking fake food, which trapped the unwary among them. So when Tim began exploring Lake Nasser, he had at least some modern lure-fishing systems in mind. Of course, he quickly developed a whole new range of techniques, and these eventually became a veritable revolution.

The Influence of Safari Anglers

Tim has always maintained that the improvement of fishing techniques on Lake Nasser was brought about by experienced anglers who came to Lake Nasser and passed on their knowledge to Tim and his Nubian guides.

Tim was brought up in the central Kenya bush, and from a very early age spent as much of his spare time as possible hunting and exploring, accompanied by a local tribesman, a reformed African poacher employed by his father to make sure his beloved son was not run over by a rhino or something equally aggressive. Tim learned valuable lessons about bushcraft, but hardly anything about fishing. Later in life he had the opportunity to do quite a lot of deep sea fishing from the Kenya coast, and went fly fishing for trout and salmon in Northumberland alongside his father, a keen fisherman since he was a boy.

Therefore although Tim had the experience and bush knowledge to set up a safari operation in the wilderness of Lake Nasser, he was at a disadvantage in that he had no real experience of modern fishing techniques and watercraft. However, he learned this skill from constant observation, and in particular from watching the skilled visiting anglers who came on safari with him, often from the UK.

The Nubian guides on Lake Nasser also went through the same learning curve as Tim. Their original fishing experience merely covered the necessities of life, which was to catch fish as a food source, and the techniques they used could hardly be called sporting: their original objective being to catch as many fish as possible in a short time, they used such methods as nets and long-lines. But they quickly adapted to modern sport-fishing methods because they really enjoy fishing for sport, and get a real thrill from seeing an angler catch his fish of a lifetime.

LEFT: *Tim Baily with a fish of 186lb, one of the early giants.*

BELOW: *Tim with a gigantic Nile perch of 155lb.*

6 MODERN TECHNIQUES AND TACKLE

You may have got the impression from the previous chapter that with the notable exception of angling on Lake Victoria, fishing for Nile perch was a bit of a 'hit and miss' affair – and there is some truth in that before Lake Nasser came on the scene. Even on Lake Victoria, trolling techniques may have been a little stereotyped – though this may not matter in the early days on a fishery. In this chapter we want to give a flavour of the basic bank and boat techniques that we have learnt over the years, coupled with the approach work necessary to succeed.

Bank Fishing

So you are on the banks of Lake Nasser for the first time, surrounded by wall-to-wall sunshine, and for most of us the water is BIG. You may not be able to see the opposite bank. So where do you start, and where on earth are the fish in such an expanse of water? The answer is: under your feet. For most of the time the Nile perch, like its humble British cousin, likes to hug features such as rock piles, overhangs, individual large boulders, sunken dead trees, or sunken islands or drop-offs.

Many fish are very close to the bank, and if you know where to look you may see small groups of very large fish mooching around within a yard of the water's edge. Barrie well remembers one early trip in which Tim took him to a cliff overhang: they peeped, very cautiously, over the edge and there below them were half a dozen fish averaging 60lb each, and a monitor lizard of 6ft long swimming with them. Barrie was moved carefully into position by Tim, about 30yd along the bank. His first cast, with a Rapala Super Shad

Walking the dog!

Rap in perch coloration, was taken with violence, and the result was a spectacular fight and an 80lb fish. The fish became airborne several times, as well as making long, deep runs, which somehow managed to evade boulders about the size of a small car, and was eventually landed.

That, then, is tip number one for bank fishing: look for the fish. Tip number two is to tread quietly and be as inconspicuous as you can be. Sometimes there may be no cover except rock walls at your back, and in those circumstances avoid sudden movements and wear clothes that blend into your surroundings. Generally there is enough cover in the form of boulders or rock ledges, but you must always tread lightly and try to avoid dislodging loose debris (also for your own safety).

The basic bank-fishing technique is, therefore, to use your eyes and creep around carefully, casting into likely places close to the bank. What are likely places if you haven't been lucky enough to see fish? Well, rocky overhangs and steep rock walls are well worth a try, as are ledges of rock running out into the lake, or piles of boulders just offshore. For all this you need only a rod, and a bag or bucket full of lures, plus, of course, a camera and a pair of pliers to unhook the fish.

You will rarely be on your own: almost always one of the team, a Nubian guide, will be there to lift the fish out of the water. The actual landing and handling of the Nile perch forms the subject of another chapter, because it is very important and has its own problems.

On the boats you can carry all manner of extra equipment that you wouldn't dream of lugging along the bank – boxes of lures, for example, or butt pads. You will also have weighing equipment, a box of weights, traces, swivels and so on. You will, in fact, have everything you need, because as a rule you'll be sleeping on the boat: it is your home for a week, or more.

To improve your watercraft one of the first lessons to be understood is that most fish are not as dumb as you might think they are – especially Nile perch. It is a well known fact that many species of fish quickly learn to avoid hooks and lures – and not just the fish that have been hooked, either. Our freshwater fisheries' biologist friends in Australia publicize the fact that barramundi are famous for their ability to learn the danger posed by anglers. The barramundi is one of the closest scientific relatives to the Nile

perch, which leads us to conclude that Nile perch have a similar survival instinct. Although Australian fisheries' biologists fully support and encourage 'catch and release', they also point out that 'catch and release' is starting to cause problems on some barramundi fisheries in the Northern Territories, where populations of uncatchable barramundi are increasing. These uncatchable barramundi survive, and grow to sizes that create a lot of damage to re-stocking programmes because they eat large numbers of introduced fingerlings.

In a wild fishery such as Lake Nasser, 'catch and release' is critically important to the survival of the fishery. But Tim believes there is a huge number of uncatchable Nile perch in Lake Nasser that are a contributing factor to the decline in catch rates on the lake. Nature has given Nile perch, like any other wild animal, a basic survival instinct without which a species would not survive. This survival instinct works against the angler who in reality is the 'super predator' – and we are doing it just for fun! Fish swim in shoals, and may have a communal warning system: when one fish gets spooked, the rest may get spooked in exactly the same way as a herd of deer, which without any hesitation will follow a warning signal given by a member of the herd, all taking off in a panic until the danger has been recognized.

Understanding this survival instinct will help you catch more fish. Part of it is to try and think

A big Nile perch could engulf your head – easily.

A big double: two fish over 150lb each for two German anglers. (Olivier Portrat)

like a fish; not that a fish actually thinks: it reacts and its survival instinct quickly teaches it to avoid potential danger. We have seen very many examples of this phenomenon of Nile perch learning about the danger posed by lures, and also the sound of boat engines: there is absolutely no doubt about it.

There are many hotspots on Lake Nasser where it is very obvious the Nile perch have learnt about lures and boat engines. One particular shore-fishing hotspot comes immediately to mind, and that is Maharaga, a beautiful peninsula of mainland and rocky islands about an hour and a half's boat ride out of Garf Hussein on the southern shore of the huge Wadi Allaqi. Here you can walk up a small hill from the beach where we park the fishing boats, and when you get to the top of the hill you can look down about 80 to 100ft (25–30m) almost sheer, into the lake, and see huge Nile perch basking in the

margins. Talk about a knee-wobbling event – it's unreal! Just imagine looking down and seeing four or five Nile perch of between 50 and 100lb quietly swimming backwards and forwards below you. On rare occasions we have counted up to twenty of these big fish enjoying the warmer water in the verges just a foot or two below the surface.

Lures and Baits

In the early days when we started a safari at Garf Hussein Tim used to boast to the anglers: 'One of you is going to catch a big Nile perch on the first cast of this safari!' – and sure enough it worked almost every time! There are still quite a few areas on Lake Nasser where one can climb across the top of shore-fishing areas and look down and see Nile perch basking, and then stalk

ABOVE: A giant Nile perch being released…always a good moment.

BELOW: This big fish gives you some idea of the size of its head and mouth – which could engulf yours easily. (Olivier Portrat)

them to pit your skill against their natural survival instinct. We are trying to look after these areas by not fishing them too heavily, and when we do, we fish them carefully, causing as little disturbance as possible.

Nile perch have a simple lifestyle, and there are basically only three main themes throughout their life: eat, reproduce and survive. Of the three, eating is the most important because basically if they don't eat, they die! To be more successful an angler needs to understand two of the Nile perch's life themes, namely eating and the survival instinct. So why do fish react to one particular type of lure? Is it movement, vibration, colour, shape, size, or something else, and how does the fish find the bait?

A lively topic among anglers is, 'Do fish see in colour, or do they just see in shades?' The most accepted theory is that fish only see in shades. How many times have we all fished exclusively with one particular coloured lure, convinced that it is its colour stimulating the strikes? Hundreds of times, and we all have our own favourite colour – but is it really *colour* that is making a difference, or is it a shade of grey, seen in a particular light? Then we might ask ourselves the question, 'Why then are prey fish camouflaged?' Has nature provided them with a colour camouflage, or a shade camouflage? It is more likely to be a shade camouflage. One of Lake Nasser's favourite lure colours is gold, but is a Nile perch really stimulated by a *gold* fish, or does this colour provide a more visible shade in lower light conditions and thus fool the fish into striking?

In the water sound and vibration travel faster than in the atmosphere, and this must play an important part in the fish's sensory system when they are hunting. Fish can feel their prey quite some distance away, through their lateral line which is linked to their central nervous system. This leads us to believe that one of the first ways a predator detects its prey is by the swimming movement, which creates a vibration they quickly become aware of. So now we have a Nile perch that is lying in ambush and has been stimulated by vibration and is tensing up ready to go for it. Vision then plays a part, but in low-visibility water vision is limited to only a few feet and is probably used to confirm the target at the last moment.

By this stage the fish is committed – so is the colour important? Probably not, if we have agreed that colour makes hardly any difference. We then have to start thinking about the other methods Nile perch use to locate their prey, or for that matter a lure. We have come to believe that Nile perch do most of their feeding and hunting at night because they are following *Tilapia niloticus* (bream), which are in the habit of spending the daylight hours in deeper water, and then converging on the weed beds in shallower water at night (Lake Nasser's species of *Tilapia* are weed eaters). This night feeding is borne out by the local fishermen who fish mostly at night and tell us the same story about the tilapia's feeding habits.

So how do we explain Nile perch locating their prey at night? Is it colour? We don't think so – humans cannot really see colours in darkness, it is mainly shades that are seen. The first thing that would draw the perch to its prey would almost certainly be vibration, or some sort of sound, and finally a dark silhouette against the low surface light.

An unsuspecting tilapia (or tigerfish) swims into range, and the ambushing perch darts out and grabs it, then goes back to the rock and waits for more food. This particular ambush has taken place in about 10 or 12ft of water, and next a lure comes into range. First, the ambushing perch will have sensed/'heard' the lure swimming into range, and when it looks up it will see a silhouette with no particular colour, just shades reflected by the light from the surface of the water, similar to the tilapia that it has just eaten. Will our perch, waiting in ambush, grab the lure in the same way that it did the unfortunate tilapia? This will depend on several issues.

If he is hungry, the likelihood of a strike is much higher, especially when our ambushing perch realizes it might have competition from other perch waiting nearby. Competitiveness

> **Scent and Catfish**
>
> With some species of fish, smell plays an important part, for example catfish, but we don't think smell is of great importance with a predator such as Nile perch. Catfish are scavengers and rely on their sense of smell to locate their preferred rotting food. When fishing for Vundu catfish on Lake Kariba in Zimbabwe the most popular bait is a chunk of the local blue soap, and the reason for its success is because part of the ingredient for making this soap is an animal fat that slowly dissipates, giving off a 'smelly' slick that is picked up by Vundu from some distance away.

has been the downfall of many perch, even those that have become lure shy, and it is a strong instinct with the smaller perch that have to eat a lot to grow quickly. There have been many, many occasions when an angler is fighting, say, a 10 to 15lb perch, when suddenly the fighting perch becomes twice as strong – and when the angler has eventually got the perch within sight they will be amazed to see not one, but *two* fish hooked on the same lure. This happens when a competing perch spots something hanging out of the first fish's jaw and darts in to pull it away, and then finds itself hooked to the end of a protruding lure.

To return to our perch still waiting in ambush and now watching a lure swimming past – is it going to dart out and grab the lure? As it looks up at the silhouette, might it be unconsciously assessing the shape of its intended prey? Most lures have a fish shape, and the ones that look most like a tilapia are the Rapala SSR and another lure recently added to the African Angler lure arsenal, the Manns Stretch Imitator Junior, with a deep body and a perfect tilapia shape.

Nile perch are also keen on a tigerfish meal, so the Depth Raiders and Rapala Magnum series, and many other lures of elongated shape, will emulate that of a torpedo-shaped tigerfish. Then there is the swimming action of the lure,

'I'm keeping the lure,' says this veritable giant in excess of 150lb. (Olivier Portrat)

and the more it looks like a wounded bait fish the better, because that signifies easy prey. We do not need to worry too much about vibrations, although our perch will already have detected them, because when we fish it is daylight and the prey has already been sighted.

Next, the size of the lure might be considered. If the ambushing perch is small, the size of the prey will not matter very much, but our ambushing perch is big and well into the 100lb category. Without being conscious of its mental reactions, our big perch is now assessing the value of chasing the prey – why? Because of the high water temperatures perch have a high metabolic rate, which means the more they move, the more they will have to eat to replace used-up energy. Exactly the

same instinct exists in mammal predators: you will never see a pride of lion dashing around chasing antelope all over the place.

The size of the lure looks reasonable and it's close, well within striking range, and will be worth the effort for the protein energy return. All these instincts flash past in a second because the predator has to act quickly before the prey has a chance to escape.

So far things are starting to look good from the perspective of our perch lying in ambush, and it's starting to tense up for a strike. But wait a moment, what is that movement on the bank? Old survival instinct comes into play, inherited through its gene system from the time it was a speck of a fingerling. Danger on the bank –

herons, monitor lizards or a crocodile – but this shape is much bigger! Then any thought of its meal is forgotten as every instinct tells it to get away as fast as possible. And the angler on the bank retrieves the lure, blissfully unaware that they have just missed hooking a 100-pounder.

Our account of a big perch lying in ambush covers some of the main issues that might lead up to a strike. Other circumstances might include curiosity or aggression. Anything that swims is potentially edible and worth assessing for its food value, and because fish do not have a pair of hands to pick up and inspect things with, all potential food will go straight into its mouth – and if it is not suitable, it will be quickly regurgitated.

While fighting a Nile perch, the angler might get the impression that the fish has just thrown the hook when they see something fly out of its mouth: but often this is the fish's natural reaction for trying to get rid of the lure, by emptying its stomach of its contents, and what the angler has seen is a half-digested fish from the perch's last meal fly out of its mouth.

Proud of his dad. A family affair as a giant is returned. (Olivier Portrat)

Tackle

As you can see, the Nile perch needs a canny and thinking approach, but the tackle has to be basically sound as well, so let's have a look at that next.

At the outset it is important to realize that Nile perch in most waters are accompanied by one major problem, and that problem is called a tigerfish! The Nile perch has no teeth, only a rasping plate or two, whereas the tigerfish has very serious teeth that you will do well to avoid. But the tigerfish takes the lures intended for Nile perch, and sometimes more frequently than the latter. If you had only Nile perch to contend with, then you wouldn't need a trace of any kind, and you could fish on monofil or braid straight through to the lure.

Or could you? We do need to digress very slightly to discuss mono and braid. You still hear it said that braid is abrasion resistant: it isn't. At least, it is not as resistant as mono in similar breaking strains, and we have tested this in the laboratory as well as in real fishing. Put it this way: take an 80lb braid and an 80lb mono piece, and rub them against the corner of a brick. You will find that the braid gives up relatively quickly

compared with the mono. In real fishing situations braid cuts through on rocks in a flash, when the same breaking strain of mono gets you out of trouble. So whatever else you do in terms of your end rig, you cannot fish braid straight through to the lure: you need a mono trace of about 6ft length. We'll return to the manner of its connection to the braid line if you happen to be using braid (for example, for its casting abilities from the bank).

The Link Swivel Problem
In the early days on Lake Nasser we used a wire trace up to 5ft or so long. This was helpful in the rocks, and also prevented tigerfish from biting through the line down near the lure, but the trace had to be attached to the reel line and this we did, quite sensibly we thought, by means of a swivel. But it turned out to be not a good idea, because the tigerfish also attacked the swivel and, naturally, they immediately bit through the line, be it braid or mono. Picture this: you are trolling along quite happily, the Rapala Super Shad Rap throbbing away beautifully, and suddenly, with barely a tap at the rod end, the line goes slack. You reel in to find nothing but a severed end – and a few moments later an RSSR pops up to the surface. At least you get your lure back if it's a floater, but if it's a sinker you've just lost a tenner.

So what next? Some of us put transparent plastic tubing over the swivel, pushing it into a firm fit. This does work, but it is seriously ugly. The tigerfish still attack it, but all they do is gradually shred the plastic, and you are unlucky if you get a bite-off, fishing like this. So yes, this is a method you can employ.

But – and there is always a 'but' in Nile perch fishing – the one thing we have avoided mentioning so far is the actual attachment of the lure to the trace, whether the latter is thick mono (say, 60–100lb bs), or wire. Again, quite naturally one would think, anglers used heavy-duty link swivels, and for a while at least many got away with it; but Nile perch make mincemeat of even the toughest swivels – and we are not exaggerating here. Swivels with a breaking/

straightening strength of 180lb have been mangled as though they were paper clips. This is not because the fish impart a pull in excess of 180lb, but because the Nile perch battle involves the fish diving, spiralling and twisting. It is the twisting that does the damage, especially if the fish is close to being landed and it couples twisting with airborne antics and serious thrashing of the water. You can test this at home, not with a Nile perch but with a pair of pliers: first, try a serious straight pull on a giant swivel: the chances are that you will be quite unable to straighten the loop. Now take a pair of good pliers and twist it – and you will find it easy to twist out of shape, and from then on it's a short journey to being opened up.

You can see now the sorts of problems we are getting into. On the one hand we have twisting Nile perch, and on the other hand the tigerfish. Of course, we are not trying to dismiss the tigerfish as an inferior species, and we, and many others, fish for it regularly (we touch on this elsewhere in the book).

So what can you do about the link swivel problem? Well, one thing we have tried, which works well, is to tape it up with insulating tape. This is a fiddle, but it does prevent the swivel from being twisted out of shape. Barrie has used this method extensively, and so far has not lost a fish through the link swivel being damaged.

There is a down side, however, in that the tape needs to be about ½in wide and 2in long. That is easy enough, because insulation tape comes in rolls of the right dimensions, but each time you change the lure the very advantage of a link swivel – quick change – is lost because it takes a little while to get the old tape off, and a little longer to put on the new piece. All this discourages you from changing lures when you know – or sense – that you should do so. Even worse, having put on the new lure, you forget to put on the tape, or can't be bothered – and then you could be in trouble with the next fish you hook. It is perhaps worth emphasizing that it does not need to be a big fish in order for a link swivel to be damaged: a fish of 20 or 30lb could easily do it. This method of taping up the link swivel is also rather ugly. Even so, it does work.

What else can one do? The lure can be attached directly to the trace line (let us say it is 100lb bs mono) by means of a Rapala knot. This knot has the advantage of allowing the lure a very free movement (as do the best link swivels, but not all of them), and it doesn't take too long to tie. We have used this a lot. OK, it is a bit of a discouragement to changing a lure, but it is not too bad.

We should also mention that even if you are using a link swivel, you still have to knot the trace line to it. Under these circumstances, Barrie uses a half blood knot. Although this is decried in many angling circles, the wet strength of a half blood knot properly tied is around 90 per cent. Barrie once had about 1,000lb of Nile perch in a week on one half blood knot, and it wasn't retied in the whole of that week. You can add a blob of superglue to such a knot if it worries you at all, but properly tied it will not slip. Or you can use the more popular grinner knot that the inventor – Richard Walker – always claimed was superior to the half blood knot.

By now you will have noticed that we have not discussed joining the mono trace to the reel line, whether the latter is mono or braid. There are various knots used for joining two bits of line – such as the widely used overhand knot – especially if the diameters are different. One might expect, for example, that the braid reel line will be of smaller diameter than the 100lb bs mono trace. Or if you are bank fishing with mono reel line, again, the trace will be much thicker than the reel line, which might be only 30lb bs line. Once again, though, the half blood knot – or rather, two half blood knots, back to back – can be used. This is a highly efficient way of joining two lines of even quite different thickness. You can add a drop of superglue if you are not sure about it.

This very last point brings us almost full circle in our arguments, because lines so joined do away with the need for a swivel, and hence also do away with tigerfish attacks on the join – tiger-

fish don't seem to attack knots very often. So far, so good…

At this stage we should mention the bimini knot for attaching a lure to the trace line. This knot was developed in big game fishing, and it is the favourite knot of some of our Nubian guides in Lake Nasser. Tim has very considerable experience of using it. Probably its only down side is the time it takes to tie it, which must surely inhibit its use if a lot of lure changing is envisaged or becomes necessary.

None of what we have written about so far has been covered by anglers fishing for Nile perch elsewhere, but on Lake Nasser huge catches have been, and are made regularly, and this has been going on for about fifteen years.

When huge catches are made (Barrie had fifty Nile perch on his first trip to Lake Nasser) the weaknesses of traditional approaches are soon exposed: you really do not want your line bitten through frequently by tigerfish, or the swivel mangled by lively Nile perch.

So where have we got to? First, do not use swivels to join the reel line to the trace: use a knot such as the overhand, double half blood or grinner, or any other knot in which you have confidence. Second, do not use link swivels unless they are seriously protected from being twisted open. You may prefer a Rapala knot, a bimini knot, or a half blood knot. Third, use a monofil trace of quite thick mono, say 60–100lb bs, and preferably closer to the latter. If you could get fluorocarbon traces of around 100lb bs, and as long as these were not prohibitively expensive, it might make the best material of all.

This still leaves us with the problem of the tigerfish that attacks the lure itself – and make no mistake, this happens often. If the lure is very large – say, a Rapala Super Shad Rap, or even larger or longer – then the danger of a bite-off is relatively low, except on a bad day; but if you are using smaller lures such as rubber jigs, then the risk is proportionally greater. Tigerfish often hit the lure amidships, which also lessens the chance of a bite-off – if you look at the tooth marks on a lure they are nearly always amidships. Having hit the lure the tigerfish will often cartwheel spectacularly, and at this stage its teeth may tangle up with the trace mono – but you'd be unlucky if that happened. This is where we are now: most of us prefer to take a slight chance on a tigerfish bite-off and attach the trace to the lure by means of a rapala knot, a half blood knot or a bimini knot, or sometimes by means of a taped-up link swivel of substantial proportions. But surely the best thing would be for manufacturers to devise a link swivel that could survive twisting?

In 2006 Barrie tried another means of attachment, and this does have possibilities: it is Ad Sweir's spiral steel wire trace for pike fly fishing! It is a 6in length of piano wire, stiff, with a loop at one end (to which the monofil trace line can be attached with a half blood knot) and a turn-back of wire at the other end, which is wrapped in a spiral around the shank of the trace wire. To attach the lure you simply hook up the lure nose ring, and spiral it to the bottom of the trace where it clicks into the final loop. So far we've had no problems with this, but it has only landed a few fish up to 40lb weight, so it is early days.

Just before release: checking all is well.

The Reel Line

Now we are on somewhat safer ground. There is, of course, a choice to be made between monofil and braid. On the bank, braid is probably the best bet because you can fish strong lines of reasonably small diameter, and still be able to cast well. For example, a braid of 50–60lb bs can easily be cast from the bank, whereas a mono of that breaking strain could not be. Furthermore, the heavier braid gives a better chance of landing a really big fish. Barrie's best bank-caught fish was around 120lb, but the shore record is nearer 200lb, so very big fish can be expected from the bank, and fish of over 50lb are *often* caught there. Similarly, when casting from a drifting or anchored boat, braid is probably the best bet, simply because of the extra casting distance obtained from the same breaking strain.

When trolling, however, the matter is not so clear cut. Many prefer to use braid, but heavy monos of 50–60lb bs can easily be used, and they have the advantage that if a perch goes round a headland of boulders, then you at least stand a chance with mono – with braid you've had it. We're not going to talk brands with respect to either braid or mono: at these breaking strains it probably doesn't matter a great deal. We prefer clear (mono) or dull colours rather than the garish colours that sea anglers seem to use these days. Given that there may be plenty of weed or algae around, then a dull green mono is a good alternative to clear mono.

Some anglers prefer lighter lines than the one we have mentioned, sometimes going down to 20lb for shore fishing. We are uneasy about this, not least because the fish can be very big. Barrie's first big fish from the shore was an eighty-pounder, and he seriously doubts if he would have landed it on anything less than the 35lb bs used at the time: it gave a tremendous fight and had to be steered clear of boulders as big as lorries. John Wilson, in his videos, is shown using lighter lines, but he is very experienced, more so than either of the authors. In fly fishing, too, there is a certain amount of worry as far as bank fishing goes. It's not so much the fly line itself, but the leader. The main line is strong enough as a rule, but the leader surely needs to be 30lb bs at least. This is discussed further in the chapter on fly fishing for Nile perch.

Finally, we should mention the backing line. This can be dispensed with, of course, and the spool simply loaded right through with the reel line. Alternatively, a longer length of slightly weaker line can be used, say 30lb bs mono or 40lb bs braid. Generally this will not be called upon, but you never know… One lady angler had over 200yd of line stripped off against the clutch before the line finally snapped on the retaining knot. The line was found floating, because it was braid, the very next day, was reattached to the reel, and a Nile perch of 95lb landed. So allow for trouble and have a good length of backing.

Choice of Reel

Once again we are on relatively safe ground here, although personal preference is important. There was a time when all boat fishing was done with multipliers, and bank fishing with either a multiplier or a fixed spool reel. We now know that fixed spool reels are perfectly satisfactory for trolling, just as they are for shore fishing – but if you prefer using a multiplier, then use one. We use both, as the fancy takes us. You'll see some rather strange idiosyncrasies. For example, a bank angler will use a left-hand wind, fixed spool reel for bank fishing, and then a right-hand wind multiplier on the troll. It doesn't make sense. If you are right-handed, then the multiplier handles should be on the left, and not the right (and the opposite if you are left-handed). On the boat this may not be so critical, and if an angler prefers to lever a big fish with his non-drinking arm, then that's his business – but from the shore it's a different matter. The take and initial run of a big Nile perch is so fast that any delay caused by changing the rod from one hand to the other

can result in a fish lost in the rocks. You do have to be 100 per cent ready and in action from the word go, and simply may not have time to swap hands. Naturally, quite a few experienced anglers can manage in ambidextrous mode, but it should be admitted that that is just what they are doing: managing to cope.

Again, we do not want to mention particular brands of reels because everyone has their favourites, and most major brands are fine. It pays to use a fairly big fixed spool reel, but you can use, for example, a Shimano Bait Runner that you'd use for pike fishing. That gives you some idea. Multiplier reels do not need to be big game types, but they do need to be much larger than those used on single-handed bait-casting rods. Nor do reels need to be expensive: Barrie's fixed-spool reels are big sea reels that cost around £20 each, which is hardly bank-breaking.

Clutch or Backwind

This is a difficult matter. The best starting point is to emphasize that, on the strike, the Nile perch accelerates away so fast that one simply cannot rely on backwinding. On the other hand, a clutch set too light can result in tens of yards of line disappearing off the spool far too quickly: every yard gone takes the fish closer to snags. When Barrie's clutch has been set by someone else it has almost always been set too light, and the only fish he has lost on the initial run (three fish) have been with the clutch set incorrectly by someone else. Set the clutch fairly firm so that the fish has to work for the line, and keep the spool spindle well oiled (some clutches need oil or grease as well); this will also have the effect of helping to set the hooks, because the initial jaw clamp of a Nile perch may actually prevent the hooks moving a fraction. If there is little or no clutch resistance when the fish runs, then the hooks will not shift into purchase position. On the contrary, cause a little drag and the hooks will not only shift position, locating a hold for one or more hook points, but the fish will have greater difficulty throwing them.

You can still have backwind as a standby, as we have done on many occasions. Sometimes, when the rod is really hooped over, the clutch mechanism can seize up, and at that moment backwinding can save the day. It goes without saying that you cannot backwind if the anti-reverse lever is in the 'on' position, so if you habitually keep this in the 'on' position early in the fight, then you should turn it off during the fight or you will lose the fail-safe facility of backwinding.

In terms of boat fishing and clutch setting, there is one further matter, and that relates to the speed of the troll and the ability of the boat handler to bring the boat to a standstill. If the boat travels forwards 20–30yd after a strike, and the Nile perch runs 30yd in the opposite direction, that's up to 60yd *in seconds* between you and the fish. Sixty yards of free line increases the chances of the perch reaching a rock or sunken tree – where he may have struck out from in the first place, as we explained earlier in the chapter. Sometimes you have to troll fast, and sometimes slowly, but if the former the boatman should be ready to slam on the brakes, so to speak, even if he has to turn the boat sharply at the same moment. Anything else is loose fishing. A clutch set too light, lines that are too weak, rods too soft (*see below*), all lead to prolonged playing of Nile perch, and is at least contributory to over-tired fish. Personal preferences come into play, of course, but try to remember the fish at all times: bully it in, and it will be fine on its return.

Choice of Rods

This is an interesting subject, but we have reached a measure of consistency in recent years as a result of a great deal of fishing. Let us consider bank fishing first. Here a longer rod is preferred because the margins can be – and usually are – very rocky, and maybe with a weed fringe. You can manage with a short bait-casting rod, and many do, but the problems arise as the fish nears the bank for landing, when you have much less control with a shorter rod. There is also a point early in many fights when to get the rod up high helps to keep the Nile perch away from snags and sunken bushes. Generally, then, we prefer a longer rod. To give you an idea, any of the 12ft rods normally used by pike anglers, with a test curve of 2½–3¼lb, is about right, can be used with braids up to 60lb, and is powerful enough to land almost any fish from the bank, bar catfish perhaps. If your preference is for a multiplier reel then you may want to opt for a shorter rod, possibly 9 or 10ft, though the advantages to you of the multiplier – smoothness and accuracy – may be lost as the rod is shortened, as we pointed out above. It becomes a matter of preferences, confidence and of balancing one variable against another.

On boats, the whole business may become reversed: that is, most prefer shorter, pokier rods down to around 7 or 8ft. Even so, our own experience is that the long, 3lb test-curve bank rod will suffice, and we have seen several Nile perch in excess of 100lb landed on them. They enable you to keep the lure just outside the bubble and turbulence trail of the outboard motor, although they do have the drawback that the rod tip bends quite a bit on a fast troll. On the other hand, should you wish to change from casting from a drifting boat it is much easier to do this with the long rod than the short, especially if the latter is coupled with a non-bait-casting multiplier. And similarly, you may wish to do a quick session on the bank, and here also the long rod comes into its own. Many of us have both types of rod on the boat, and simply switch from one to the other. (This does mean carrying more rods through the airports, though most safari firms do hire out rods and reels.)

The short rods need to be a bit stiffer than the long rods, and usually are, of course. Sea rods of the 20lb–30lb class are fine (test curves are not usually given for sea rods). Our preference is to use them with a multiplying reel (but *see above*), and braid for reel line. A great deal of braid can be loaded on the spool, the braid cuts a bit deeper in the water than does mono of the same breaking strain, and you can feel the bump of rocks or the drag of weed rather more easily than you can with mono. Nor do you have quite the same worry with bankside rocks when on the boat, although a big Nile perch will head there given half a chance.

7 PLAYING AND HANDLING NILE PERCH

Barrie's actual average weight of Nile perch caught on Lake Nasser is just under 22lb. From the boats he has had three fish in excess of 100lb, and from the bank one such fish, his biggest, of 120lb. With weights like this, how you handle the fish is clearly an important matter.

We'll begin by discussing striking and playing, before going on to the actual landing of fish. In effect the angler doesn't strike: the fish does – and how! As a rule the lure is hit with great speed and ferocity, and before the angler can react, the fish is running, fast. You are never in any doubt that you have a frantic fisherman at one end of the line and a vigorous problem at the other. You should clamp down on the fish as soon as possible: make it work for its line. If it seems to be going deep, then get the rod up high because the chances are it is heading for a sunken rock or two.

You can always tell if the fish is about to leap, and they do so frequently, because you can feel the line coming upwards with quite a surge. It is best to lay the rod over somewhat so that when the head goes airborne it is dragged over. This keeps the line tight, and it may – may – stop the perch shaking its head in the air. When they shake their heads they often throw the lure. In part this may well be because the fish is not actually hooked. Nile perch have very powerful jaws, which you can feel for yourself by putting your hand in the fish's mouth and letting it close (don't do this if there is a lure in there!). So what happens is that when they hit the lure, they simply clamp it in their jaws. They may not be able to shake it loose when the line is taut, but they can do so if they create a little slack line when shaking their heads. However, when a Nile

Tim Baily demonstrating how to handle a big fish at the boatside.

perch leaps very close to the landing spot, say a couple of yards away, it may be better to *create* a little slack line rather than keeping it taut. After all, the fish will be hooked by then, the hooks with a good purchase, and keeping the line tight on such a short line may result in the hook straightening or the link swivel (if in use) twisting out of shape. Either way, it's a lost fish.

Bearing in mind what we have said about the fish not necessarily being hooked, it is clearly important to keep a very tight line, and if the runs slow down, to effect a moderate strike. This may not always be necessary or, indeed, possible. It also follows from this that you do not want the clutch set too light. We dealt with this matter in the last chapter, so will merely emphasize here that the fish should be made to work. This helps set the hooks, and also tires the fish more quickly, which, as we shall explain below, is preferable to having a long drawn-out battle (from the point of view of the fish, that is).

Correct and Incorrect Procedures for Handling Fish

This chapter is really all about what the Americans call 'catch and release'. A sports angler on Lake Nasser does not intend to kill captured Nile perch, which is why we are now going to devote a whole chapter explaining how to keep

perch in good shape in order to return them to their habitat in good condition. A Nile perch is too valuable a resource, and a personal commitment to conservation adds a lot more fun and meaning to fishing. Almost all sport fishing venues around the world now practise a 'catch and release' policy, and nowadays all sensitive anglers get upset when a big fish they have caught dies. Much of what we write about in this chapter is a matter of common sense, which most anglers understand and appreciate. There is also another side, which is the scientific research that has been conducted into the correct or incorrect procedures for handling fish – especially bigger fish. The bigger they are, the gentler you will have to be.

The Gassing-Up Problem

A few years ago, Tim had the good fortune to meet up with a group of senior freshwater fisheries biologists who work for the Queensland

Weighing a big fish is always carried out in weigh slings.

TOP: *It's not about to eat him! Olivier Portrat just let the fish go, and it swims off safely. (Olivier Portrat)*

ABOVE: *Barrie with a big bank-caught fish 'on the lead', allowing it to recover before photographing it.*

Government Department of Primary Industries. These biologists are responsible for fisheries research covering the huge barramundi farming and leisure industry in Australia, and as part of their studies they have also carried out research into the possibilities of farming Nile perch. Much of the research these Australian biologists have conducted concerning barramundi also applies to Nile perch – and this includes the gassing-up problem.

Sometimes Nile perch are a problem in this respect after landing. *It doesn't happen very often,* but very occasionally the fish is unable to swim away. It has a buoyant look about it, and is unable to dive. If it is nursed gently in shallow,

71

well oxygenated water, it may well recover and swim off – but only about 50 per cent of the time, which is not good enough: so why does this happen?

Barrie feels the most common factor is that the fight has lasted too long, so the fish is exhausted. This is similar to the problem some British and Irish pike anglers have experienced, where the consensus of opinion is that the pike has come up too quickly from too great a depth, which has caused it to 'gas up'.

This also happens to Nile perch that are hooked in deep water. The reason is, that perch are not always able to vent the expanding air from their swim bladders when they are played up quickly from deeper water. We believe that one reason they do not have this venting ability is because they have evolved to live in river systems as opposed to lakes – although this cannot be the full explanation because Nile perch will sometimes strike a shallow-fished lure from deep down, coming up from depth very quickly.

On the whole, it is man who has been responsible for introducing Nile perch to lakes – as in Lake Victoria – or he has built them a lake, as in Lake Nasser. The natural exception is Lake Chad, which is a 'young' lake in evolutionary terms; it is also a very shallow lake. The only other natural lakes are some small ones in Ethiopia, and Lake Turkana in northern Kenya, fed by the Omo river, which introduced Nile perch to Lake Turkana from the Ethiopian system.

The gassing-up problem is more common during the winter months on Lake Nasser, when the Nile perch are living in deeper water and are often caught from depths exceeding 30ft. They need time to adjust the air pressure in their swim bladder, and when fighting a big Nile perch you may not have enough time to give the fish an opportunity to equalize its swim bladder air pressure. This is another argument for a quick fight, which will keep the fish strong enough to endure the process of removing the air from its swim bladder. Obviously this 'gassing up' is a very important subject, and one we will discuss in more detail later in this chapter.

Playing Big Fish the Correct Way

Getting back now to playing big fish the correct way, both Barrie and Tim believe it is best to bully the fish in – as far as one can, with a very large fish! If a fight takes too long, the fish is exhausted, whereas the quicker you can land your catch, the fresher it will be when you are unhooking and photographing it. A quick fight gives the big fish a far better chance of survival. You can often tell when the angler is being too 'light' on a fish because the rod is hardly bent, with just the rod top tapping away. If the rod is not well bent, then the fish is not being made to work and the 'fight' may last too long for the wellbeing of the fish. In short, put some real effort into the fight.

An issue that follows on logically from this, and one that we find difficult to write about (being unwilling to condemn the actions of our fellow anglers), is that some anglers deliberately target big fish with light tackle in order to 'get a better fight'. This is surely wrong. By 'better fight' they usually mean a longer fight, with longer runs. As we now know, this unnecessarily tires a fish that you are supposed to be returning to the water in good condition.

We are also uneasy about the concept of line class records, when the angler uses lighter and lighter gear in order to obtain a 'record' fish. Of course, in experienced hands light tackle is less of a risk than it is in the hands of a beginner, but many of our safari guests are beginners to fighting very big freshwater fish, and it is perhaps better if we encourage them to use tackle that will get the Nile perch on the bank as quickly as possible. We realize that when you go fishing for Nile perch most of the fish you will catch are not monsters, and that if you are always using heavy tackle the smaller fish are not much fun – similar to hauling in a small fish with a crane.

The best way to solve this problem is to use three sets of rods: first, use heavy gear for targeting big fish – from our own experience, these are found in areas we have come to recognize. A lighter (but still fairly substantial) rod should be used for lighter fish (and for tigerfish that live in another habitat, where they avoid contact with very big fish, which would eat them if they had half a chance). Then a light tackle rig, mostly used for catching small tigers for deadbait or for just having fun. Use the right tool for the right circumstances.

You are probably starting to think that we are quite dogmatic in our view as to the best way to fight Nile perch. I suppose it's because after seeing literally hundreds of magnificent fish in the 100lb-plus bracket caught, you tend to get quite emotional and upset when one dies. In the early days when we were catching a lot – and we do mean a lot – of very big fish, the individual fatality rate was much higher than it is now, in 2007. This was our fault, and mainly resulted from ignorance and complacency. We thought, quite wrongly at the time, that the supply of big fish was endless, and we didn't fully realize that damage was sometimes being done.

Tim recalls when he was a boy, sitting listening to his father and friends discussing hunting plains game in Africa, and a remark that often came up in these conversations: 'They will never shoot out all the plains game in Africa. There are just too many of them, the herds are endless.' In a smaller way this is what is happened to the great 'pods' of very big Nile perch on Lake Nasser. Maybe it is a case of closing the stable door after the horse has escaped, but now our strong reaction is to protect, as best we can, the many magnificent fish still remaining. Commercial fishing is also to blame, possibly more to blame, but we will discuss this problem elsewhere.

'Pods'

We call a group of big Nile perch a 'pod'. This word is normally used to describe a group of whales, but we feel it is also a good word to describe a group of huge freshwater fish, better than the word 'shoal'. Nile perch tend to gather in loose groups of up to ten, or slightly more, big fish. This sort of number does not seem to warrant the word shoal, but nor do they swim around in unison.

Securing a Big Fish

When you get the fish close to the bank or next to the boat, what then? After all, most of us cannot lift out 100lb in a straight lift, or we'd be representing our country in the Olympics at weight lifting. However, it is worth remembering that in most circumstances you'll have a guide or companion with you, so it becomes a two-man job, making things easier. The problems are not simply related to the weight of the fish, but to the

One of the most exciting moments of most Nile perch battles is when they attempt to go airborne.

facts that the lure may have three sharp treble hooks on it, and the shoreline may be rocky. On boats it is a little easier, as we shall explain below.

First you have to secure the fish, and it is important to handle it properly when securing it with a stringer. Use wet hands or gloves to hold the fish, then turn it on its back and cover its

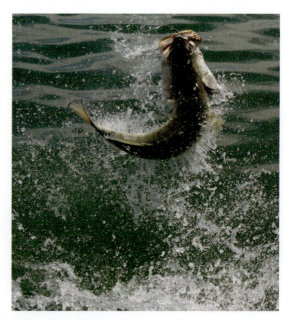

LEFT: *Almost clear of the water…*

ABOVE: *Fully clear of the water.*

BELOW: *Head-shaking, which can fling a lure clear, accompanies all leaping of Nile perch.*

eyes with a wet towel to calm it. Don't put your fingers in its eyes or gills. Larger fish can be kept in the water by holding the leader with a glove, or by slipping a gaff through the lower jaw. Avoid removing mucus or scales, and protect yourself from injury by handling the fish carefully and correctly.

Fish weighing over 50lb should be gaffed through the lower jaw where the skin is soft and heals easily. You are probably doing the fish less damage by putting a hole in its mouth than by securing it with, say, a stringer through the gills, which might easily damage a gill raker.

Once your catch is secured on a stringer, the next stage is to remove the hook. Try to back the hook out the opposite way it went in. Use needle-nose pliers, to work the hook and protect your hands. For a larger fish in the water, slip a gaff around the leader and slide it down to the hook. Lift the gaff upwards as the angler pulls downwards on the leader.

Once the hook has been removed and the fish has been secured on the stringer, allow it time to recover. Always be patient when you come to resting your big fish, which may be worn out after giving you a hard fight. Handle your Nile perch as little as possible – it has never been 'groped' or 'fondled' in its life before, and excessive handling will add to any stress factor.

With big fish, the longer you leave them in the water the better – but be careful not to leave them just that bit too long, as Tim once experienced, to his embarrassment. He was on safari way down at the bottom end of Wadi Allaqi fishing a favourite hotspot, and the angler with him had just caught the fish of his dreams: a Nile perch that must have been 130lb plus. They got the fish to the side of the boat and secured it with a stringer. The next stage was to slowly drive the boat, with the huge fish still in the water, to the closest stretch of shoreline where they could beach the boat and weigh the catch.

Whenever possible, it is much better to take a big fish to the shore, rather than haul it into the fishing boat for weighing and photographs – although it is hard work for the person responsible for holding a big fish in place alongside the

A crucial moment when the skill of the guide takes over.

boat as it slowly motors to the shore. Holding a 100lb-plus fish upright in the water when you are draped over the gunnels of a boat is quite an interesting experience, and it requires a certain amount of muscle power and a good sense of balance to keep everything under control.

When Tim and the angler eventually got the fish to the shore it looked to be in good condition, but Tim suggested they should let it rest for a while longer to make quite sure it was all right. The Nile perch was secured to the side of the boat on the end of a stringer, and immediately swam under the keel of the boat and sulked there. After about half an hour or so they were ready, with cameras primed and the weighing sling and scales all set up to record this fish of a lifetime, and went to get it to put it through its weighing and photo ordeal before releasing it. But this Nile perch had other ideas: as they waded into the water, the perch under the fishing boat gave their approaching feet and groping hands one look and took off at great speed – it reached the end of the stringer and 'snap' – and the last they ever saw of this fish of a lifetime was a huge silver-grey shape taking off, then stopping for a split second as the stringer parted, and finally disappearing into the green depths.

The first reaction was to think, 'How did it manage to break through such a tough stringer?' When the stringer was retrieved, the ragged end showed that the break was very close to the knot. The fish had been stringered through a gaff hole in the soft skin just under its lower jawbone, and what seemed to have happened was that the Nile perch's rasping, file-like jaws had weakened the stringer to such an extent that it just broke under the pressure of the 130-pounder's frantic escape charge away from the boat. So there were no photos of the guest's most memorable fish of a lifetime, thanks to Tim being too cautious about the perch's well-being.

Landing Nile Perch from the Shore

The first rule for shore fishing on Lake Nasser is that you must have a companion or guide with you, especially if you have never had any experience of handling and unhooking big fish. Trying to unhook a big Nile perch on your own is dangerous, with particular risk from the large, sharp treble hooks that might be flying around in all directions, especially if the fish is still green. To be on the safe side, landing a big fish from the shore needs two people, one to hold and secure the fish while the second person removes the hooks from the safely secured fish.

The Nile perch is not built delicately. It has scales like a coat of chain mail, is 'dry' to the touch, not slimy, and is clearly built for hunting in the rocky environment in which it lives. So you don't have to worry too much about the fish bashing itself on rocks. In reality a Nile perch does not flap around too much on the bank, and you can hold them down with two hands if they show any inclination to flex. If the fish is still green and making a fuss, then always keep in mind that if you cover its eyes with a damp cloth, the darkness will help calm it. A quickly removed 'T' shirt is always an option, though make sure you wet it first: you can always rinse it out afterwards, and you can count on it drying out quickly in the desert climate.

So how do you get them on the bank or into a boat? We have tried nets in the past, but have given them up – even the big Wels catfish nets. One obvious problem is that the net would need to be very large, and then they are too cumbersome, to say the least. Barrie's 120lb fish was 1m 60cm (5ft 4in) long, and Nile perch in the top 100lb can grow to over 6ft long. Smaller Nile perch hardly need a net, and can be lifted carefully.

On Lake Nasser, perch of up to, say, 30lb are normally hand-landed using a pair of gloves; this method is used extensively, and is still preferred by most guides. The larger Nile perch of 30lb or more should be secured by using a gaff. The gaff point is slipped under the very point of the jaw and pulled through the soft skin; once the fish has been securely gaffed the gaff itself is then used to hold the fish steady while the hooks are removed. Once this has been done, the hole created by the gaff is used to thread the stringer. (Note that the hole made by the gaff is not large and will heal quickly; there is no evidence of any lasting damage that we have seen in fish that have been recaptured: the gaff hole heals up quickly, and eventually there is hardly any evidence that the fish has been gaffed in the past.)

Threading a stringer into a gaff hole is a practised art, and has to be carried out quickly and

Families enjoy the Nile perch safaris as much as anyone. (Olivier Portrat)

efficiently – fumbling might lose the fish. This procedure is best done by two people, though many guides are quite capable of doing it on their own. The fish is held by the jaws by a gloved left hand (if you are right-handed), while the other hand removes the gaff and quickly inserts the pointed end of a pair of long-nosed pliers through the hole; the pliers are then opened to grip the end of the stringer, which is pulled through the hole and then secured.

Tim uses a slightly different gaffing technique to most. He rests the point of the gaff at the very point of the Nile perch's jaw, actually resting it on the bone, as above, but is able to lift even quite large fish inboard or on to the bank without the gaff point penetrating the fish. We have

never seen anyone else able to do this, and it is clearly a great and useful skill.

As we have already mentioned, hand-landing Nile perch can be dangerous (as can all hand-landing of fish), not so much for the fish, but for the angler, with all those flying trebles. The trick is to lift the fish at one of its quiet moments. Every experienced angler can spot this moment, when just for a second or two the fish lies quiet, mouth agape – so in goes the glove, carefully avoiding any trebles, and the fish is quickly lifted or slid up the bank. With a very big fish two hands may be needed, and with a colossal fish, such as the many, many 150 to 200lb-plus monsters that are landed, four or more hands may be necessary.

Landing from Boats

Getting big fish into the fishing boat correctly is critical for its survival. With this in mind, always try to keep your fish well supported in a horizontal position using either your hands or a sling. Also, do your very best to take big fish to the shore for weighing and trophy shots, rather than hauling them into the fishing boat. This can only be done if the shore is reasonably close and of suitable structure – a sandy bay, say. The jaw is gripped by gloved hands while the boat driver gently noses the boat shoreward until it beaches. Pulling the fish slowly through the water also causes water to flow over its gill rakers. This method is much, much better than manhandling a big fish over the gunwales, and is the preferred method of today's Nasser guides. Aside from giving a big fish a much better chance of survival, there are other advantages with taking big fish to the shore. First, the fish will be spending most of the time in its natural habitat, giving it an opportunity to regain its strength. And then the all-important trophy photograph is so much better with a natural shoreline backdrop to the picture rather than perhaps the boat engine or an untidy cabin as a background.

You will have to get into the lake with the fish, which means getting wet, although more often than not this is in fact a pleasant experience in the desert heat. It is much easier to handle big fish when you are in the water with them. Your trophy shot will also look more natural if you only have to lift the fish a short way from the water into your arms – and who knows, if you are lucky and have caught a real monster you might well need the help of one, or even two other people to lift a catch that could be anything up to, or over, 200lb.

Often, however, you will not have the chance of taking your big catch to the shore, and it will have to be lifted into the fishing boat. While in the fishing boat, the correct method for lifting a Nile perch of, say, 30lb upwards is to use a big weigh sling with lifting handles. These weigh slings are specially designed for landing big Nile perch and are based on the same pattern as the weigh slings/unhooking mats designed for the giant European Wels catfish. To get the fish into the fishing boat, it should first be secured on a stringer and then held steady alongside the boat. The weigh sling is immersed in the water in front of and just under the fish, then the sling is gently slid under its belly until it completely supports the fish. Finally, lift the fish into the boat using the handles attached to the sling.

All the above methods are great in theory and when the conditions are favourable, but there are times when it is just not practical, and maybe even dangerous to try and land the fish – for example, when you catch a big fish in rough weather and the boat is bouncing all over the place, making it almost impossible to stand firmly in one place. In such circumstances it is best to photograph the fish at the side of the boat and then let it go without trying to land it.

Unhooking Big Fish

Unhooking perch is usually straightforward enough. The mouth is big and not too difficult to open, and a pair of long-handled pliers does the rest. (Artery forceps, so commonly used by British anglers, are not really strong enough for the job with big lures.)

There is a case for carrying the hook snips so beloved of British pike anglers, because if a treble really is badly located it can simply be snipped to pieces. The demand for such action would be rare but it would occasionally be helpful. The 'hook snips' you will need to carry for Nile perch hooks will have to be heavy duty wire cutters because almost all manufacturer's hooks on standard lures should have been replaced with some of the toughest hooks in the world, such as the Owner 4 × Stinger trebles.

Every boat on Lake Nasser is supposed to have a set of these heavy duty wire cutters because they are sometimes needed to snip through the arm of a hook that is embedded in a guide or an angler!

Some big lures probably have too many big trebles, and it is now common practice amongst Nile perch enthusiasts to cut the number of trebles on a lure to two at the most. At a stroke this cuts the frequency of difficult and messy hook-ups almost to zero. When bait fishing it is more common to use a large single hook, so unhooking the fish in these circumstances is even easier, partly because the bait itself always seems to have been 'blown' away, ejected by the perch with some vigour.

When weighing a fish it should be placed in a weigh sling to fully support its body before lifting it up to the balance. Make sure there is plenty of clearance between the balance and the deck to weigh any size of fish. Small fish – say, under 30lb, are rarely weighed, but a good guide can estimate these weights to within a couple of pounds (on Lake Nasser in 2006 we tested the Nubian guides out several times, for a bit of fun, and they were rarely more than 1lb or so out with their weight estimate).

Stringers are an important tool for correctly handling big fish; in fact we can't imagine what we would do without them! All this tool consists of is a 6–8ft length of strong parachute cord with a loop tied on one end. This loop is used to thread the opposite end of the stringer through, which means you do not have to tie a knot. Once the fish has been correctly stringered it is much easier to control because it is attached to the end of a strong piece of cord.

Regardless of whether you are landing a fish from the shore or from a boat, it will need to rest for a while before weighing and trophy photographs. Recovering in the water at the end of a stringer is much less stressful for the fish. If the fish has stopped swimming and is lying on its back, you will have to support it in an upright position and then gently move it backwards and forwards to get water flowing over its gills. When you are on the shore we call this revival method 'walking the dog', which involves getting into the water with the fish and then gently leading it around on the end of the stringer, in

In rare instances the guides can de-gas a fish to ensure its survival (see page 80 for the full story).

much the same way that you would walk your favourite dog.

The local fishermen on Lake Nasser use stringers, but unfortunately not for the same reasons as an angler. One of the problems they experience is to keep their catch fresh until it can be sold to a passing ice boat (this is the name we have given to the fish-collecting boats on the lake because their holds are full of blocks of ice – sometimes a vital source of ice for keeping our beer cold). So what do the local fishermen do? They string the Nile perch they catch, sometimes keeping them on a stringer for several days. It is interesting that they nearly always attach their stringers through the perch's nasal holes. It is a sad sight, but effective for keeping the fish alive until the ice boat arrives.

Solving the Problem of Gassed-Up Perch

It will be of interest now to tell you more about some of our earlier attempts at solving the problem of gassed-up Nile perch. One of the earliest methods, when we think about it now, sounds really quite crazy, but at least we were – even fourteen years ago – getting concerned about killing big fish, and were already making an effort to try and save their lives. In those early days (1994/95) we would nurse a gassed-up perch on the deck of a fishing boat whilst making a mad dash back to our camp – assuming the camp was close enough. When we reached camp someone would leap over the side of the boat and 'walk the dog'. Someone else would be collecting longish straight sticks (quite a difficult task in the desert), and when they had enough, a cage consisting of two walls of sticks would be constructed in water 3 to 4ft deep. The Nile perch was then placed in an upright position in the cage and left to recover on its own, with anxious anglers paying frequent visits to see if the fins were moving. Strangely enough this method sometimes worked and the fish would eventually swim away – maybe a bit groggy, but at least alive.

Tim remembers one particular night in the early days when they were still using the 'cage procedure'. In the late afternoon a big Nile perch had been caught in deep water and was gassed up. Luckily they were close to camp so they set up a cage to revive the fish, and then stopped fishing for the day. After dinner on the shore (yes, in those days we used to camp on the shore as mother ships had not yet been introduced) they gave the perch one more inspection before going to bed. Its fins were moving slightly and there were reasonable signs of life, though not quite enough to give them the confidence to release the big fish from its cage; so the decision was made to leave it in its cage overnight. This seemed to be a good decision, made after several beers and a bottle or two of red wine, when getting wet while releasing the fish didn't seem to be a very good idea.

At some time in the early hours of the morning there was a lot of splashing in the camp, which went on for several minutes and eventually woke everyone up. There was a bit of shouting between the fishing boats, and torches were shone around where the cage was, but nothing could be seen below the surface of the water. No

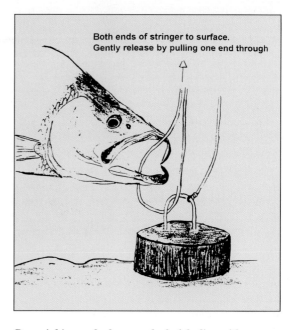

Deep sinking and release method of dealing with so-called gassed-up fish.

one was willing to get out and see what had happened to the Nile perch – probably just as well. So they all went back to sleep.

The next morning they found that the cage had been completely wrecked, hardly any sticks remaining in an upright position. It seemed very unlikely that the Nile perch had caused all this damage, because if it had recovered enough it would have gently nosed its way out of the cage and swum away. So what was the reason for the devastated cage? A crocodile attack seemed to be the most likely explanation.

As the above story is being written (May 2007) Tim is on safari, with his computer connected to an efficient small generator – a much better way of doing some work than sitting in a stuffy office. Last night, while Tim and the anglers were having dinner on the mother ship overlooking the lake, all brightly lit by a full moon, one of the guides spotted a huge crocodile lying in the water only about 250ft (75m) from the mother ship. Even after everyone stood up and went to the rails to get a better look, the big croc remained in the area for some time. The Nile crocodiles in Lake Nasser are the only 'natural' predator of bigger Nile perch, but out of necessity they will also feed on smaller dead fish. Tim believes that these crocodiles get quite used to boats and will often hang around near local fishermen, who fish a lot at night, to pick up the rejected dead fish they throw back into the lake.

Another method we used extensively in the early days – and one that is in fact still used by some Nasser guides – was to return the gassed-up fish to deep water using an anchor to take it back to the bottom. This involved attaching the fish to the anchor using lightweight monofilament line, not more than 10lb breaking strain. Then the fish attached to the anchor was gently lowered into the depths, and the end of the anchor rope was attached to a life ring and then left for some hours while the anglers continued fishing. When they returned they would often find the fish had broken the light retaining line and swum away. On the down side, for the other 30 per cent of the time, they found a dead fish

attached to the end of the anchor. This was a method also tried by pike anglers in Ireland.

Then some of our visiting anglers started to tell us about a method that involved piercing the swim bladder with a needle. At first we were sceptical, but two professional anglers eventually persuaded us to check the bladder-piercing method by seeking the expert advice of Olivier Portrat who has spent more than six months, in total, fishing Lake Nasser with us, on some ten safaris. Olivier was the first angler to start using the needle-piercing method on his safaris, and he taught our senior guide Ramadan 'Fox' the method. Ramadan was immediately persuaded when he saw how easily the fish recovered and swam away. However, we were still not 100 per cent sure where to insert the needle. At this time we thought the trapped air was in the body cavity and were inserting the needle into the fish's belly, which, in retrospect, was probably doing more damage than good – though we have to say that air was still coming out, and the method seemed to work.

The second expert angler, fondly known as 'Captain Cranky', an Australian character who captains a luxury marlin fishing boat off the Queensland coast for a living, had come on a safari to find out for himself if all the stories he had been told about giant Nile perch, which were said to be rather like a barramundi on steroids, were true. C.C. is also a keen barramundi angler, and had been reading the literature provided for leisure anglers in Australia about how to look after landed barramundi and then return them safely to their habitat. He had successfully used the needle method himself with barramundi, and reassured us it worked – and even went to the trouble of giving us a practical demonstration on a fish we had kept for the table. He dissected this Nile perch to show us exactly where the swim bladder was located. He explained that the Australian fisheries biologists had approved the method and claimed it had about a 75 per cent success rate for the long-term survival of a fish treated correctly in this way. This is also a method perfected by England's pike anglers back in the 1990s.

The Barramundi Lessons

Tim's second home is Australia: his safari company is an Australian-registered company. Tim and his brother, Peter, who run the company, were both brought up in the equatorial climate of Kenya; when the time came to move on, they found that Australia with its wide open spaces, easy-going lifestyle and the Ozzies' great sense of 'fair play', was the very best place to live.

On a visit to Australia in 2003 Tim made a point of flying from Sydney to Cairns to stay with John and Jennifer Mondora who are 'true blue' Ozzie and generous to a fault, in the Australian tradition. John and Jennifer had both been on a couple of Nile perch safaris, and were interested to help Tim as much as they could. John is a well known fishing journalist in Australia, and both he and Jennifer are skilled anglers. Amongst their friends to whom they introduced Tim was Alf Hogan, who works for the Australian Queensland Government Department of Primary Industries as a senior freshwater fisheries biologist. Alf and his team of biologists are responsible for the scientific study in support of the huge barramundi farming and leisure industry in Australia.

As part of their studies they have also carried out research into the possibilities of farming Nile perch. Initially this research was conducted because Nile perch spawn in freshwater, whereas the barramundi need brackish estuary water. In the end they discovered economical methods to breed barramundi, and abandoned the Nile perch project.

There are several species of the Nile perch genus (*Lates*), and perhaps one of the most important – or at least, the one we know most about – is the barramundi (*Lates calcarifer*). Much of the research that the Australian fisheries' biologists have made into barramundi also applies to Nile perch, and the information in the following paragraphs is from research results carried out by Alf Hogan and his team of Australian fisheries' biologists.

Alf Hogan has produced a DVD entitled *Handling and Releasing Big Fish*. This DVD presentation explains the results of some of the research that Australian fish scientists have done into the correct methods of handling big barramundi, which can grow, at the top end, to 80–90lb. At the time, Australian fisheries' biologists and anglers were starting to realize that far too many captured and released barramundi were dying some time after they were released, although they had evidently been handled correctly, and had swum away strongly at the time of their release. Alf and his team of biologists set out to try and find out why this was happening, and came up with the following advice. The first is that you should never hold up a big barramundi suspended vertically by its jaws: always hold it horizontally, fully supporting its body (in fact it is not easy to hold a big fish vertically).

In his DVD presentation Alf takes us through an experiment to help explain why this is. He takes a freshly caught 10kg fish (approximately a twenty-pounder, only an average fish on Lake Nasser). Before the fish is taken from the water, its jaw is firmly secured to the top end of a long tray, which has a tape measure on the bottom. The fish is measured while lying in the tray horizontally in the water, when its length from the tip of its nose to the end of its tail is 93.0cm (36.6in). The same fish is then measured again while it is held vertically supported by its jaw: the length of the fish is now 93.3cm (36.7in), which means it has stretched 3cm (just over 1in). To most people this will not mean very much but if a human spinal column is stretched by as much as 3cm it could well result in serious disability. Also, because there are only nineteen vertebrae in the spinal column of a barramundi (or Nile perch) this damage could be serious.

Anyone who has had the misfortune to suffer a back injury, will know that a stretched spinal column is a very painful and inhibiting experience, and one that requires a lot of therapy. Alf admits that a lot more research needs to be done to prove conclusively that holding a fish vertically might eventually kill it, but as he says, 'Why take the chance?' It also seems logical that because a fish spends its life suspended in a much lower gravity, water, their organs and spine will not build up a supporting muscle system in the same way as, for example, a mammal living on land, which has a far greater gravitational pull on the mammal's body parts. It seems that this is not as critical where smaller fish are concerned because they have a more compact body mass. Of course big fish leap, in the wild, so gravity is not too constraining for short periods.

In Australia it is fairly easy to keep track of fish that expire after having been captured and released by an angler. First, in Australia most fish are tagged; and second, the lakes and fishing areas are much smaller bodies of water than Lake Nasser. On Lake Nasser we do not tag captured fish, and we only fish each area for a few hours before moving on to a different part of the lake – it is often some days before we return to the same fishing area for another try. So we would not notice any dead fish as a result of our capturing them.

Some years ago we were considering starting a tagging programme, and even went so far as to purchase a tagging system. But when we looked into the practicalities of starting it, we realized it would not work. The biggest problem was the sheer size of the lake: with only eleven fishing boats in this huge area we were never in one place long enough to get any returns. Also, sports anglers on Lake Nasser only account for a very small number of Nile perch as compared to the local fishermen. There are some 2,500 fishermen on the lake, and to get their co-operation for returning tags would be an impossible task without launching a major and costly project.

Earlier in this chapter we explained how a Nile perch's swim bladder may become gassed up because it may not be able to vent when it is caught in deep water; and apparently barramundi have exactly the same problem. Here is a little more detail on how to de-gas fish. Use the largest hypodermic needle you can find (#10 or larger), and remove the plunger so that you are just left with the needle. The idea behind this is to insert the hypodermic needle into the swim bladder and release the trapped air. Some schools of thought suggest that if you stick a long pin into a fish to let the air out you will cause damage to it, and that although the fish swims away, it has a

stab wound that might slowly kill it. However, a majority agrees that piercing the swim bladder will not cause damage – *as long as* the procedure is carried out correctly.

Although you have to use a big hypodermic needle, the actual hole you create is very small, and the body tissues of the fish will quickly contract to seal this hole. Many fish are known to heal quite serious wounds in a matter of a few days. It certainly works with pike. Fish in a wild environment are remarkably resilient and are capable of surviving extraordinary body damage, much more so than a mammal, and much more than an angler inflicts. Also, think about all the needles that doctors stick into humans!

It is important that you pierce the fish in the correct place. Insert the hypodermic needle for only about $\frac{1}{4}$in at an angle of 45 degrees, under a scale, near the tip of the pectoral fin. Then squeeze the fish gently and you will hear the trapped gases escaping. Make a needle-clearing tool from a piece of stainless leader wire to clear any tissue and so on from the needle, and leave this tool in the needle between uses. Sterilize the needle with iodine or alcohol after use, and store it in a safe place.

'Catch and release' comes with both a moral and an actual price tag. Looking through the newsletters sent out to Nasser anglers over the years we came across the following statement: if safaris had killed and sold the 106 Nile perch weighing over 75lb that were caught during the season between 15 September 1998 and 15 January 1999, we would have been paid £1,950.00 by the many black market fish-collecting boats on the lake. The same fish, once they had reached the Aswan retail market, would have fetched £9,450.00.

If we had also killed and sold all the Nile perch, regardless of what weight they were, that were caught during the same season, this income would probably have doubled. We believe that by the techniques we have developed and described in this chapter, we are nurturing a major sporting resource, and at the same time are able to continue careful studies of the ecology of Nile perch.

8 ADVANCED BANK FISHING

Barrie Rickards playing an 80lb Nile perch on a standard pike rod near Maharaga camp.

For many anglers who visit Lake Nasser for the first time, taking on a big fish from the bank will be one of the ultimate experiences of their angling career, and this first experience can have long-lasting effects. For example, Barrie's first experience was in the early 1990s in the company of Tim – in fact it was his first experience of Nile perch at all. They had been cruising down the lake from Aswan for most of the morning, heading south under a glorious sun, Barrie setting up his tackle on the boat as they went. First stop was to be a small island surrounded by deep water, and it was a well known bank-fishing spot. Just before lunch they nosed the craft into a small sandy bay on the lee shore, and the adventure began.

Tim and Barrie each fished a small cove into the wind, the water falling away to tens of yards deep within a yard of the rock overhang. Barrie's Rapala Super Shad Rap was heaved well out, maybe 30yd, and wound back fairly quickly to get it to its working depth. Just as Barrie's lure was being lifted from the water, first cast, a huge fish materialized from the depths at his feet and just missed the lure as it left the water. It sat there: Barrie stood there. Then releasing the clutch, and without moving a muscle, he let the lure drop on to the surface again. In a flash the Nile perch grabbed it and dived. In went the strike, of sorts, and the fish simply continued down, down, down, with the clutch squealing away.

'Tiiiiiiim!' shouted Barrie. Tim was half way there when Barrie had some line back on the reel and was pumping the fish upwards, or trying to, against repeated dives – and then all went slack. When things go slack with big fish it's best to keep winding fast because they have often simply created slack by swimming directly towards the angler; but this one had created slack permanently, and what could have been a quite magnificent start ended in momentary dejection. Just think, a 50lb fish on your first-ever cast for Nile perch!

In that first week several lessons were learned about bank fishing. One was that Nile perch have strong jaws and can clamp on the bait, holding it very tightly, without actually being hooked. So you have to hold the rod firmly and then at some stage try to establish a strike – but mostly the fish will hook itself as it dashes away in panic.

Barrie had fifty Nile perch that week, which was his first on Lake Nasser. This was during August, not usually regarded as a good month. The biggest fish was 37lb on the troll, but most of the fish were caught bank fishing, and quite a few were small. It was an inauspicious beginning, bearing in mind other very successful trips.

Retrieve Speed

The second important lesson learned about bank fishing, unfortunately realized only late in the week, was that the average English pike angler is naturally inclined to retrieve his lure much too slowly for Nile perch, and the best advice we can now give is to reel in fast. A Nile perch can overhaul anything you throw at it, at any speed, but a slow retrieve seems to give them time to inspect the lure and maybe have

Lake Nasser shore-caught record by Frenchman Bernard Bru, at 179lb.

Nile perch mooching around trying to look inconspicuous to tilapia and small monitor lizards.

second thoughts about striking. This was finally brought home to Barrie when he was casting from the rocks, using a Gudebood Sniper in bright yellow. The cast was made alongside a ridge of rock that ran out into the lake, just under the surface, so that the ridge had a foot of water over it, and then dropped away to one side into perhaps 12ft. He could see the lure wobbling along, at pike-retrieve speed, just above the drop-away point. Then a huge shape was following it – and that's all it did. It followed it almost to his feet, and then turned away in distain. Having had several fish of 100lb since then, Barrie now knows he was looking at one of them.

It was only when he saw Tim bank casting that he realized that his own retrieve speed was much too slow. Having realized this, they discussed the retrieval speed, and the combined opinion was that it is a mistake to let the Nile perch get suspicious of his potential meal: it was better to make the fish think 'I had better grab this, even if it looks a bit strange, before it gets away – after all, I can always spit it out.' A fish doesn't have hands to grab hold of and inspect a potential meal: it has to use its mouth, and its biology enables it to reject anything that is not good for it. In this way new food opportunities

are discovered or rejected as the case may be. Barrie speeded up the retrieve to very fast, and later in the week took several nice fish with far fewer rejections.

All the perch family can get suspicious of artificial lures if they get a good look at them, and on Lake Nasser the water is so clear that a chasing fish will easily see the lure. The only lures that we find can be fished slowly are the soft plastic or rubber varieties with the wiggly tails, or jigs of various types – though on these, the body parts such as the tail do move quickly. These baits are especially effective when retrieved correctly with quick 'wounded fish' jerks.

In short then, don't give the perch time to think, make it feel the lure is going to escape, and prompt it into immediate action.

What about retrieve style? This is very important in all lure fishing, and usually varies from species to species, as well as on particular days with one species. With Nile perch it seems that some sort of erratic retrieve works better than the straight, steady retrieve. Again, the latter is often favoured by pike anglers. Barrie learned this from his own experience, which is usually to retrieve steadily – that pike experience again. Tim had a go at him several times in those early visits, and eventually, belatedly, he gave it a try by moving his rod tip from side to side to make the lure look as if it were darting about in a panic. The steady retrieve does work, but much more often the lure needs to be worked so that it changes direction often, and depth, too. You can stop and start the retrieve, use jerkbait tactics, and so on. Perhaps as an aside almost we should mention here that jerkbaits *per se* have not, so far, been a success on Lake Nasser. This may mean that they have not been tried thoroughly (or when the fish were 'off', anyway), or it may indicate something more subtle about the way Nile perch feed and hunt.

When bank fishing on Lake Nasser, the best method is to find rocky features with fairly deep water around them, and then work your lure past the crevices and boulders. Small fish hide in shallow water avoiding bigger fish that live

Mandy Lyne bank fishing from a high vantage point – with help.

below them in deeper water. As the smaller fish grow bigger they gradually move towards deeper water. So, generally speaking, the bigger the fish, the deeper the water it prefers to live in. Nile perch are good at ambushing their prey, and will hide amongst the rocks and wait. The bigger the fish, the deeper they will position their ambush point, because bigger predators need bigger prey.

Hunting Tactics

One of the first things one learns about hunting is that movement is the biggest giveaway of your position that there is. Even the best camouflaged animal will reveal its position by a movement: just the flick of an ear will suddenly make it appear out of its camouflage, as if by magic. Camouflage is a protection, but movement reveals all, and that very much includes the angler on the bank. Keep in mind while you are pursuing the bigger, more experienced Nile perch that they got bigger by being smarter than the others, which ended up as a meal.

Sight casting is an exciting pastime on Lake Nasser. There are literally hundreds of miles of rocky shoreline that you can walk along (or climb in some places) and watch for Nile perch. One of our tactics, especially when fly fishing, is for the guide to go ahead but much higher up than the angler, and then direct his casts to any fish he can see from above.

If you spot a big fish or two there really is no point in scrambling down over their heads and casting at them from 3ft away. They'll be long gone, gliding away into the gloom in a manner at which they are expert. No, mark their position carefully, and then work out how you can get into a casting position some distance away. That distance will depend on the conditions. It's nearly always brilliant sunshine so you can't creep close under dull conditions, but you can go a little closer, moving very slowly and steadily, especially if the water is choppy, because the waves break up the smooth surface and make it harder for the fish to see what is going on.

Large monitor lizard and Nile perch in the 40–80lb bracket, photographed from the cliff top. Nile perch mooch along the margins looking for tilapia to eat.

in the margins – and then he spotted what he thought at first was a log of wood floating in the water quite close to where the perch were swimming, blissfully unaware. However, he soon realized it wasn't a log but a crocodile of about 8 to 10ft long. Tim sat very still, watching this scene for some ten minutes. The crocodile seemed to be completely still, suspended just on the surface, but as the minutes stretched on it was obvious that the drift of the croc was taking it gradually closer to the perch. Although Tim was some distance away he decided to try and take a picture of the unfolding events, and gently laid his rod aside and reached into his pocket for a compact digital camera he was carrying. But this small movement alerted the crocodile, which immediately dived with a splash – in a moment the water was still and both crocodile and perch has completely disappeared. Just that one small movement had given Tim's position away and triggered a warning.

By now our reader might be starting to think that we have been exaggerating the point about how important stealth is. But what we are really referring to is 'hunting', in the proper sense, for the big fish that have become the wise old survivors. Also, this advice refers to swims where the fish have become lure shy. With smaller, inexperienced fish or fish that have little experience with lures you can get away with a lot more. But with big fish you will have a lot more success if you 'hunt' them properly.

Always move slowly and carefully, and take your time. If you spot a fish, freeze, do not move a muscle, not even your rod tip, then carefully observe the fish until you see it turn away from you before moving forwards or making a cast. Also, make sure the fish you have spotted is the only one in the vicinity, and that there is not another fish around that will see you stalking its partner. If you are spotted by one fish, in all likelihood the warning will go out and all the fish will fade away – but not always in a panic if you are not moving.

If you have spotted fish and they have faded away into the deep they might not be fully spooked, so wait a few minutes, keeping still, then move into position slowly. Attach a sinking lure or plastic fish, and then cast well out and allow the bait to sink almost to the bottom before you retrieve. You will often pick up a fish that has quietly glided down into deeper water.

Tim recalls once watching a crocodile hunting perch. He had very quietly approached a swim where he was sure he would find perch basking in the verges. He was still some way off, but sure enough, he could just make out perch

ABOVE: Barrie Rickards with the then unofficial bank record of 80lb taken on a perch finish, Rapala Super Shad Rap.

BELOW: Barrie with a big fish from the bank in typical rocky country beloved of Nile perch.

Camouflage is a debatable issue, especially if we agree that fish only see in shades rather than colours. Tim feels that it is a question of being camouflaged by the right shade of colour, which will blend into the background. In the old days we felt it was important not to wear white or bright-coloured shirts because we felt that Nile perch could see very well through the clear water and that a bright shirt moving against the sandy brown of the rock background would easily be seen. The best advice is to wear colours that are neutral and blend into the background.

With a sighted fish, don't frighten it by casting directly at it. What would you think if your roast chicken dinner started to chase you? This is what a fish must feel like when an angler casts a lure and then frantically reels it in, aiming it directly at the target fish – but prey fish are not in the habit of chasing predators. So cast to the side, and retrieve the lure at an angle from behind and away from the target, so that it catches the target's attention out of the corner of its eye. At frequently fished, shore-fishing hotspots, avoid using lures with flashing silver diving vanes, for example most Rapala Magnum lures, as we feel the bright flash caused by the sun's reflection will eventually start to act as a warning signal to spooky Nile perch. Try painting silver diving vanes a neutral colour to match the body colour, or paint them black with a magic marker.

Sometimes choosing the wrong lure will spook a fish, especially if it has had previous experience. Try and start with the correct lure: ask your guide which are the best lures at that moment, or that day, or in that week. If they know, they'll tell you quickly. For more information on

this subject, refer to the chapter about lures (*see* page 99).

It is not often that you will be bank fishing without a guide in attendance. One good plan, having spotted the Nile perch grouping, is to leave the guide in place, watching them: not only will he be able to tell you exactly where to cast, but he can alert you to any fish movements and tell you how the fish are reacting to the lures you are casting. If the fish look nervous, then stop immediately and give them some time to settle down, and if necessary, take this opportunity to change the lure you are using.

Most of the strikes you get from the shore will take place just a few yards from your feet. What seems to happen is that the perch follows the lure in from deeper water, and as the lure gets closer to the rocky shoreline the chasing Nile perch will get the impression that the meal will soon be lost in water that is too shallow for it to swim in – so at the last moment it will make a lunge to swallow the lure before it can escape. Or you will see the perch just behind the lure and nothing happens. One very useful tip is to raise the lure to the surface some yards from the bank. This can also have the effect of making the Nile perch think it is about to lose its meal. But if it comes short of the lure for whatever reason, it does not see you, the angler. It may take the lure, of course – that is the object of the ploy – but if it doesn't do so immediately, it may do so as soon as you continue the retrieve towards the bank.

Beware of this last-moment follow up. There you are, convinced the cast was a failure, you are about to lift out the lure, and may be half turned away preparatory to the next back swing, and you glance down and see a huge Nile perch right at your feet. You didn't see it arrive, but my word, you'll see it go. And then you may not see it again... not good for your heart. In these circumstances, with a fish at your feet, you can crouch down very slowly and lob a recast to the fish, when it will sometimes take with a vengeance.

Playing a big fish to the bank does not always spook the rest of the group; in fact you will often

have other fish following the one you have on the end of your line. And as luck will often have it, the following fish are much, much bigger than the one you have hooked. When this happens, take a chance by keeping your fish swimming in the water by giving it some line, and then call a fellow angler, if they are fishing within calling distance – often they will have a very good chance of hooking one of the following fish. This follow-up by other fish also happens quite often while you are casting from a boat or even trolling.

Another thing we have noticed when fishing to a group of Nile perch that have been detected lurking near the bank is that sometimes these fish may not be actively feeding or even interested in feeding, so you may not be able to induce a strike, but – and this is the odd thing – on occasion there are deeper fish, beneath the surface group, that will feed. So if the targeted group shows little interest, try a deep-fished lure underneath them and a bit further out into the lake – this tactic is often highly effective.

Another important matter when bank fishing is to check, before you cast, where you are going to land any fish. Much bank fishing is done by casting from restricted spots, not precarious exactly (or they shouldn't be), but awkward. If you are 6ft above the water you cannot easily land a big Nile perch: you need a route down to the water.

Barrie's Biggest Ever Bank Fish

Let us give you an actual example, which paid off in the form of Barrie's biggest ever bank fish. He'd been dropped off on an island and was on his own, and the guide had motored away to help a couple of beginners about half a mile away.

Having worked the windward shore – into which the breeze was blowing – without getting a take, he moved round to the sheltered bank, which, as it happens, was over deep water about 40ft straight off the edge. He was casting from horizontally bedded sandstone and was balanced 6ft above the water – a good place to keep a lookout from. But the sandstone was stepped

Kalabsha camp: where possible, camps are chosen with good shore fishing in mind.

down towards the water, and the bottom step was in about a foot of water and maybe 6ft wide.

Barrie could have stood on that submerged point, paddling, and done the casting, but the elevated position allowed him to watch the banks for cruising fish. In actual fact he saw none, but if he hooked a fish on his deep retrieve he'd know exactly where to go to land it. He did hook a fish, and after a quite modest fight a huge Nile perch showed itself a few yards from the bank, in a big slow roll. It was a lazy fish. Barrie crept down the steps, keeping the rod well bent, reacting to runs in the usual way, and eventually found himself in that foot of water on a flat, safe slab of sandstone. For some reason this fish didn't fight much at all and in five minutes it slid on to the sandstone shelf next to Barrie. Suddenly the 6ft square of space became full.

Unhooking was easy enough, but Barrie had no scales to weigh the fish, the big balance having been left on the boat. For a while he sat there in the water, the big and fairly docile fish at his feet. Obviously it might be an hour or two by the time the boat returned, so he decided to measure it. This was accomplished by snipping off a length of fishing line and using it to stretch along the length of the fish, then snipping off when the length reached the tail end. It was both easy and reasonably accurate. The length, measured later, was 5ft 4in which, given the condition of the fish (it was one of the long 'tubular' ones, rather than the deep ones), was calculated to give a weight of around 120lb, although Barrie's original estimate was 90lb upwards.

The fish in retrospect was clearly well over 100lb at this length, so this seemed a very likely figure. It was a very solid fish, but not deep. Had it been deep as well, the weight at that length could have been nearer 150lb. The fish slid away quietly when returned, and dived deeply immediately.

The cast after the big one produced a fish that fought very hard indeed with a great many heart-stopping runs but no aerobatics. It was eventually beached, and was estimated to be around 50lb in weight. If this smaller fish was to be judged by its fight, it should have been twice as big as the big one.

Perhaps Nile perch are a bit like us humans, in that the older you get the heavier you get, and you slow down at the same time. Nile perch from about 50lb to, say, 90lb seem to the strongest fighters and must be in their prime. However, like humans, there are some really tough old veterans out there.

Fishing the Windward Shore
Earlier we mentioned fishing the windward shore as opposed to the lee (or wind-protected)

shoreline. As a general rule, a windward shore provides the best Nile perch fishing, and there are several possible reasons for this.

When there is a constant prevailing wind, the windward shoreline will have the roughest margins, since the boulders, undercuts and so on will have been cleared of sand by wave action, leaving ideal Nile perch living areas and ambush points. Also, any shore into which the wind blows has more highly oxygenated water, especially in low pressure regimes where oxygenation due to turbulence may exceed loss of oxygen as a direct result of lower pressure.

The prevailing wind seems to liven up the food chain, by washing up algae and plankton for the smaller fish to feed on, creating a biomass with the Nile perch at the top of the food chain. Generally, then, go for the windswept bank as a starting point when shore fishing and also trolling.

Lake Nasser's Weed

Lake Nasser is an unusual lake because the level of the water rises and falls each year by anything up to 15ft to 20ft (4.5–6m); this is caused by the annual flooding of the Nile. During the summer months when the level of the lake is at its lowest there is a lot of marginal weed on the shoreline. In the winter months when the lake is at its highest level this weed is submerged, and as with most water weed, is growing from the bottom up towards the light. When the levels drop, the weed comes to the surface and forms into mats of concentrated vegetation. The weed, although of the 'soft' variety, is actually quite tough. Even so, any snagged-up lure can usually be pulled free easily enough.

Weed is one of the places where the small fish like to hide, as long as it is not too thick and matted. Also, tilapia feed on a particular variety of weed. Living amongst the weed is a host of tiny water insects and other creatures, in particular a small freshwater shrimp, all of which is good fish food. However, generally speaking, the Nile perch that are found close to weeds are generally the smaller ones, probably due to the fact that weeds tend to grow in shallower water and the bigger Nile perch prefer the reassurance of deep water close by, that they can escape into. Barrie remembers getting six Nile perch out of one small gap in thick weeds, simply by working a small Rapala jig through the gap. They were not big fish, but several were over 10lb.

There is one final consideration connected to bank fishing: because bank fishing spooks Nile perch much less than the presence of fishing boats, one of our techniques is, after locating a pod of fish by trolling, and perhaps having had a strike or two, the boat backs off and pulls into the shore some distance away, and the fishers proceed on foot back to the taking zone. This can be a highly productive approach, with fish after fish being taken on occasions. The danger is that, with fish after fish coming to the rods, the anglers can become less cautious and careful than they should be – and that is when a giant fish puts in an appearance.

In this chapter, we have only dealt with lure fishing from the bank, but livebaiting also works well, as we have described elsewhere in the book (Chapter 11). In fact, in some circumstances it may be the best approach – if you have the bait. Bank-fished deadbaits, suspended beneath a float, have produced more tigerfish for Barrie than they have Nile perch. And deadbaits on the bottom are usually used for cat fishing at night, at the camp or in its vicinity. It would be interesting to discover whether or not a daytime bank-fished deadbait would regularly work in a known and 'going' Nile perch hotspot.

One of the great pleasures of bank fishing at the end of the day.

9 ADVANCED BOAT FISHING

The start of the day: fishing in glassy calm conditions, so typical of Lake Nasser.

Generally speaking you will catch most of your big Nile perch whilst trolling, because trolling covers a larger area of water and, as a result, puts the lures in sight of more fish. Landing big fish is also much easier from a boat than it is from the shore, due to the heavier boat tackle used and the advantages of playing fish from a moving boat, not to mention the very close assistance of a Nubian guide.

There is not really a huge amount of further information that we need to give you about trolling, because compared to bank fishing it is a relatively sedate and straightforward pastime. The *modus operandi*, for the most part, involves making sure that your fishing tackle is correct, that you have the right lure for the circumstances, and that you let the lure out behind the boat for the correct distance – then you just sit there and wait for something to happen – not

forgetting to work the lure, and being sure that you hold the rod: most certainly, that you hold the rod! We must emphasize, too, that trolling is *not* boring, not on Lake Nasser.

Almost all the skill required for trolling is down to the guide who has to drive the boat, then find the fish and present your lure to them. You do have to work, but not a lot; indeed, trolling seems to be a mind condition of comfortable anticipation. On the down side, Tim has become convinced that 'experienced' Nile perch now associate the activities of the boat and the sound of the outboard with signs of danger. This subject has been discussed already, but we will mention it briefly again: because of our catch and release policy (which we will never change) the released fish are returned to the lake, but because of their experience they will instinctively associate the sound of a boat engine

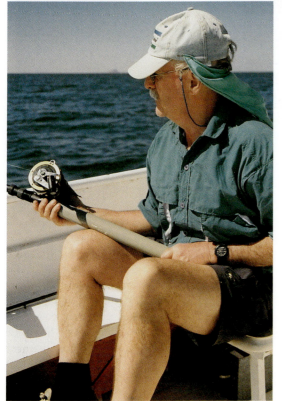

ABOVE: All prepared – all the boats have echo sounders (fish finders) and rod holders.

LEFT: Barrie trolling with lure and trusty Policansky multiplier. Rods are held all the time for Nile perch, and are not *fished in rod holders.*

with danger. This problem was recognized many years ago, and at the time Tim instructed the guides to cut the motor as soon as a reasonable size fish was hooked, and then let the angler fight the fish from a drifting boat (as long as the conditions were safe and there was no danger of going aground). He also told them to pay a lot more attention to shore fishing, and to give the trolling swims more time to rest.

On a normal safari as much as 80 per cent of the time is spent trolling. This is probably largely due to the fact that trolling requires very little effort, and would be considered safer than shore fishing by many newcomers who in the back of their mind might be concerned about hazards on the bank such as loose rocks, crocodiles, snakes and scorpions – the unknown. In fact the

ABOVE: Boat in the wilderness, one of the great pleasures of Lake Nasser.

BELOW: Temporary and useful storage of lures on the gunwales of the trolling boat.

shores of Lake Nasser are safe, and except for the occasional scrapes and near misses, in fifteen years we can't recall anyone who has been injured badly enough to be taken off the lake.

Trolling Techniques

Trolling for Nile perch is not the same as deep sea trolling when you follow a straight line. Nile perch trolling is either close to deep rocky drop-offs or following underwater contours and out-crops where the perch live, which involves a lot of manoeuvring by the boat. This in turn means the angler must be alert, and keep an eye on what his lure is doing, and make sure that it has not got tangled up as a result of the boat turning a corner.

When the trolling boat turns a corner, a slack loop will be created in your trolled line, and rather than just allowing it to straighten out itself, it's a good idea to take up this slack and *work* the lure round the corner, giving it the occasional twitch, because corners are often a strike zone. You can also twitch the lure and change its speed and depth whilst sitting there waiting; this often gets results.

Pay attention to the action of your lure, and make sure it is always running true. From time to time the hooks on your trolled lure will pick up weed, and this will stop the action because you will just be dragging a lump of lure and weeds behind the boat. So although it is a bit of an effort, reel in the lure and clean it, because Nile perch don't take salad with their meal!

The height you hold your rod tip above the water level will, to a certain extent, affect how deep your lure is running. From time to time the guide will shout 'Rods up!', which means he has seen from his fish finder that the boat has just gone over a shallow patch, perhaps an underwater promontory or just a shallower area. Then you must hold your rod way above your head so the tip of the rod is as high as possible. This will bring your lure up in the water and hopefully take it over the snag. Again, it can be a good time for a take as it dives again.

Downrigging

We have done very little about downrigging on Lake Nasser simply because we have never real-ly felt that we needed to use this system of trolling. Also, downrigging is a very 'finicky' method that needs a lot of attention, and it always seems as if you have spent most of the time untangling the weight from submerged bushes, rocks or nets. We have lures that can quite easily be fished down to depths of 30ft plus, and that is probably about as deep as we need to get for regular fishing.

However, we now believe there is a use for one particular style of downrigging, and that is to slow-troll deadbait downrigged or float-trolled to about 6 or 7ft – in some areas you could downrig a bit deeper, but too deep and you will start to get snagging problems. Float trolling will have the same effect, no doubt. This works well during the summer months when the Nile perch are in shallower water and the Nile perch's favourite food – tigerfish and *Alestes* – stay close to the surface. As bait, small to medium-size tigerfish of 6 to 8in are ideal; these are easily obtainable from local fishermen.

When fish leap close to the boat – and they may do several times – slacken off a whisker. (Olivier Portrat)

ABOVE: *Attila Portrat, then aged eight, exhibiting one of his father's fish. (Olivier Portrat)*

BELOW: *Playing a big perch from the stern. Note the large mouth – this is a fish over 100lb.*

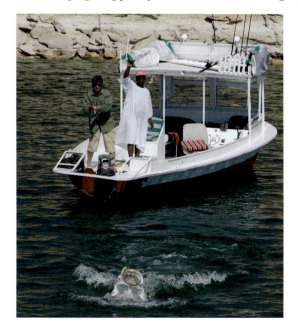

Looking after your Lures

One of the neglected areas of trolling is the care of your lures and their accessibility. It may be important to change lures frequently, and they need to be within reach – but safe. Do not, therefore, leave them lying about on any decks or the beds. Arrange them in rows on the gunwales, but not where someone will accidentally get hooked up on them. You can keep them in the usual custom-built lure boxes, but these are hardly quickly available. You have a lot more gear around, in addition to the lures, and this should always be kept in a tidy state to improve the overall efficiency of your lure fishing. It is a neglected art! If you need a treble, or tape, or pliers, it doesn't help at all if you can't find them: being too casual is the bane of the would-be troller.

ABOVE: On the way to camp, and supper…probably the last troll of the evening.

RIGHT: We never tire of the vista of rock and sand dunes. This is real wilderness fishing.

Angler 'Hook-Up'

Fish are not the only ones in danger of getting hooked. Leaving lures lying around the boat is not a good idea, especially when anglers are not wearing shoes. One day Tim was fishing with John Wilson, casting from a drifting boat, when they hit a pod of perch: they had a double hook-up, which resulted in a lot of action and running around the boat. In the course of the action Tim stepped on a closed lure wallet, and a hook came through the canvas side and attached the wallet to the heel of his foot. It must have been quite a sight to see Tim hopping around on one foot playing a good fish with a lure wallet dangling from the other foot. Two fish were on, so there was no immediate help at hand – and John was quietly having hysterics while playing his fish and watching Tim. When both fish were landed, John straightened up from releasing his fish and reached for a pair of pliers. With a wry smile and an expression that clearly said 'This is going to be interesting,' he said to Tim 'OK, let's get it over with!'

The soles of Tim's feet are very leathery and tough (in fact they are somewhat disgusting), but the hook was in deep and the barb well embedded. After Dr Wilson had made his inspection he said, 'Sorry, Tim: the only way is a straight pull.' To this day when John tells this story he claims that Tim squealed like a stuck pig: this Tim strongly denies, maintaining he was quiet and manly throughout the 'surgery'.

10 LURES

Lures, baits and flies are perhaps the most talked about subjects between anglers, and this is certainly the case on Lake Nasser. Each season has different lure requirements: broadly speaking, in winter they need to be bigger and to go deeper, and in summer, slightly smaller and shallower. We will give you our opinions about the best lures to use, but keep in mind that conventional wisdom changes with time and gained experience, as Tim once remarked:

> As a keen angler I learnt long ago that the more you get to know about a particular style of fishing and the baits involved, the less – you come to realize – you actually know. After fifteen years and countless personal captures of Nile perch over 100lb you might think I am an expert. Maybe I know a bit more about it than most people, but I still have a long way to go and a great deal still to learn.

We will also discuss, where appropriate, the correct hooks, split rings, knots, swivels and terminal tackle.

Since Tim's first day's fishing on Lake Nasser on Sunday 17 January 1993 until the time of writing this book, almost all the fishing on the lake has been with lures and plastic soft baits. This means that Lake Nasser has developed as a conventional fishing venue simply because the perch have been so much easier to catch using lures or baits as opposed to more challenging fly-fishing techniques (discussed in Chapter 14). But as any experienced angler will realize, circumstances and fishing conditions are changing all the time, and to keep up a good catch record, attention must be paid to introducing new ideas, and new lures.

With fifteen years of experience one can start to analyse lure-catching patterns with some

Barrie using his alternative comedy mode of lure storage.

confidence. But this has been a slow process, because the Nubian guides on Nasser tend to favour particular lures that have caught big fish, often making the mistake of excluding all other lure options. The reason for this reluctance to experiment is the pressure to catch fish for their guests, and if one lure has worked before, then the guide is disinclined to 'waste' the angler's time trying a new lure or colour that might not work as well.

ABOVE: Many bank anglers prefer to use a multiplier reel with their lures.

RIGHT: Big Nile perch chewing a jointed Depth Raider.
(Olivier Portrat)

Tim and Barrie are always experimenting with new lures and methods, but a huge amount of experimental contribution has been made by anglers who come on safari with us. We have a debt of thanks to these, and to many other skilled anglers, for contributing their experience to experimenting with new lures, and teaching our guides to be more imaginative.

The Type of Lures used for Nile Perch

Although most of the information provided in this chapter is about lures that work on Lake Nasser, it is also good advice for catching Nile perch at other fishing venues, such as Lake Victoria and the Nile river in Uganda. We have researched the type of lures used, in particular on Lake Victoria, and have found strong similarities with the lures now used on Lake Nasser.

It is difficult to list Nile perch lures and plastic baits in order of importance because different lures are used for different occasions, such as the seasons, weather conditions, time of the day, the mood of the Nile perch, and especially when Nile perch are starting to become 'lure shy'. Your best chance is when the Nile perch are hungry and competing with each other, and then they will throw caution to the wind and grab almost everything. But it's when they are indifferent about feeding that we have to pay more attention to detail, and try to find ways to make them respond to a lure.

The most successful lure on Lake Nasser, the Rapala Super Shad Rap, here with a tenuous grip on a large fish. (Olivier Portrat)

There is a great saying: 'It's not the lure that counts, it's the jerk behind it' – and there's a lot of truth in this. You can have the very best equipment and all the right lures, but your catch results will always be in proportion to your fishing skills. Strategy and presentation are all-important for good catch records, especially when bank fishing, while trolling skills and finding the fish are more the responsibility of your guide.

When Barrie arrived on the water in 1994 the popular lure was the Rapala Super Shad Rap (RSSR) in various colour patterns, although the perch colour seemed to produce the most consistently; perhaps it resembled tilapia most closely. On occasions a bright orange lure worked, and sometimes a blue and silver. One common factor seemed to be that those lures with a bright red or orange flash under the belly worked best. Interestingly of all, of the lures used on Lake Nasser the RSSR continues to work well – though not as well as it did in the early years. Ringing the colour changes really can pay off, and it is as good from the bank as from the boat, and the red or orange flash still seems important. So the RSSR is a good bait to have at all times.

On Barrie's first trip, whilst the RSSR was the 'in' lure, many others were still being tried. Spoons and spinner baits did not seem to work too well, and were soon abandoned. Although on that first trip Barrie had fifty Nile perch up to 37lb (disappointing Tim at the time!), only a few fell to the RSSR because the fish seemed to be taking small lures – quite a number fell to Canadian Wigglys in bright red and orange colours. These are sinking metal plugs only about 3in long. The Gudebrod Sniper in bright yellow, one of Barrie's favourite pike lures, also succeeded quite well (including with tigerfish occasionally). Strangely, this lure did not succeed on subsequent trips, and it is now left at home.

Of course, these early trips were coloured by the fact that we were all just learning. For example, Barrie's retrieve speed when bank fishing was far too slow, and resulted in a number of very good fish coming short at the lure. He tried all manner of pikey lures, but eventually realized that the Rapala range, including the sinkers, countdowns and so on, were about the best.

On Barrie's second trip, fishing with Geoff Neville and Russell Manning, things were making more sense and they had a full range of RSSRs, several very large Nilsmaster Invincibles, a fistful of Canadian Wigglys, the Rapala range of floating divers and countdowns, and a few small Rapala jigs. Russell caught a fish of 80lb on a large red and white Nilsmaster Invincible, and on their very last day, Barrie and Geoff got in amongst good fish in the 60–70lb bracket, all falling to RSSRs in blue and silver with an orange belly. They were beginning to try some deeper diving lures on that trip, although it is worth noticing that a big sinking Rapala goes deep, as does the Nilsmaster Invincible. The latter also fishes well from the bank, even though it is difficult to throw it more than 20 yards.

It is interesting that the Rapala jigs were not widely used. Several times they produced a few nice but not big fish, and on one occasion several puffer fish – including one to Barrie of 5½lb, which, when deflated, looked like quite a decent carp; but jigs didn't catch on at that stage. By 2006, however, they were about the very best of lures. These jigs were not hard plastic, however, but were made of latex with extremely realistic colouring, soft feel, and very waggly tails. What is interesting to Barrie about this, is that in the

It is this vigorous fighting and twisting that mangles all except the toughest of trebles. (Olivier Portrat)

This is when the lures are shaken free. Keep a tightish line unless the fish is close to the boat: if it is, then slacken the line a little. (Olivier Portrat)

previous year he'd taken out a selection of them, but the Nubian guide on that occasion simply refused to cooperate in testing them. This is most unusual on the part of guides, but one or two of them do worry if you are not catching, not realizing that many experienced anglers really don't care in the least whether they catch or not, as long as they are doing what they want to do.

Quite early on it was realized that many Rapala treble hooks were not man enough for the job. Nowadays, guides insist on replacing doubtful trebles immediately, but this may be a little over the top, because you can certainly catch a fish or two before you need to change them! We'll discuss this further, later in the chapter.

The next phase, in about the year 2000, saw greater use of deep-diving or sinking lures with a very robust, vibrating swimming action, such as Ernie and Depth Raiders and similar actions in other brand names. Coupled with the repertoire developed early, primarily Super Shad Raps and Rapala countdowns, it began to look as if everything was being covered – shallows, deeps, and the fish-feeding vagaries too (sometimes up top, sometimes down below, sometimes hugging the shore rocks).

Thus by the early 2000s, the following range of lures was in use at various times by most serious anglers: Shad Raps (various); other Rapala lures in the Magnum range, and countdowns (CD) were more popular than floating – CD14, CD18 and even the deep sea CD22s were popular; Canadian Wiggly; Ernie; Grandmas, Depth Raiders; Russelures and Nilsmaster (especially Invincibles). Other lures used as standbys or on trial included Renosky's Natural Super Shad (preceding the present soft bait boom), Renosky Lurker Minnow, heavier Quickfish, various Yo-Zuri, electricity generating/flashing lures (good for tigerfish), and various surface poppers (these did not seem to work very often).

At that time jerkbait fishing had transferred to the UK from the USA, and was very successful with pike, so it was natural that UK anglers tried it for Nile perch – but it didn't really work. Fish have been caught on jerkbaits, it is true, but they haven't taken off at all in a big way. It is possible that they have not been used widely enough. Barrie has had considerable success with the Salmo Slider jerkbait, designed by Bert Rozemeijr, a lure that also works well with tigerfish. It casts like the proverbial bullet and can be fished shallow or deep, but is not a fast-retrieve lure in the floating version; however, other jerkbaits haven't work for him – yet.

Next to arrive on Lake Nasser were the Bulldawg and Invader brands, and similar types from other stables. These did, and do work. They have a fair bit of soft rubber, especially in the wiggly tails and rear of the body parts, so it is possible that the Nile perch hang on just that bit longer on occasion – longer than they might on a hard plastic plug. Bulldawgs can be trolled deep, and also fish well when cast from the bank. We do not have a feel yet for the best colours and sizes, though those with bright orange tails have done well. Then most recently we have seen the advent of the latex lures/jigs with the vibrating wiggly tails, as mentioned above. Those are still working well as we write.

ABOVE: *The new breed of rubber lures. Puffer fish bite lumps out of them!*

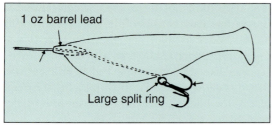

1 oz barrel lead

Large split ring

LEFT: *Rigging a Renosky Super Shad rubber bait.*

In short, it is difficult to stay ahead of the Nile perch. It has to be said that this business of them going 'off' particular lures is not in the mind of the angler: it is real. A lure they have never seen before is likely to work for a while as long as its action is good, the speed is good, and the resemblance to the prey fish is a reasonable approximation – or if the colours contain the essential triggers to incite a Nile perch to move, namely some red or orange (even if seen as shades of grey). Lures that have been successful in times past may come again, at least for a short while, whilst some, such as the RSSR, are evergreen, if browning just a little with the passage of time.

The search, then, is on for a new lure to succeed Bulldawgs and latex jigs, because they, too, will fall out of favour as the Nile perch wise up to them. As the years passed it became more and more obvious that the Nile perch were wising up to the lures we were using: fish are not as dumb as we think they are, and Nature endows each species with a strong 'survival instinct', otherwise it would soon be exterminated by its predators. This survival instinct is very much present in Nile perch that have survived – literally – for millions

In recent years the use of rubber lures with waggly tails has proved very successful.

of years. They soon learn to avoid danger – lures, hooks, boats and fishermen, and boats that were trolling noisily through the swims.

It also became evident that bank-fished lures also started to lose their effectiveness if the Nile perch saw them often enough. Perhaps none of this is surprising, for two reasons: one, by this stage several thousand Nile perch had been returned to the water; two, in most other spheres of angling, predatory fish eventually wise up to artificial lures (if not to natural bait as well).

A tip worth mentioning was introduced by Andy Davis. Andy, an experienced Nile perch angler, had held the then IGFA-approved 'all tackle' world record for Nile perch for some years, with a fish caught on Lake Victoria (until Adrian Brayshaw broke the first of three 'all tackle' world records to be broken on Lake Nasser, with a Nile perch of 213lb). We were shore fishing in a normally productive hotspot where the resident perch were spooky and were taking off at the first sight of Andy's Rapala magnum CD18, which had a standard silver diving vane. After an expert cast at a sighted fish that took off as soon as it saw Andy's CD18, he gave a mild curse and said, 'I am sure it's the flashing silver vane that is spooking these fish.'

When we got back to the fishing boat, magic markers were used to blacken and camouflage the silver diving vanes on our CD18s, and to this day Tim is convinced this works better and increases the effectiveness of the Rapala Magnum series. The logic is that the sun reflecting off a flashing vane will attract the perch's attention: great to start with, but as perch grow more lure shy the flash will start to act as a 'keep away' warning. We were also starting to notice that other lures – for example, Depth Raiders and Ernies with clear plastic vanes – were working better.

Lure and Bait Reports from the Past

In this section we have reprinted a selection of comments about lures taken from our news-letters published over the past few years, where Tim was summarizing current opinions, based on results. These reports really do show how ideas about lures and baits have changed

---

Small Lures and Big Fish

This is a story from 1993, only one year after we started fishing for Nile perch on Lake Nasser. Browsing through a dusty file labelled 'research', Tim came across some old notes scribbled on a faded bit of paper, 'words of wisdom' about a red-hot lure of the 1993 era: *Shore Lure: Formu Rat (Japan), slow retrieve – good deep runner weight on vane, Floating to jump over obstacles, Strong hooks* (or so we thought then).

The Formu Rat was a great lure that caught a lot of fish, but it was too small for bigger Nile perch: anything over 70lb inhaled it like a pea, resulting in deep throat hook-ups. Also, the hooks were totally inadequate and many bigger fish were lost – although at that time we were very laid back at losing big fish: not very satisfactory, but then, we still had a lot to learn.

In the early days we had a lot of crazy Formu Rat fights with big fish – and Bob Kimber had a fight that Tim will always remember. They were trolling along a steep rocky drop-off, as they did most of the time in those days, when Bob had a heavy strike – the sort that gives you the impression a boulder has been snagged, until the boulder starts to move and you can feel the thump of a big tail. Bob was fishing very light – absurdly light, to be honest. This fish was just taking line steadily, emptying Bob's reel; so the decision was made to chase the fish in the boat. Bob, an experienced fisherman, was doing all the correct things and holding on the best he could with the light tackle he was using.

This huge fish was just staying down deep: it did not give the impression it was panicked, but just carried on at a steady pace with the boat following, and Bob applying as much clutch as he could afford. Half an hour had passed and they found the fish heading into a small, deep, steep-sided bay; it gradually worked its way right into the middle of this bay, where it seemed to literally anchor itself. Bob tried everything to raise the fish, but it had obviously decided it was not going to move under any circumstance: he would work it up a couple of feet, and then it would win all the line back again. This went on for what seemed like hours, when at last something gave and the line parted. Poor Bob was gutted – every angler knows that bitter feeling when you have just lost something amazing, and you know you will never find out exactly what it was.

Throughout this story we have referred to what Bob had on the end of his rod as a 'fish', but to this day we are not sure what it was, and there has been a lot of speculation as to what it might have been. There are several theories, so you can decide for yourself. We don't think it was a perch, because it didn't fight like a perch, which will normally come to the surface, even if it doesn't actually jump. On the other hand, Nile perch are capable of growing to something like 550lb (250kg), so maybe it was a very big perch? Tim is convinced there are still some huge perch living in deep water feeding off bottlenose bream and big tilapia, which tend to stay in deeper water during the daylight hours.

Or was it perhaps a big vundu or a giant bagrus catfish? This is more likely than a Nile perch because of the way it behaved, digging deep and probably ending up in the middle of the bay burrowing its head into a bed of weeds. It couldn't have been a sunken fishing net because nets do not move for something close to half a mile, which whatever it was had done so on its way to the small bay, where it broke off the line.

Who knows? It is interesting that these experiences with the Formu Rat tally with Barrie's early success on Canadian Wigglys (also too small) – and of course, big pike take tiny lures quite often, as everyone knows.

LEFT: *Perhaps the most successful of all Nile perch lures, a selection of Rapala Super Shad Raps.*

LOWER LEFT: *Rapala Magnums CD22, CD18 and CD14, fitted with Owner Stinger 3/0, 2/0 and 1/0 hooks.*

BELOW: *The Rapala range – or part of it – of count-downs and deep divers.*

over the years, and it makes interesting reading with Barrie's observations, and comparisons with fishing for pike – the great European predator.

May to July 1997

For this time of the year the lures that were the most successful whilst trolling were not a surprise. Looking at our records, floating and jointed Depth Raiders and Super Shad Raps (RSSR) caught equal numbers of big fish. Some of the new Depth Raider colours were great (especially the pikey one), and the new metallic Rapala SSRs were good, except we discovered that the hooks on the latest RSSRs seemed to have a lot softer temper than previously: so these hooks needed to be replaced.

For shore fishing, the Rapala Magnum CD has reigned supreme, especially the CD18 right down to the CD9. We also discovered another use for the Russelure (5½in version), which is normally just used for trolling: they are excellent for shore fishing in deep water. They cast well, sink rapidly and, most importantly, hold their depth. They have three attachment points, and we found the middle attachment to be the best. The only disadvantage is that they are hard work to retrieve – but it is worth the effort.

October to December 1997
As we expected, during the winter months most of the big fish were caught on deeper diving lures. The sinking Depth Raider was the most widely used deep runner, but some very big fish were also caught using Rapala Magnum CD18s; also the 6½in version of the Russelure was a good catcher.

The choice of colours for all these lures seems to be entirely subjective, but perch-coloured sinking Depth Raiders were the flavour of the month. On the subject of Depth Raiders we strongly advocate replacing the hooks supplied by the manufacturer with the stronger Mustad 5Xs or similar.

We believe that when a lure has a set of three hooks it is preferable to remove the middle hook. In our opinion this does not lessen the chances of landing fish, but it definitely reduces the damage inflicted on fish, and eases the landing and unhooking process.

(Note: This comment about removing the middle hook from a set of three was eventually proved to be completely wrong advice. It was some time later that we discovered the best method was to remove the top hook and leave the second and last hook attached to the lure. We refer to this method, and why it works better, later in this chapter – and incidentally, this also works well with other predatory fish in other countries.)

Report October to December 1997
Through October to mid-November the weather on Lake Nasser was more akin to that of summer to mid-autumn, and the fishing tended to reflect this. When the lake was like a millpond, the fishing could be slow; but as soon as the wind picked up, the fish went crazy.

As water and air cooled, the perch dropped deeper in the water. The big fish grouped together and the smaller fish seemed to disappear – a very similar tale to the last couple of years. Once again it was a case of off with the Shad Raps and on with the Depth Raiders!

Virtually all the biggest fish have come on the troll. This is largely because we are exploring offshore areas out of shore-fishing range. This is just as well, as some of the fish being hooked would unfortunately stand little chance of being landed and returned successfully from the bank.

The trolling has been exceptionally good, with most big fish falling to deep lures. The Bucher Depth Raider is by far the most widely used deep runner, but some very big fish have been caught on Magnum CD18s, and the Russelure (in the 6½in size) is catching.

The choice of colours for all of these lures seems to be entirely subjective, but perch-colour sinking Depth Raiders are the flavour of the month!

Report March to June 1998
This season started steadily with plenty of good fish being caught. Early in March most of the better fish came on the troll and to deeper lures: Depth Raiders, CD18s etc. The morning/early afternoon periods were particularly productive, but the traditional hot time of late afternoon and early evening could be dour. However, as the weather and water warmed up, so the evening sport improved. The warmer water also brought fish into the shallows, and Shad Raps and other shallow lures became equally effective.

In general, the months of March to the end of June have been similar to those last year. The trolling has been good, at times excellent, and the shore fishing dynamite. Although as always we have had quiet spells, there is no overall sign of the fishing tailing off.

Report Summer and Winter 1999
Most anglers have a strong instinct to repeatedly use a lure (or colour) that they have been told catches, or which they have seen catch, an exceptional fish. Our Nubian guides also follow this same instinct. If the angler they are guiding catches a big Nile perch they will always strongly recommend the lure that caught this fish – time and time again, safari after safari – and the bigger the fish, the more the lure is recommended. It is not uncommon to have a group of six to eight anglers all using the same brand of lure and even perhaps the same colour, to the exclusion of almost all other baits.

Results are important, and when a particular lure is working it makes good sense to continue using it. On the other hand, we have often found that in a hotspot that has been heavily fished with one make of lure, a change produces better results. For example, during the winter season, in places where the Depth Raider and Russelure have been used extensively, we change to the Rapala Deep Sea Magnum CD22, with very satisfying results – although the two big double hooks that come fitted to the CD22 are designed for a different type of fish, and we recommend they are replaced with 3/0 or 4/0 trebles. When the perch are not lying very deep, a good lure to have available is the Nilsmaster 25cm Magnum, a great lure but one that doesn't dive as deep as the similar size Rapala CD22.

During the 1999 winter season a lure that particularly impressed was the Reef Digger. We wouldn't mind betting this lure will become one of the hottest lures on the lake for the big fish. The Reef Digger was introduced by two experienced American anglers, George Liska and Charles Patrasek. On a two-week safari in October, between them they caught eighteen Nile perch over 75lb.

The Reef Digger is a big lure about 10in long, with a prominent vane that takes the lure down to about 16 to 17ft, a bit deeper than the Depth Raider. The swimming action is erratic and there is a rattle, both good strike signals for a big perch. The available colour ranges are the same as what we are used to with the Rapala and Depth Raider ranges. The Reef Digger is an American lure, and to date we have not discovered where to buy them.

We are starting to agree with the old saying 'size counts', in particular when it comes to the size of lure used to catch Nile perch of 100lb, especially during the winter months. Mammal predators will not expend a lot of energy and vital protein chasing small prey if they can conserve their energy for more substantial meals that can better stock up their energy reserve, so why should predatory fish be any different? This can also be true of other predatory fish, such as the pike.

During the summer months we reduce the size of the lures and also lighten up a bit with the rod and reel to take advantage of the excellent sport from smaller Nile perch from 30–50lb plus. During mid-March to late April the tilapia and other species start spawning, mostly in shallower water, and this draws the Nile perch out of deep water into depths as shallow as 8 to 10ft. For some reason, in summer there are many smaller (30–50lb) Nile perch in evidence. Summer is the season for excellent sport shore fishing, as opposed to winter when the shore fishing can be difficult and slow. The big Nile perch are still around but much more spread out than they are in winter.

The all-time Nasser summer favourite is the Rapala SSR that swims at about 7ft deep. This lure has the shape of a small tilapia and a very alluring swimming action. We tend to have a preference for more natural-looking colours and recommend the metallic silver and bronze. The fire tiger and redheads are also good catchers.

The Rapala CD14 ranges are also very popular with top Nasser anglers and produce good results shore fishing and casting from a drifting boat. Just one size bigger and, in our opinion, almost as effective is the Rapala CD18. Both the CD14 and CD18 have interesting colour options. The purple and orange colours work well.

You will have noted that we are constantly referring to CD lures (countdown) as opposed to F (floating lures). The beauty of a CD is its versatility: if you cast it into shallower water and immediately retrieve, it will swim at its designed depth, but if you find a deeper pool you can cast and count down approximately one foot per second and get down to the fish lying in deeper water. On the other hand, a floating lure designed to dig in and swim deep is useful because when you hit a snag you simply stop reeling and the floating lure will rise and clear the obstacle. You can use the same trick as the bank is approached.

A floating medium-deep diver we have been testing is the Little Ernie. Its big brother Big Ernie is already a popular lure alongside the

Depth Raiders. Ernie lures are designed for catching musky in America, and are made by an American company, Musky Mania Tackle. The Little Ernie is 5½in long, and really digs in deep with a good swimming action. It's a tough lure, except that the eyes drop out, so we call our favourite catcher 'Nelson'. A useful feature of the Ernie is that it has a built-in rattle. The results of field tests prove that this lure is a good catcher, and we can recommend it as a summer shore-fishing lure.

Lure and Terminal Tackle Tips from 1999

Experienced anglers will have developed their own terminal tackle methods, which work for the species of fish they are normally targeting. When you go fishing for Nile perch do not underestimate the perch's ability to do incredible damage to lures, treble hooks and split rings that are designed for normal angling. Note also the following words of advice:

Depth Raiders: We advise that the treble hooks supplied with Depth Raiders are replaced with stronger Mustad 5Xs or Gamakatsu trebles. Remember to bring a hook sharpener, because Mustad trebles will need to be sharpened frequently.

Hooks and split rings: We recommend changing hooks and split rings on all lures with the exception of the Russelure and the bigger Rapala Magnums. We have started to find that the hooks provided with recently manufactured smaller Rapala lures, RSSRs and Magnums from 18cm or smaller are not as strong as they were in the old days, and we now recommend these trebles are also changed. You might only have one chance at the big one, so it's better to be safe than sorry. Wolverine split rings are reliable.

Nilsmaster Invincible: Possibly because it imitates a tigerfish, the big Nilsmaster Invincible has been catching well, and is a useful middle rod lure running to about 12ft. As with other lures with three hook attachments, we prefer to dispense with one treble. A new lure that runs to a similar depth – perhaps a bit deeper – is the Musky Mania Ernie. It looks very tough, has a great action, and so far has caught plenty of fish.

We feel it is a mistake to get obsessed with particular lures. Many anglers feel that in winter if you're not fishing a Depth Raider you won't catch, and in summer the same blinkered attitude is applied to Rapala SSRs. The important thing is to match the lure to the season, and to have confidence in your own 'gut feeling' and try something that nobody else is using. Many anglers who visited the lake last June and July can attest to the efficiency of Depth Raiders in high summer, and on several occasions in winter we caught on RSSRs and floating Magnums when Depth Raiders produced nothing.

For shore fishing the Rapala Countdown range, from the tiny CD9 up to the CD18, is probably the most successful, in particular the CD14, which is sometimes used almost to the exclusion of anything else! Sinking Depth Raiders are also great, particularly when casting into deep water, as are Russelures. Both of these lures require heavy rods and will make your arm ache! The Luhr Jensen Fingerling and the Manns Stretch 25+ are both floating deep-divers that deserve more use. They must both be refitted with stronger hooks and rings.

When attaching a lure we do not have confidence in cross-lock swivels: there have been far too many occasions when even a heavy duty cross-lock swivel has failed. We recommend two methods: either the Rapala knot, or a simple but very tough paper-clip type attachment, similar to an elongated split ring. Importantly, both these methods allow the lure to swim in the way it is designed to. Heavy terminal tackle can seriously affect the swimming action of lures if not connected up correctly.

The Renosky Super Shad is a lure that has been really effective, especially for spooky fish, or fish that you can spot-cast to. The Renosky Super Shad in the largest (205mm) size is good when mounted with a large treble and a lead weight. The 'smelt' colour is the exact image of a tilapia in the water, while the 'brown trout' resembles a puffer. To rig a Renosky Super Shad, push a pair of forceps or an eyed baiting needle into the vent of the rubber fish, up through the body and out of the mouth (*see* page 104). Grasp the 80lb mono, and pull it back through and out of the vent. Tie on a big split ring and pull it flush with the vent. The split ring will help stop the hook being pulled into the rubber fish and the hook points being embedded in the rubber. Attach a big (4/0), very sharp treble. At the other end of the 80lb mono cut off the trace about 8in above the fish – the short trace means you can just attach it to your normal wire or mono shore-fishing trace. Slide the barrel lead down the line from this end, and push it into the head of the rubber fish. Tie on a swivel to the top of the trace. When fishing with a rubber fish it's worth taking a pair of long pliers, as the perch sometimes engulf the whole lure.

Favourite Lures 1998–2007

We all have favourite lures, some that seem to catch consistently and others that have produced perhaps only one fish but a memorable one. Our guides are fishing on Lake Nasser for up to eight months every year, so we decided to ask some of them to select two lures for summer and two for winter, and finally, if they were only allowed to have one lure to cover both winter and summer, which one would they rate as the best all-rounder. This question was first asked in a newsletter published in 1998. Each guide gave his answer separately from the others, and didn't know what the other guides had said. Without reminding the guides what their preference was in 1998, we asked them the same question in 2007 – ten years later. The following is a comparison of their replies ten years apart.

Red-head lures of various kinds are reliable at various times, especially dusk. This lure is a Manns Stretch 30+. (Olivier Portrat)

Ahmed 'Bushera'

1998: The lures that catch the most Nile perch change with the time of year. In the winter months when the fish are deep, if I had to select only one trolling lure, it would be a sinking Depth Raider, and the colours I like best are silver bait fish and perch because they look most like the fish in the lake.

In the summer months when the Nile perch are in shallow water, my favourite is the Rapala Shad Rap (RSSR) and the big Nilsmaster as middle or outside trolling lure. Because the water is less clear (because of algae bloom) in summer I like brighter colours – with the Shad Rap, the best is natural roach because it looks very like a *sardina* (local name for an *Alestes*, which is a large sardine look-alike). For shore fishing Shad Raps are good, but the best all-rounder is the sinking Rapala Magnum CD14 and CD11 (CD countdown or sinking).

If I could have only one lure for both winter and summer, I would take a sinking Depth Raider in natural roach colour.

2007: My first thought, when you ask about selecting only two lures for the winter months, is a Manns Stretch 30+, in colours silver bait fish or a redhead. A very close second would be the

big Reef Digger, the one that has two connecting rings on the diving vane. One ring will take the lure to 20ft and the second to a depth of up to 30ft, depending on the type of line used; colours would be fire tiger and perch.

For the summer season my first lure is the straight-floating Depth Raider in the colour silver bait fish. This lure has a good action and does not run too deep when the perch are in shallow water. My second choice is a Rapala SSR, and the colour – well, I am not sure what you call it, I don't think they're making them any more: it has a dark silvery colour with an orange belly and a black dot on each side. (This is the lure that Barrie and Geoff Neville once did so well on.)

If I were allowed only one lure for both seasons it would be a Rapala sinking RSSR, probably the perch colour.

Shaban 'Shabby'

1998: I have to choose the jointed Depth Raider in silver as my favourite. All the Depth Raiders are good, but the jointed one has the best action. CD14s are excellent for shore fishing, but I also like to troll with them. They're a nice size and they run a little bit deeper than Shad Raps. Probably the orange one is my favourite. Shad Raps are great, too, particularly the redhead. From the shore, as well as CD14s I like CD11s in grey, especially if the fishing is hard. When you can actually see the Nile perch shore fishing, the rubber fish (Renosky Shad) is very good.

If I were only allowed one lure for both winter and summer it would be the Rapala CD14 or 18, coloured orange.

2007: My favourite lure for the summer months is a Rapala SSR in perch and redhead colours, because most of the Nile perch are in shallower water close to the bushes and weedbeds. The second lure would be a big Ernie, again perch and fire-tiger colours. The perch colour looks like a small tilapia.

In winter I would take a sinking Depth Raider and a Manns Stretch 30+. These two lures will give me both deep and medium trolling depths,

and the Depth Raider will be good for countdown shore fishing.

If I were allowed only one lure for both winter and summer it would be a small Ernie in the dark perch colour.

Mohamed 'Elephantine'

1998: For trolling all through the year I really like Depth Raiders. In my opinion the best is the straight floater in perch or pike colours. For deep trolling, particularly in the winter, the biggest Russelure in either green or silver is brilliant. It runs deeper than Depth Raiders, is really strong, and swims very strongly. The CD18 in orange is another good winter lure and is also very useful from the shore. My favourite Shad Rap is the brown one (Crawdad); in the water it looks just like a small tilapia.

If you are casting into deep water from the shore I would again choose a Russelure. I also like rubber fish – they look very life-like.

If I were allowed just one lure for both winter and summer? The Rapala CD18 in orange.

2007: My first choice for summer is the sinking Rapala SSR in perch colour because it looks like a tilapia and I like the orange belly. I would also take a redhead Manns Stretch in summer, to get at some of the bigger fish that like the deeper water.

In winter my first lure will be a big Ernie colour yellow and brown, because it has a medium to deep running depth and can also be used from the shore. The second lure will be a Manns Stretch 30+, but I also like the Halco Crazy deep which quickly gets down to 20ft plus, and the colour would be red nut – a great lure, but it needs stronger hooks for Nile perch.

If I could have just one lure for both winter and summer I would take a Rapala sinking SSR in perch colour.

Ramadan 'Fox'

1998: At this time of year – in the summer – I use Shad Raps a lot. The redhead is always a good colour, but the gold ones are even better, I think. As well as the Shad Rap I also like floating Rapala Magnums, again in redhead. They dive to the same depth as the Shad but have a different action and seem stronger. When the fish are deeper, the sinking Depth Raider is the best. I would choose perch, pike and redhead. Sinking Depth Raiders are also very good shore-fishing lures, but the CD14 is probably the most popular.

Just one lure for both winter and summer? The sinking Depth Raider in perch colour.

2007: This summer some Australian fishermen introduced me to a new lure, which caught a lot of good fish. I think it is called a Big Boss. The two colours I like are the redheads and another one that is blue and white. You must get some for the tackle hire. This lure has the same action as a RSSR, but maybe runs a bit deeper. The second lure for summer will be a Little Ernie, which is good for both trolling and casting from the shore.

In winter I would take the Manns Stretch 30+, either redhead or the silver-blue colour. My second lure would be a Big Ernie in perch or fire tiger; this lure has a good action and swims deep for winter, depending on whether mono or braid line is used.

If I were allowed only one lure on Lake Nasser I would take a redhead Manns Stretch 30+. This is an unusual choice, but I have found that most of the big fish tend to prefer deeper water, and big fish are what the *hawager* (visiting guests) are interested in. (This is not strictly true, and to many British anglers 30lb is big!)

Will Wragg

Depth Raiders and Shad Raps are great lures, but I'm always on the lookout for something new or different. The Musky Killer Ernie is a good-looking new lure, and I've caught a lot of fish on the rainbow trout colour. Like Ramadan, I often use the floating Magnum 18 in place of a Shad, but my favourite colour is orange, especially early morning or late

evening. For the winter, the Russelures are an essential lure and they seem to be unbreakable.

When shore fishing I will generally have on either a gold Russelure, or for stalking, a Renosky Super Shad. If the going gets tough I may change to a drab-coloured CD11.

Barrie Rickards

1998: In 1998 I was still following pikers' methods and types of lures. I tried hard with spoons and spinnerbaits, but quickly reverted to Super Shad Raps. Even my Gudebrod Snipers were abandoned as too slow for Nile perch. For deeper work I used Canadian Wigglys, and these did work, but my early trips were in low water conditions so really deep-water work was unnecessary. I always tried a range of lures, and changed my lures regularly. You can't succeed for long by sticking with one lure.

2007: In 2007 I used the whole gamut of deep and shallow lures, including all the usual CDs and Depth Raiders. Unlike 2006 when rubber lures worked well, I didn't do so well this time, but the Nilsmaster Invincible came into its own again – but so did Rapala SSRs. Again, I tried all manner of new lures, such as beautiful tilapia look-alikes, and I'll keep on trying new ones, and I'll keep on changing lures regularly.

Tim Baily
('Mr Tim', alias 'Tum Belly' according to the Nubian guides)

1998: I feel more confident using a lure that resembles the natural prey as closely as possible, in both shape and colour. I also believe vibration and swimming action is important, so a lure with plenty of 'activity' is preferable. I am always looking for new ideas, and at the moment some of the Australian barramundi lures have my attention. I have favourite lures and colours for different seasons and times of day.

In reply to the question 'If you were only allowed one lure, which would it be?', for both trolling and shore fishing I would take a sinking Rapala Magnum CD14, in silver-grey colour.

2007: My opinion has only changed slightly since 1998 about using lures that closely resemble the 'real' prey. I still believe this, but have also come to realize that most fish don't just take a lure because they are hungry, and other instincts also come into play, such as aggression and curiosity.

My preference is shore fishing as opposed to trolling, which means my choice of lures favours casting, rather than the bigger trolling lures. In summer my first choice would have to be a sinking Rapala SSR in either fire tiger or gold. The second lure would be a sinking Depth Raider (or Big Ernie) in the black perch pattern.

In winter, when I am fishing by myself, I still prefer bank fishing, and my choice will be the same as the summer season because I would be using sinking lures that can reach the depths I will need in winter by counting the lure down.

If I were only allowed to take one lure on safari it would be a sinking gold Rapala SSR. Rapala have (at last!) introduced a sinking version (2004) of their RSSR, which is great for countdown fishing from the shore; it's also a good trolling lure.

Lake Victoria Lures

We sent an email to Paul Goldering who operates Nile perch-fishing safaris through his company Wild Frontiers on Lake Victoria out of Uganda, and asked Paul the following question: Please can we have some information about the most effective lures you use for Nile perch? It will be interesting to make comparisons with Lake Nasser. He replied:

The most successful lure on Lake Victoria (Uganda) in the last ten years is the Manns Stretch 25+. We have used all shapes, colours and size of lures. Some odd lures have worked well for a period. My best lure in 1997 was a Stump Jumper, an Aussie lure with a replaceable

lip. It hammered the fish when all else got a 'dilly wash'; a client lost it on a fish. So at £8 a shot we ordered ten from a smiling Mr Harris. Bloody things have not caught a fish since! At other times one particular lure gets constant action, and the same lure on the next door line, same colour, not even a sniff. In no particular order we use the following lures: Rapala CD18 – Depth Raider – Russelure – Halco Sorcerer – Nilsmaster – Rapala Super Shad Rap.

Australian Magic

Tim Baily is continually testing new lures for Nile perch on Lake Nasser, and the range he has been interested in are Australian lures that are the Aussies' favourites for barramundi. The following is Tim's report from 2003:

Over the past few months I have been extensively testing the Halco Tackle Company Scorpion 150 DD, which Halco claims to be the ultimate big barramundi lure. The Nile perch like it, and I have had exceptionally good results when using this lure for shore fishing.

The Scorpion 150 DD is 7in in length, which is a nice tempting size for a medium-size Nile perch. This lure casts easily, hardly ever tangling, and dives to approximately 15ft. I was impressed with the diving action of this lure: it has a determined air about it – 'let me get down there and sort those fish out' – and off it goes, straight down into action. It is also a floating lure, which at first gave me second thoughts because I like a sinking lure that can be counted down into the holes where Nile perch are lying slightly deeper than normal. But in fact, I found that because the Scorpion floats, it was very helpful when the lure hit an underwater rock – a slight pause on retrieve, and the lure floats up a foot or so and clears the obstacle.

Lake Nasser's current favourite lure for shore fishing, in the same size range as the Scorpion, is the Rapala CD14 (CD – countdown). Rapala CD14s are really good lures, tough, dependable and with a good tight action – if anything maybe just a little too tight. The Scorpion 150 DD has an appealing body roll and a light rattle. I am almost positive that Nile perch are attracted by this extra body action, and especially the light rattle. The advantage of slightly exaggerated body movement in a lure is born out by the big success of two Nasser trolling lures, the Russelure and the Depth Raider, both of which have an exaggerated body action. The rattle in the Depth Raider is also, I am sure, a big plus.

The remaining big question is, is the Scorpion tough enough for Nile perch? I can't say for sure about fish over 75lb, but I have been impressed with the overall strength of this lure.

I am careful about changing the treble hooks on most lures in the Nasser lure armoury. I have not changed the Scorpion 150 DD hooks, and to date (and they have landed a lot of Nile perch) I have not had a Scorpion hook straighten out on me. This lure is adequately tough enough for the job of catching the smaller perch in the 15–50lb range, and it hangs on really well with big fish – but ultimately it is not a big fish lure, but a killer of medium-range Nile perch.

I have found that I am not losing as many Scorpions on the rocks as I do the Rapala CD14. One Scorpion that I have been using extensively has caught twelve Nile perch between 15 and 40lb, and is still looking positively ready for more action.

In conclusion, we now have an exciting new shore-fishing lure in the Scorpion 150 DD: good diving efficiency, an appealing body action, a light rattle and comfortable casting ability (I cast with a Calcutta 400 multiplier rather than a fixed spool reel). I will be including this lure in our tackle box that we hire out, and will also recommend the Scorpion 150 DD to anyone coming on safari with us. I would not mind betting that this lure will also appeal to the British pike. The latest models include the 'crazy deep' version.

Hooks, Split Rings and Snap Lock Swivels: 2008

You can see from the picture on page 54 the damage that a Nile perch can do to a lure. The Rapala SSR shown in this illustration eventually landed an 85lb Nile perch. The hooks are still intact because the original manufacturer's hooks were replaced with Owners ST-4X Stinger trebles – the original hooks would not have held under the pressure, and the fish would have been lost.

Tim changes the hooks on almost all the lures the African Angler provides in the tackle boxes they hire out to anglers. The hooks used are Owners ST-4X Stinger trebles, which are considered the strongest and sharpest on the market (they are also the most expensive). Other types of hooks are also sufficient, for example the Mustad 4X, but these hooks seem to need sharpening, which can be a hassle. Extra strong Gamakatsu trebles are also reliable.

Avoid treble trouble. Occasionally we've had to remove deeply embedded trebles from anglers' hands, legs, and even a nose. These hooks are big, which makes removing them from an angler a most unpleasant and painful experience, and one that could have been avoided. When you are shore fishing your guide will be on hand, and it's his job to land and unhook fish for you. Guides are good at unhooking because they have already learnt the hard way, most of them having already been 'hooked' themselves.

If you intend to do a lot of shore fishing on your own you must come well prepared. It is very important that you bring a strong glove (left-handed for a right-handed angler, and vice versa) and a good set of long-nosed pliers. The glove should be worn for landing every fish, whatever the size. Indeed, smaller fish are more dangerous than bigger ones, because like Jack Pike they can lever up their entire weight and flip, causing trebles to fly uncontrollably around. Rather than lugging around huge tackle boxes on precarious rocks, the best way to transport gloves, pliers, stringer, spare lures and so on, is in a bum bag, which is comfortable and doesn't affect your balance or ability to cast.

Tim does not like gloves because he is worried the big, super sharp Stinger trebles will go clean through the glove and into the hand, causing an even greater problem getting the hook out of your hand. Maybe you should take Tim's advice, because he has unhooked many hundreds of perch of all sizes and has some experience. His rule is to make sure the fish is properly secured and lying quite still before any attempt is made to remove the hooks, and he always uses pliers with long handles.

Tim has also removed many hooks from other anglers. Perhaps the most amusing was when he had to extract a Rapala CD18 from the nose of a Frenchman. You might well ask 'How the ... did he manage to get hooked up in the nose?' It all happened while taking a trophy photograph, and the Frenchman decided to display in the same photo the lure that had caught the fish: he placed it on to the head of the 'still green' perch in his arms, but the perch lunged, and threw the lure up into his face – and very fortunately it landed on his nose. Tim said he quite enjoyed extracting this hooked Frenchman, because they had just beaten the English in the World Cup!

It is also important to replace the split rings on most lures. The split rings now used on Lake Nasser have three twists instead of just two; they are made by the Wolverine Tackle Co. in America, which claims they are the strongest split rings in the world – which might well be true.

Rapala SSR and the Rapala Magnum series have strong enough split rings, but change the hooks. The split rings on the RSSR shown in the picture are the original Rapala split rings, but the hooks have been changed. Change the split rings on all Depth Raiders and Ernies, as well as most other Nile perch lures that are used to target big fish.

The size of split ring will depend on the size of the lure, but for most Nile perch lures – Rapala SSR, Depth Raiders, Ernies and so on, size #7 split rings are the size to order. The Wolverine rings are available in black and stainless steel; we suggest you use the black split rings, although they are not as corrosion resistant as the silver ones, which are made with zinc and nickel. Corrosion will not be a problem if you are only using your lures in freshwater, but the silver ones will be better if you plan to use your lures for sea fishing as well.

We suggest you do not use cross-lock swivels for trolling or shore fishing while you are targeting big fish. It is more efficient to tie your monofilament leader directly on to the lure attachment ring using a version of the Rapala knot. Any good guide will also be able to show you how to tie this simple but very effective knot.

Knots

When we first started fishing for Nile perch on Lake Nasser we rigged our terminal tackle in the traditional way by attaching the main line to a Rosco 80lb swivel and then attaching the 80lb or 100lb monofilament (or wire in the very early days) trace to the other end of the swivel; then finally we attached a heavy snap-lock swivel to the end of the trace. It was quite a long-winded method making up traces, and you had to make absolutely sure all your knots were correct.

Many anglers get set in their ways, and when one method works, see no reason to change: if it seems to be working, then it is OK. Our original method of rigging terminal tackle worked quite well and we had a high measure of success and landed a great many big, heavy Nile perch; but we were also losing a lot of good fish due to tackle failure. We have mentioned in several places in this book the quite amazing terminal tackle destructive ability that Nile perch have. Knots would fail, and as mentioned, snap-lock swivels would straighten out, but it seemed this was all part of the hazard of taking on big fish. Now that big fish are not as plentiful as during the early days, we are a lot more careful.

By far the greatest part of our learning curve in the early days on the lake was fed by the experience of the many anglers who came to fish with us. Quite literally we had expert anglers coming from all parts of the world: English, American, Australian, Europeans, Russians, Czechs and even the occasional Japanese 'fishing Samurai'. Many of these men are top anglers who travel the world looking for big fish, and in their travels they have picked up a lot of experience. We were beginners, so listened avidly and learned the lessons from them.

One of these men was Larry Dhalberg, a top American television angling personality well known for his unique fly the Dhalberg Diver, who came on safari with us in 1997. Larry took one look at the way Tim was rigging his terminal tackle, and politely remarked:

That rig looks OK, but personally I find it too complicated for what we want to achieve, and that is to cast a lure, not to spin it. You are using lures, not spinners and spoons, which will twist your line if swivels are not used. You don't need swivels because all good quality lures will run true without swivels, and I find there are also other advantages not having swivels.

Larry uses a multiplier for casting, but the method he showed us works equally well for fixed spool reels: he attaches his main line to a long 80lb leader with a bimini knot, and then the lure is attached to the shock leader with a version of the Rapala knot. Larry's rig looked very neat, and the bimini knot slipped easily through the rod eyes with no problems, which allowed him to have a nice long leader without the swivel constantly getting snagged in the top eye of his rod.

There were only two knots involved with Larry's rig, giving simplicity and strength. Best of all, his system worked very well for casting, and ever since that day Tim has never used a swivel or a snap-lock swivel for either casting or trolling. Mind you, as we have said, spinning is another matter. And maybe now, Tim is set in his ways and others might not completely agree with his or Larry's method – but then, that is fishing, where there are always many different opinions, which only goes to make fishing the fun that it is.

Another problem you must be ready for, especially when shore fishing but also while trolling, is having your line dragged over rocks and snags and then breaking. While fighting at the end of your line, a Nile perch will not actually go and hide among rocks and crevices: rather, they will swim past or through rocks, dragging your line

Correct Lure Placement

Placing your lure correctly needs a special mention as it is one of the keys to catching more fish. It is seldom the objective to get as deep as possible or to cast as far as you can, but instead to get the lure to where the fish is located, and present an opportunity to strike.

The actual maximum running depth of a lure will vary, depending upon several factors: the length of the cast (from rod tip to lure), the diameter of the line (the thinner the line, the deeper it will run), and to a lesser extent, the speed of the retrieve or troll (a faster retrieve or troll results in a deeper running bait). Basically speaking, longer casts with thinner line will make the lure run deeper, whereas shorter casts with heavier line will result in a shallower track. While trolling, additional weight can be added 3–5ft in front of the lure to attain extra depth; the speed of troll will also affect the depth achieved.

behind them and putting it at grave risk of being broken. We add some insurance by doubling up the main line for about 5 to 6ft from where it is attached to the shock leader; this doubling up will give extra strength when it is dragged over rocks or through bushes.

The knot Tim now uses is to twist both ends of the line and shock leader over each other (eight to nine times at each end), leaving an opening where he starts in the middle; then he passes each end of the line and shock leader back through this loop and tightens the two together. Barrie uses the Rapala knot, a link swivel (protected by tape), but his preferred knot is the half blood knot. Although this knot is out of fashion these days, it really is still a knot to be reckoned with.

Recommended Lures and Baits for 2008 and the Future

(See also Chapter 16)
From what we have learned over the years we have put together a list of lures and baits that are the current recommendations for 2008 and beyond. These lures presently work on Lake Nasser; other venues such as Lake Victoria and Murchison Falls might vary slightly, but not by a great deal. No doubt in a year or so some of our recommendations might well change, as we make progress by improving our strategy.

To correctly field test a new lure you should test it thoroughly through many different fishing conditions. But when it comes to the bottom line, the best method is to follow 'gut instinct', and this should come from someone who has had a lot of experience catching Nile perch, or other larger predators for that matter. The Tropic of Cancer bisects Lake Nasser just south of Aswan and so puts much of the lake into the northern hemisphere, giving it the seasons of spring, summer, autumn and winter (unlike Lake Victoria, which is located on the equator and has no seasons except for a rainy or dry time of year).

Lures marked below with two or three asterisks **/*** show our level of recommendation,

thus: must have ***; recommended **. Following this list of super lures you will find a more detailed breakdown of their features and use. They are presented in alphabetical order:

Depth Raider, straight and jointed **
Fox Replica *
Halco Crazy Deep and Sorcerer *
Mann's Stretch Imitator Junior *
Mann's Stretch 30+, 25+ and 18+ **
Musky Big Ernie and Little Ernie **
Rapala:
    RSSR floating and sinking **
    Magnum series, CD14, CD 18 and CD22 *
    X-Rap Magnum 30 *
    X-Rap Jointed Shad *
Reef Digger 7in straight and jointed *
Renosky Super Shad **
Russelures - 6½in and 5½in *
Storm Deep Thunder 15 *

Depth Raiders, single and jointed, go down deeper than Shad Raps, and so come into their own when the fish are deep.

Depth Raiders work best from a boat where again, a multiplier is often preferred, although it is not crucial by any means.

Depth Raider, Straight and Jointed ★★

The Depth Raider is one of the most successful trolling or casting lures in use on Lake Nasser. The sinking version produces big fish from the shore, but it needs a powerful rod to cast this 2¾oz lure properly. It comes in both straight and jointed versions, either sinking or floating.

The Depth Raider has been designed for fishing around heavy cover such as weeds and boulders, and for bottom bouncing. The built-in, tail-up buoyancy of this lure, combined with its large triangular diving lip, allows it to bump into almost any cover with minimal hang-ups. To maximize its effectiveness, always work the Depth Raider with a high rod angle, whether casting or trolling, and whenever the lure collides with cover, immediately drop the rod tip (creating a momentary slack line). This allows the Depth Raider to float up backwards from the snag. Most of the time the diving lip is the first to contact the snag. The sudden reverse rising motion backs the lure out of most snags.

Halco deep divers, Scorpion (right) and Crazy Deep (left), possibly the world's deepest divers for their size. A shallower version is in the centre.

Resume your retrieve or troll with a sudden rip forward of the rod tip to free any rubbish still clinging to the lip or hooks. This rubbish-freeing tactic can often trigger strikes. The straight form comes in either floating or countdown versions, and the jointed Depth Raider is a floater.

Key Points
Hooks: Change the manufacturer's hooks.
Split rings: Almost good enough but not quite – change them to be sure.
Recommended colours: Silver baitfish, black perch, natural perch, redhead.
Swimming depth: 6 to 12ft.
Lure length: 8in.
Lure weight: 2¾ oz.
When to use: Trolling; and when bank fishing, use a heavy casting rod. The sinking model is a useful lure for fishing deep drop-offs from the bank.

Halco Crazy Deep and Sorcerer ★

Halco Sorcerer 150 XDD – Crazy Deep will dive to 26ft on 18lb (8kg) monofilament line. Designed for barramundi, it's a great shore lure, casting over deep drop-offs. This lure is very effective for catching smaller Nile perch, but is perhaps a bit small for the big Nile perch.

Key Points
Hooks: Change the manufacturer's hooks.
Recommended colours: Mullet, orange chartreuse, green tiger, redhead.
Swimming depth: to 26ft.
When to use: Can be used for trolling, and is very effective for bank fishing.

Musky Big Ernie and Little Ernie★★

Ernie lures have a natural fish-shaped body, a rattle and good swimming action, and are effective trolling lures that dive to about 15ft. The smaller Little Ernie is proficient for shore fishing and for summer trolling.

From the left, the two smaller lures are Musky Little Ernies, and the two larger ones are Musky Big Ernies.

Key Points
Hooks: Change the manufacturer's hooks.
Split rings: Change the split rings.
Recommended colours: Perch, black perch, Tennessee shad, fire tiger.
Swimming depth: to 15ft.

Mann's Stretch Imitator Junior ★

This is a relatively new lure from Mann's, which mimics the outline of a tilapia, a popular food fish for Nile perch. Dives to 20–25ft, and needs to be trolled slowly; if it is properly used, it works well.

Key Points
Hooks: Probably strong enough.

Split rings: Strong enough.
Recommended colours: Tinker mackerel, bleeding bunker, croaker.
Swimming depth: to 20ft plus.

Mann's Stretch 30+ and 18+ ★★

Deep-diving lures with a good action; very useful during the winter months when the Nile perch are lying in deeper water.

From the left, Manns Stretch Imitator with two smaller Imitator Juniors; very successful slow trolling lures.

Manns Stretch 30+, another important lure recommended in the text.

Key Points

Key Points
Hooks: Probably strong enough.
Split rings: Strong enough.
Recommended colours: Pearl/black, chrome/black, redhead, green mackerel.
Swimming depth: to 25ft.

Rapala

Rapala lures have been the most popular make of lure for thousands of anglers who have fished with us over the past fifteen years. Up to about three years ago the Rapala Magnum series – with 14cm, 18cm and 22cm lures – was very popular, especially the two smaller sizes, but now they seem to have taken second place to lures such as the Depth Raider and Ernie.

The most effective lure we have ever found for Nile perch is the Rapala Super Shad Rap (RSSR). For many years this lure was only available in the floating version, then in 2004 Rapala introduced the sinking version of the RSSR, which gave this lure an important new dimension: it could now be used for counting down to fish lying in deeper water, and this has increased its overall effectiveness.

There are several more technical reasons for Rapala popularity:

Reliability: Tough, durable lures that withstand massive punishment from strong fish with a reputation for destroying ordinary lures. Although a 140lb Nile perch can practically rip an RSSR apart, the tough through-wire still holds and the angler can land his fish of a lifetime.

Action: Excellent, panicked prey action that is enough to fool any predator – often, anyway.

Shape: The all-time favourite is the RSSR, which has the same shape as Nile perch's principal prey, a small tilapia. The second most popular lures are the CD18 and CD14, which represent the minnow shape of young tigerfish that the Nile perch love.

The only criticism is that over the past four or five years the strength of the fitted treble hooks is not what it was in the past. We now have to advise anglers to change the hooks on all Rapala lures.

Rapala Super Shad Rap, Sinking and Floating ★★

Key Points
Hooks: Change the manufacturer's hooks.
Split rings: Strong enough.
Recommended colours: Perch, blue, gold, 'tilapia', redheads.
Swimming depth: to 12ft on the troll, maybe 10ft from the bank.

Rapala Magnum CD18 and CD22★

Many regulars use a CD18 instead of a CD14 for shore fishing. The CD18 is also a good trolling lure. Tip: paint the silver diving vane black.

Key Points
Hooks: Change the manufacturer's hooks.
Split rings: Strong enough.
Recommended colours: Purple, fire tiger, mackerel.
Swimming depth: to 12ft plus.

Rapala Magnum Countdown CD14 ★

The CD14 is a good lure for shore fishing in deeper water – they can be counted down to where the deep fish are lying. Tip: paint the silver diving vane black.

Key Points
Hooks: Change the manufacturer's hooks.
Split rings: Strong enough.
Recommended colours: Redhead, orange, purple and fire tiger.
When to use: Bank fishing, but can also be used for trolling.

Rapala X-Rap Magnum XRMAG30★★

Good minnow shape with a massive deep-diving lip for up to a 30ft trolling depth. Great attraction features include flashy internal holographic foil, and 3-D eyes and aggressive swimming action that make them look like small tigerfish. A favourite with Nile perch; can also be used for casting from the bank.

Rapala X-Rap Magnums dive to 30ft plus, and are recommended for deep trolling or deep-water bank work.

Key Points
Hooks: Change the manufacturer's hooks.
Split rings: Strong enough.
Recommended colours: Silver, spotted minnow, bonito.
Swimming depth: down to 30ft.

Rapala X-Rap Jointed Shad★

This is a relatively new lure in our collection, and has performed well for lightweight shore-fishing casting. It features the attributes of the X-Rap Magnum, exaggerated 'wounded minnow' action, internal holographic foil, and stainless-steel wire construction with a good fish body shape.

Key Points
Hooks: Hooks are probably strong enough.
Split rings: Strong enough.
Recommended colours: Fire tiger, clown, perch, silver.
Swimming depth: down to 10ft.

Russelure

The Russelure has the longest history as a successful Nile perch lure. It was already famous for catching Nile perch long before Lake Nasser was discovered. Way back in the 1960s it was popular when Rasinga Island on Lake Victoria was the 'in' place for Nile perch fishing. It is still a very effective lure, but seems to have lost ground, in the eyes of guides and anglers, to more modern lures. We feel that possibly one reason for its decline is due to the lure's very distinctive swimming action, and the Nile perch have learnt that it is dangerous.

The body is high-strength aluminium, with solid brass and stainless-steel hardware, plus a super-tough anodized colour finish, and superior quality Mustad hooks attached with stainless-steel rings. With its unusual wobble swimming action – which can be varied from an eccentric fast motion, to a slower, smooth natural movement through three separate towing positions – you have an incredibly versatile bait for Nile perch.

The colours are either anodized or powder coated: this ensures there is no flaking or chipping, and no fading with age, and makes this lure virtually indestructible. Designed with big game in mind, this is one of only a few lures that will fish Nile perch, tuna and suchlike straight from the packet without hook and splitting-ring upgrades. Stick-on strike strips are sold

ABOVE: The Russelure in action, a popular lure on Lake Victoria. (Olivier Portrat)

LEFT: Russelures are used successfully on Lake Nasser but are more typical of Lake Victoria.

separately for those who wish to jazz up this already productive lure even more.

Key Points
Hooks: Strong enough.
Split rings: Strong enough.
Recommended colours: Green, silver.
Swimming depth: down to 25ft, depending on the size and hook-up chosen.
Lure length: 6½in and 5½in.

Reef Digger 7in Straight and Jointed Diver ★

These lures have a lifelike action for both cranking and trolling. Tip: paint the silver diving vane black.

Key Points
Hooks: Change the manufacturer's hooks.
Split rings: May need changing.
Recommended colours: Black sparkle, chartreuse shad, sucker, shad.

These are Reef Diggers, jointed and single.

Soft Plastic Lures ★★

A wide range of tails with jig heads, shads and twisters are available, and are very effective for shore fishing, especially in 'hotspots' where the fish are used to regular lures. We do not plan to give a breakdown in detail of these lures simply because of the huge range of styles, colours and weights – which is what gives them their versatility, of course. Some are too light for jigging from a boat – so choose a bigger, heavier one for easy jigging control. Some of the elongated tails have a rather weak, ripply effect which is often bettered by those with a stiffer, more curved tail which vibrates robustly. With these lures you can probably effect more changes than with any other range. A down side to them is the puffer fish, because these little chaps bite huge lumps out of them. Our recommendation is to save a couple of lures so damaged, and use bits of them, with Superglue, to repair other rubber lures. We have done this successfully.

The rubber lure with one big single, as opposed to trebles, does result in a few fish being pulled out of, or missed on the strike. Some rubbers with trebles on them have *poor* trebles and they really need changing. All in all, tough rubber lures are certainly here for a while, and could be the best way forward for a decade or more.

TOP RIGHT: A welcome sight: a fish ready to be landed. (Olivier Portrat)

RIGHT: One of the slim lures near to ejection! Note the flared gills. All leaping perch do this. (Olivier Portrat)

11   BAIT FISHING

It is possible that bait fishing is the underrated technique on Lake Nasser, simply because the use of artificial lures has tended to be so productive. Elsewhere baits, usually livebaits or spun deadbaits, have yielded results, especially in the old colonial days, and a big fish here or there. Livebaits on Lake Nasser have not yet been widely used, and what could be the most effective method of all, namely trolled livebaits, has hardly been used. Live tilapia, suspended beneath a float and fished quite shallow, have produced good fish, Barrie's best by this method being 70lb.

The catching of that fish was in itself instructive, and perhaps indicative of what is to come. A group of anglers had been fishing a known hotspot at Maharraga, using the usual range of lures, without success. One of the guides suggested trying some tilapia, of which they had a couple. A simple fixed float tackle was set up, with one single hook, and the bait lightly hooked in the root of the dorsal fin. Barrie and the guide were at the foot of a cliff, on a narrow ledge above deep water. The bait, fished about 3ft deep, was swung out about a rod length from the bank, whereupon it promptly swam quickly back to the bank. The next cast produced the same effect, but this time, when the livebait was only 3ft from the bank, and just at the feet of the two anglers, a huge swirl occurred, engulfed the bait fish, and the float disappeared to the depths. This proved to be the fish of 70lb. The surprise was the speed of the response in an area that had seen lures steadfastly refused for a couple of hours or so.

The story doesn't end there. The guide was weighing the fish and posing for a photograph, and in the meantime Barrie had put on the other tilapia and dropped the rig in the water's edge; it remained there about three seconds, when the

Barrie with a bait-caught fish from the bank.

float departed in a shower of spray. This fish was about the same size as the first, but came off after a short battle when the single hook came adrift. So these fish were not spooked by the presence of two large humans and a large fish on the bank, as well as the chaos of the fight and all the splashing. But they were spooked – or had no interest in – artificial lures being drawn through the swim.

Every time we have tried live tilapia they have produced Nile perch, but often quite small fish. Clearly they have potential: find the big fish groupings and show them a livebait, and it will probably be taken. Barrie's two best fish to this method were both seventy-pounders.

We should also consider casting and wobbling a deadbait, because it is perhaps more effective than livebait fishing, only because it is easier and you can cover a lot more water with a dead fish than you can with a live one. This method is fairly simple and very effective. The bait, because it is dead and does not have to be kept alive, is easily obtainable and simple to rig with two single hooks so that it can be cast and wobbled.

The best deadbaits are tigerfish or *Alestes* (*Sardina*): both these species are easily obtained from local fishermen who are pleased to exchange a few in return for a couple of cans of Coke. If the deadbait is sizeable, say, a tigerfish of 1lb, then trebles down the flanks of the bait may be necessary in addition to a big single through the jaws. John Wilson's film *Lake Nasser Safari* contains several minutes' explanation of this very effective procedure, and has some great action shots of live hook-up footage of Nile perch to 40lb being caught using a rigged deadbait.

Livebaiting

For livebaiting, baits are hooked in the dorsal fin with one size 5/0 or 6/0 circle hook. The hook is attached to an 80lb monofilament leader about 2ft long. Above the leader, on the knot to the mainline, is a weight, and then 3 to 4ft above that is a sliding float. You need about 4 to 6ft between the livebait and the float. This rig allows the livebait to swim around below the weight and not get tangled up.

An alternative to tilapia is to catch a juvenile tigerfish with a light spinning or fly rod. The lake is full of small tigerfish that roam the weed margins, and they are relatively easily caught close to a hotspot. The best bait of all is a squeaker (small catfish species) because they are very strong.

When the Nile perch strikes the livebait the angler has to free-spool the bait for two to three seconds before striking; this allows the perch to turn and start heading away from the angler, which enables the strike to pull the circle hook back into the fish's scissors.

Setting yourself up to fish livebait efficiently is a time-consuming operation; you have to be well organized with a suitable livebait tank equipped with an aerator. Collecting the livebait itself is also difficult; this has to be done using a net or catching the livebait individually with a rod and line. Then you have to transport the livebait, keeping them alive and healthy, to the fishing area. Another disadvantage of using livebait is that you have to place your bait where the fish are, and get this correct the first time because it is difficult to move around and at the same time keep the bait alive. With a lure or rigged deadbait you can fish an area and then if you have no luck, move on to a new location without 'killing' your lure and making it ineffective.

We believe that one of the ways forward will be to equip stealth boats with livebait tanks and then use them to drift quietly over known hotspots pulling livebaits behind the drifting boat. This, and trolled livebaits, which also produce results, are methods for the future.

Trolled deadbait, beneath a trolling float, possibly has great potential but has been too little used to be certain. At a time when anglers were just beginning to think about it, in 2005/6, a new lure hit the Lake Nasser headlines – namely the soft plastic jig-like lures. Eventually these will lose their effectiveness, so perhaps that will be the time to try trolling both live- and deadbaits.

We have now tried pulling livebaits behind a drifting boat, and this does work. However, it has still not been extensively used. There is no doubt at all that Nile perch will take natural baits when they have quite gone 'off' artificial

John Wilson with a lovely 30–35lb fish off the bank, aided by Mohammed Elephantine.

baits. (As we have pointed out in Chapter 10 'Lures', fish will go 'off' particular lures, but they can also go 'off' all lures except the ones they are totally unfamiliar with.)

Deadbaits

Deadbaits, whilst much more convenient than livebaits, are a trickier proposition in certain respects. Firstly, baits fished on the bottom are more likely to catch catfish than Nile perch. Suspended deadbaits will take tigerfish too, as well as Nile perch. These methods have not been widely tried, except the use of bottom-fished deadbaits, at night, for catfish. They have probably caught very few Nile perch.

We are fairly sure that Nile perch are just not interested in deadbait unless it is cast and wobbled to stimulate a live, moving fish, and there are several reasons why we have come to this conclusion. Firstly, a Nile perch is a predator and not a scavenger: in the food chain, catfish are the scavengers but they are also opportunists and on occasions will take a lure or livebait. But then again, anglers used to consider that pike were not scavengers!

Many of the anglers who come to Lake Nasser ledger for catfish at night while at an overnight camp; this is a common procedure that has been practised by one or two anglers on almost every safari over the past fifteen years – and we can't recall a Nile perch being caught with a static deadbait even once, no matter how tasty it might seem to a catfish. Also, the local longliners tell us that a Nile perch will not take one of their baits unless it is alive and moving energetically.

12 SUCCESS STORIES AND SPECTACULAR EVENTS

Lake Nasser has been a success story *par excellence*, and seeing some of the home video clips of the pioneering safaris is extremely exciting with, often, fish after fish being hooked – and lost, too. Perhaps rather a lot of fish were lost in the early days because the tackle and techniques were at an early stage. Hooking up several fish at once, whether on the bank or in a boat, was, and remains, fairly common, and it is interesting to say the least, when the lines of running fish cross each other. When you think about Barrie's results, which he does not regard as out of the ordinary, with an *average* weight of almost 22lb, an average of five to seven perch per day, four fish of 100lb plus, and dozens between 50lb and 100lb, it is hardly surprising that there are some extraordinary catches, too. In this section we relate some of them.

Wilma's World Record Catch

One of the strangest trips, and ultimately one of the most rewarding, began in rather difficult circumstances. Barrie had been on the lake for a week and had returned to Aswan to see off his week's group of anglers, and was expecting to join Willie Colquhoun and Wilma Macdairmid for a second week. Willie and Wilma duly arrived on time, but for some reason their permits for the lake did not. Barrie was reluctant to go off on to the lake without them, as this was their first safari, so the three of them sat there in the Hotel Basma waiting and waiting for the permits to arrive. When eventually they did, there was only time for three full days on the lake. Will Wragg had replaced Tim Baily as chief guide and organizer, so the four of them headed

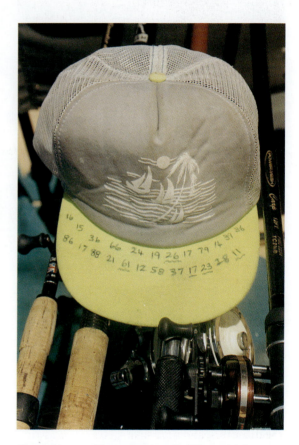

Hat, with a week's captures marked (by weight) on the peak.

south, fast. Barrie had done fairly well in the Khor Mariya region the previous week, so they headed off there first.

The wind was unusually strong, east to west, and thus the lee, on the eastern shore, would be more comfortable to fish. On the way down they trolled some shallow ledges on the western shore and were rewarded by fish of up to 60lb for Willie,

ABOVE: Terry Eustace, famous angler and tackle guru, with a whopper.

LEFT: Mohammed Elephantine with a Nile perch of 162lb caught after borrowing Tim's rod, December 1999.

and nearly 50lb for Barrie; Wilma also took some nice specimens. All fell to Rapala Super Shad Raps fished quite shallow. At Khor Mariya, however, it soon became clear that the fishing was in the doldrums, and not a take was had from swims which, the previous week, had produced some good fish. Barrie had been a little uneasy about going there in the first place, partly because it never pays to try and repeat a previous week's success, in his experience, but partly because towards the end of the previous week he had begun to develop a gut feeling. Now, all experienced anglers know about the gut feeling, nothing to do with tummy upsets (very rare on Lake Nasser), but the feeling you get sometimes that you should be fishing a particular place. These feelings should never be ignored.

Later that week Barrie was able to rationalize his feeling to a degree. He'd noticed that another party had had an 80lb fish close to a cluster of small islands on the west bank, and then they had moved on quickly further south on the lake. That place with its small islands and deep water, with both quiet and rough water depending on their disposition to the easterly blow, seemed to draw Barrie. Conditions seemed perfect, so he had a word with Will Wragg about it. Will was reluctant because the east-to-west journey across the lake would be extremely rough before the shelter of the islands was reached.

As much as Barrie persisted, Will refused, though he did eventually relent: '*Will* you stop whingeing, Rickards. If, and I *do* mean *if*, the wind drops in the heat of midday, then we'll risk

Wilma Macdairmid at an early stage of playing her 200lb world record Nile perch.

a run across. But don't say I didn't warn you.' The wind did ease up, but the crossing was still a little hairy, especially towards the west shore when the fetch was greatest. But eventually the small islands were reached, and the boat with Will, Willie, Wilma and Barrie on board entered calmer waters and began trolling with RSSRs in about 10 to 12ft of water.

On the first troll round the first island Barrie handed his rod to Will for a minute whilst he put a new film in his camera – his feelings were that strong about this place. This job completed, he turned towards the bows of the boat where Wilma was poised, rod poking over the gunwales. He focused the camera – and at that very moment Wilma's rod tip whipped savagely over, and she was in business. She was therefore also on film from the very beginning of the battle!

The fight of this fish was quite tremendous, and after a few minutes it showed itself – and the occupants of the boat each gave a very large gasp: it was huge. Not long after, it tried to leap, but it was so big that only half of it became airborne. The shots taken by Barrie at 1,000th of a second would later show that on this leap only one point of one treble, lodged in the tip of its jaw, held the mighty fish. Thankfully none of them realized this, especially Wilma. In the end – and it nearly *was* the end for Wilma, because later she confessed she was almost exhausted after twenty minutes – the fish breached the surface alongside the boat. It took both Will and Willie all their strength to heave the fish over the gunwales. Its head, as Barrie saw through the still clicking camera, was as big as Willie's chest, and once landed, it completely covered the stern deck; naturally it was easy to unhook.

They had no weighbag big enough to weigh it, so they took a canvas cover off one of the mattresses and slid the fish into that. But as soon as it was hoisted up, the canvas split along the whole of its length, and both canvas and fish slid slowly back to the deck. At that very moment the second boat on the safari rounded the point of the island and came to the rescue with a giant weighing net. Everyone proceeded to the near-by beach, and the giant fish was accurately weighed. In the sling, which was exactly 3lb in weight when wet, the big balance read 203lb. It was unbelievable, a world record Nile perch and the first of 200lb. There were ear to ear grins all round, the Nubian team just as excited as everyone else.

*RIGHT: Col Roberts, Australian television producer (*Fishing for Wild Images*), with a 140lb fish caught on a Halco Crazy Deep.*

BELOW: Wilma's 200lb world record goes airborne. Note that it is held by one point of one treble hook of a Rapala Super Shad Rap.

The whole capture was on film: thirty-six shots of the actual hooking, to the moment the big fish swam free, followed by Will and Willie swimming with it, to see that it was all right. It was, and it swam off strongly and ever deeper to its island sanctuary. Surely there cannot be many occasions when the capture of a world record has been filmed from beginning to end.

So, it was a difficult and trying beginning to a week that ended with almost unbelievable success. Since then the 200lb barrier has been broken several times (*see* Chapter 15), and no doubt with the same euphoria on each occasion. But even without the big fish, results can be staggering. In one week a small group with Barrie had over 3,000lb of Nile perch (and lots of tigerfish); although there was no fish of 100lb in this trip, there were quite a number in the range

60–80lb. The story of Barrie's giant bank-caught fish is related elsewhere (*see* Chapter 8), but there have been numerous occasions when anglers have had incredible adventures while on a Nile perch safari on Lake Nasser. Some of these hard-to-believe experiences would normally be passed off as 'fisherman's stories'…but these stories are true.

Perhaps even stranger is the sheer *number* of such events that have taken place. We'll not mention in any detail other adventures, such as two vets performing surgery on a crocodile, or hooking a 5ft monitor lizard that thought the lure was his dinner. And how many anglers have landed two Nile perch on one lure? Furthermore, what about the many, many times a tigerfish has been taken by a big perch and stripped the angler's reel clean?

A Marvellous Result

This is how John Wilson reported a marvellous result, in 'Angler's Retreat', 17 December 2000, *Daily Express*: 'In just three days concentrating upon two different areas, though both possessing the same features of weed and boulder-strewn sunken islands, our boat played host to an unprecedented ten perch of more than 100lb. In all, our boat accounted for 2,500lb, with thirty-five perch averaging around 50lb apiece.'

Now read his full account of those bald facts, staggering though they are:

Because of the River Nile's swollen waters during the past few months, levels on Lake Nasser have risen to the highest point recorded since the reservoir was created by the construction of the Aswan Dam in the early sixties. This meant we were fishing over the very same now sunken rocky islands and hilltops where I had camped and shore fished for Nile perch only six months before, while escorting a party of perch enthusiasts on behalf of a holiday company; nevertheless, the phenomenon offered enormous potential. At least, that is how Tim Baily read the situation, when he greeted Andy Davison and I

at the boat moorings following our flight from Heathrow to Luxor in Egypt, and then on to Aswan. Tim's plan was to ignore all our favourite hotspots, such as shorelines and sheer-sided drop-offs that had previously produced for us, and concentrate upon totally unfished areas created by the lake's extra depth. And how right he was with his advice!

Tim has, with the help of local guides, successfully run specialized boat-fishing trips on Lake Nasser for nearly six years now, in search of both tigerfish and the giant Nile perch. His knowledge of this enigmatic watershed is second to none. Add the fact that my friend Andy once held for eight years the IGFA all-tackle world record for Nile perch with a 191.5lb monster from Lake Victoria (until it was beaten by a 203-pounder from Lake Nasser), and you can appreciate I was in the very best company for a week's serious fishing safari for big perch.

Tim had thoughtfully installed my favourite guide Mohammed on board our 25ft trolling boat, and within just a few hours we were heading through the centre of the lake where, deep down, in the depths exceeding 300ft, the original riverbed and the ancient mysteries of the Nile lay. We, however, were more interested in depths of between just 15 and 30ft, where sunken islands of large boulders provided a raft of new ambush points.

We were using trolling combinations of large plugs, both sinking and floating divers including Rapala Magnum CD18 and 22s, Depth Raiders, Russelures, Reef Diggers and Nilsmasters on 30lb class outfits – and we struck gold on only our second location. Andy went straight into a good perch of around 80lb, which unfortunately dived under the boat and severed the line around the prop. This meant having the engine up, removing the propeller and installing a new shear pin, after unwinding the line and yet more, older fishing line. The old pin was about to disintegrate.

During this operation we had drifted into slightly shallower water where dense beds of weed growth sprouted from between the boulders. It was an area we would not normally have associated with huge perch. But when

Mohammed restarted the engine and I dropped my lure over the side, it only travelled a few yards before the rod tip was wrenched over savagely and line started to evaporate from the multiplier. Following several of those marvellous head-shaking lunges across the surface, so characteristic of the Nile perch, and a super fight, we hoisted my buffalo on the scales in a weigh sling.

All perch over 100lb are called 'buffalos' by Nasser regulars because of their distinctly humped backs. This beauty took the needle to 134lb, beating my previous best by 14lb. What

'I bet he'd fit in my tummy!'

a start! But there was more to come, and the most prolific catch of big fish in which it has ever been my privilege to share.

In just three days in which we concentrated upon two different areas, though both possessed the same features of weeds and boulder-strewn sunken islands, our boat played host to an unprecedented ten perch, each of more than 100lb.

Andy took four buffalos, the best at 139lb. I also took four, pushing my record to 141lb. Tim caught one of 129lb, and Mohammed ironically accounted for the heaviest at 162lb, using Tim's rod.

Below you will find a list of the Nile perch caught on John's safari that were over 75lb. In addition to this incredible list of big fish there were two other 'out of the ordinary' events that are worth mentioning.

On this safari, double hook-ups were a common event. On one occasion when John and Tim had a double strike they both fought 'their fish' as per normal. But after a while, both of them became concerned that their lines had crossed, or that the two fish were fighting

John Wilson's Safari, December 2000

Angler	Weight (lb)	Lure
Mohammed Elephantine	162	Rapala CD22 – Orange
John Wilson	141	Reef Digger
Andy Davison	139	Depth Raider – Fire Tiger
Andy Davison	137	Nils Master – Nubian Sunset
John Wilson	134	Depth Raider Jointed – Perch
Tim Baily	126	Depth Raider CD – Perch
John Wilson	121	Depth Raider Jointed – Perch
Andy Davison	103	Depth Raider Jointed – Perch
John Wilson	99	Depth Raider Jointed – Perch
Andy Davison	97	Nils Master – Nubian Sunset
Andy Davison	92	Nils Master – Nubian Sunset
John Wilson	84	Reef Digger
John Wilson	81	Depth Raider Jointed – Perch
Tim Baily	80	Depth Raider Jointed – Fire Tiger
Andy Davison	78	Depth Raider Jointed – Fire Tiger
Tim Baily	76	Rapala CD 22 – Orange

dangerously close to each other. Then as the fish jumped clear of the water, trying to throw the lures, they were astonished to see that this Nile perch had taken both lures in one sweep. This capturing of an 80lb Nile perch striking two lures fished by two anglers is an incredible event in anybody's reckoning, the odds being so stacked against it being possible.

The Nubian guide was Mohammed Elephantine, who has accomplished two all-tackle world records for his guests – the two biggest freshwater fish ever approved by the IGFA (December 2000). As John Wilson relates above, it was Mohammed who caught the biggest Nile perch of the safari, at 162lb. Normally he would have been driving the boat, but Tim was taking the helm from time to time, to give him a rest, and it was during one of these spells that Mohammed caught his personal best Nile perch on Tim's rod!

Two Long Fights

Here are two accounts about Nile perch that took an astonishing length of time to land – one took nine hours and the other over four hours. We can imagine the thoughts running through the minds of experienced Nile perch anglers: 'How...did it take so much time to land these two Nile perch when, for example, it took only twenty minutes for Wilma Macdairmid to land an all-tackle world record 200lb fish?' There have been lengthy debates about these fights, and no one has been able to come up with a good reason for why it took so long. It might have been some freak ability of these two particular Nile perch to use their strength sensibly to fight slowly, on what was probably too light a drag, instead of rushing off in panic when they were hooked. They might have realized that the best way was to conserve their energy by giving a steady constant pull instead of panicky energy-burning runs – though this seems unlikely.

In late April 1977 Paul Thompson was on a two-week Nubian safari with a group of his friends. He was using a 3lb test curve Steve Burke shore rod and 25lb line when he hooked into what he immediately knew was a very big fish. After fifteen minutes of playing the fish from the shore, the line snagged. His only option was to call for a fishing boat, which he clambered aboard in order to continue his fight. Everyone looked on in amazement as hour by hour passed, and still Paul's fish was not going to give in. After four and a half hours Paul was exhausted and dehydrated. Reluctantly he handed his rod over to Martin Godliman. But there was still no change...this Nile perch was not going to relent, not for Paul, not for Martin, not for anyone, it seemed. Action had to be taken: as it was, the boat had travelled over 4 miles (6km) from where the fish was initially hooked!

Those of you who have snagged lures on underwater bushes will recall the metal ring tied to a length of parachute cord. The metal ring is run down the snagged line until it reaches the lure, and then jigged until one of the lure's trebles catches. This allows you to put pressure on the lure and pull it off the bush. Well, the same system was devised in the case of Paul's fish – but there was a difference! A large treble was firmly attached to the metal ring, but instead of using parachute cord, the treble was attached to 30lb bs mono, which was rigged to a 20lb boat rod.

After a lot of jigging and failed attempts they eventually managed to connect this second treble, and hooked the Nile perch in the lower jaw. Now the fish was attached to two rods. The heavy boat rod and line made all the difference, and the fish finally gave up and was landed! This tough Nile perch weighed in at an impressive 148lb! We are pleased to report that after weighing and trophy shots the fish was successfully released in good condition. Perhaps we should just comment that a 25lb line on a drifting boat is asking for trouble, because big fish can easily move a boat with a direct pull of only a few pounds. It might have been better to anchor the boat – and the same might also be said of the next remarkable story.

For the second time in just twelve months 'Super Perch' struck again! On a week's safari in May 1998 Jeremy Wade (the author of *Somewhere Down A Crazy River*) tells the story of an epic fight between a big Nile perch and Dave Everett:

At 12.40pm, one of the trolling rods went over, and what was clearly a heavy fish chugged determinedly away, and surfaced some distance away. About 80m, was my vague impression. So why, four hours later, was it not yet in the boat?

Shaban, our Nubian fishing guide, suggested with a wry smile that a crocodile was probably hanging on to its tail. I became convinced it was foul-hooked, but at one point we saw its flickering form down deep, and the line appeared to be coming from its mouth. So perhaps we had greatly underestimated its weight from its rare surface appearances between the dogged hours of staying deep. By now Dave (in between being sluiced down with cold lake water) was pleading with the fish; but each foot of the 25lb line gained was remorselessly pulled back.

At length the Bimini Twist above the trace swivel was intermittently appearing above the water – but by then it was getting dark. We decided that the first time the 80lb mono trace was accessible, we would risk grabbing it. When the moment finally came, at 9.35pm, the fish would not co-operate – but three of us managed to haul it over the side and restrain it on the mat. A few quick pictures, on to the scales, then back over the side in the weighing sling, where it kicked free and disappeared without so much as a 'by your leave'. Then we tried to believe the weight: 'only' 75lb. The Depth Raider was hooked fair and square in the mouth. You tell me. As I said, I wouldn't have believed it unless I had been there. Five minutes short of nine hours, and landed a good three miles from where it had been hooked.

The reaction back at camp was as you would expect, after the relief that we were not lost: trying to set some ridiculously inappropriate line-class record? No. Not trying hard enough? Well, I can't vouch for the crushed gonads (nature's last-resort 'butt' pad), but certainly both groins sported impressive and colourful bruising. And interestingly, by way of comparison, Dave had a fifty-pounder from the shore three days later: same line, lighter rod, and less pressure (so as not to bring it in too soon to the rockier shallows), and inside twenty minutes it turned over on its side and was landed.

A Lightweight Safari

Several 'fish of a lifetime' resulted when Tim was on a 'good deal' with some dentist friends of his in London, trading discounted safaris for the unpleasant task of them trying to get his teeth back into shape; though he claims 'Steve Moulder and Simon Channing certainly earned their discount sorting out my fangs.' This is the story of Steve Moulder and Tim, who set out on a 'lightweight' safari in one fishing boat with a second fishing boat in support, acting as a mini mother ship. During the last week in November 1999, Steve decided to come on his fourth safari to Lake Nasser. He had not been very lucky on his previous visits, and was determined to improve on his personal best, which stood at about 60lb. Tim decided to take a break and join him.

With Shaban as the guide and a safari crew to keep us well fed, we all set out on what was, to say the least, a mind-blowing safari. For the first two days we followed the tried and tested methods of finding Nile perch: trolling rocky cliff faces and around islands, shore-fishing drop-offs, and so on. We almost blanked – just three small fish at 10–15lb.

Without the pressure of having to catch fish for other anglers, we decided to concentrate on a new method of finding the perch, which Tim had tried before with reasonable success. The strategy was to fish a small area of the lake in detail. So for five days we never left Khor Kalabsha, the big Khor running east to west, just below the famous Beacon where our first all-tackle world record was caught. (Kalabsha is about three hours by boat from Aswan.)

We stopped fishing visible rocky outcrops and cliff faces, and devoted all our attention to trolling in open water, sometimes hundreds of yards out in the lake. We were looking for underwater ridges and plateaux, about 20 to 40ft deep. We kept to the windward side of the bank, and the chains of islands that were located close to large areas of shallower water where the tilapia feed. We were looking for underwater promontories where the Nile perch would most likely be resting up during the day, ready to go hunting in the shallows at night time.

Eventually we found the first underwater promontory with big perch in residence. Shaban had reported fish on the finder, but the first real idea we had about the coming action was that heavy thump and a rod yanked down. Then... you know it's a big fish when, after the first 100 yards of line-ripping run, the old mother just settles down to a slow, steady, unstoppable pull, and you can feel the thump of its huge tail propelling it through the water – well, this happened to both Steve and Tim at the same time!

When you have a double strike both with big fish, one of you heads for the boat's bow platform, to try and keep the two fish as far apart as possible. Since Steve's fish was heading past the bow anyway, and there was nothing he could do to stop it, off he went leaving Tim to fight his fish from the stern. Eventually the two fish were brought alongside the boat and stringered. This time it was Steve's lucky day, with his fish the bigger of the two: 132lb. But with a 102-pounder, Tim wasn't complaining, either! Over the next three days we found several underwater islands and plateaux, and these produced some magnificent sport and unforgettable fish.

Between them they caught nine fish over 75lb, with three of them over 150lb (*see* table below for details). Steve broke his personal best four times over, with Nile perch of 161, 132, 92 and 78lb, and Tim broke his personal best twice with a 186- and a 178-pounder. Most of the time Tim was fishing with a gold Russelure, while Steve was sportingly sticking to Depth Raiders in order to give a good comparison of lure performance. Having said that, Depth Raiders did very well, and caught some of the biggest fish, and are still essential lures to bring for trolling and heavy shore fishing.

They were both using Harris Angling Uptide QED rods: 9.5ft, 20lb class rods, designed and tested on Lake Nasser. Steve had his rod fitted with a Shimano TLD 15 multiplier reel, while Tim was using a Calcutta 400 loaded with 40lb Fireline.

Lightweight Safari Catch Details (over 75lb)

Steve Moulder

	161lb	Depth Raider Silver Baitfish
	132lb	Russelure Gold
	92lb	Depth Raider Pike
	78lb	Russelure Gold

Tim Baily

	186lb	Depth Raider Red Fire Tiger
	178lb	Russelure Gold
	103lb	Russelure Gold
	102lb	Depth Raider Redhead
	81lb	Depth Raider Redhead

A First-Time Safari

In March 2002 Barrie, who by now was a veteran of numerous Lake Nasser safaris, invited his partner Mandy Lyne, a Cambridge lawyer, to join him there. It was Mandy's first time on safari and almost the first time she had ever been fishing. She enjoyed every moment of her desert lake trip, and subsequently brought her whole family out for safaris.

On one day, Mandy hooked a large fish that rapidly stripped all the line off the reel, and finally broke the line at the knot on the spool. Losing a good fish was enough, but envisaging it trailing 200m of line was even more worrying.

The next morning we decided to return to the same area. The plan was for Barrie and Tim to use *Kestrel*, our new stealth boat, for some drifting with livebait. Mandy was to go in the second boat with two guides, anchor, and do some casting from the boat. Everything was quiet and nothing much happening, when suddenly we heard shouting from Mandy's boat.

It was obvious that she was into a good fish, which was eventually landed.

Barrie and Tim packed up the livebait rigs and headed over to find out what was happening. They were amazed to hear that Hani had spotted some fishing line floating in the water, and when pulling it in discovered there was a fish on the end! He did some quick thinking, and attached the line to a trolling rod and reel, then handed it to Mandy, who after a good scrap, landed the same fish that she had lost the previous afternoon! Hani estimated the weight at more than 90lb and less than 100lb, so they settled for 95lb.

In April 2002 Tim went on a two-week safari with Andy Davidson, to look for new fishing areas on the lake. The area they were exploring was Wadi Allaqi, concentrating on shore fishing and casting from a new stealth boat. Normally with a two-week safari they arrange to have a resupply half way through the safari, which would have meant travelling back to Garf Hussein to pick up fresh food. Instead they planned to buy a sheep from the local Bedouin who graze their flocks on the shore of the lake.

The big perch caught the day after it was lost.

Holiday of a Lifetime

This is a story about people, and describes perhaps every dedicated male angler's dream, to find that perfect partner who loves fishing and its associated adventures as much as the lucky man does himself. The letter from Phil Spackman tells it all:

Dear Tim,

Just a quick line to say thank you, to you and your team, for giving us such a fantastic holiday. We can both honestly say that this was the best way to spend the first week of married life.

We couldn't have been looked after any better, the food was excellent and we were short of nothing, and the safari staff were extremely courteous and respectful at all times; what a great way to see Egypt, and that is without the fishing, which when the weather came good was absolutely fantastic. Lucy managed a 61-pounder and lost a 100lb+ fish, my best was 65lb – not big for Lake Nasser, but my biggest fish to date, although I managed a 35lb catfish. What a fight!!!

You know that you have had a good holiday when you feel quite sad when flying home – and we both certainly were. Which brings me on to my next points: can we come again? Possibly early April, which fits better with our workload. What lead time do we need to book another safari, and if possible can we book the same guide (Ahmed), and possibly leave from Gulf Hussein and therefore fish a different part of the lake. I don't know how this would work out logistically, but it would be nice if it were possible.

Thanks again for making us feel so welcome and giving us the holiday of a lifetime. If I can be of any more help with fish finders or any other supplies, don't hesitate to ask.

Sincere thanks and regards.

An Encounter with Bedouin

Arriving deep in Wadi Allaqi, in an area our safaris had never reached in the past, we noticed there were quite a lot of camel herds, which in turn meant there were Basharia Bedouin in the area. Eventually we spotted some sheep and goats, and decided to take the boat to the shore and find out if we could buy a small sheep for our kitchen. As we closed with the shore we spotted two young Basharia herders – but when they saw us approaching, they ran off into the desert in a panic. After travelling further along the shoreline we spotted the Bedouin camp and pulled up close by.

At this point we were approached by several angry-looking men armed with daggers and swords. There was a lot of shouting in Arabic between Yousef our guide and an impressive-looking Bedouin, whom we later found out was called Ali and the sheik (headman) of the Allaqi

Bedouin. When Yousef eventually had a chance to translate, we found out that they were angry with us for terrifying their teenage boys, who had never seen a white man before – especially two half-naked ones (we were only wearing shorts). This really brought home to Tim the adventure of a Lake Nasser safari – there can't be many places left in the world where some of the local people have never seen a white man. Another thing, for sure, there was not a television set within 100 miles or more of where they were.

After apologizing suitably to Ali and his supporters and putting on our shirts, we were invited into their camp for a cup of coffee. The camp was divided into two sections with a fair distance between them, and as I started walking up I was quickly stopped by some of the Bedouin: I was heading for the women's camp, which for all the time we were with the Basharia remained strictly off limits.

Fifteen or twenty Bedouin men sat chatting in a large shady tent with a top but no walls, cross-legged on camel-hair carpets spread on top of reed mats. Unfortunately our Bedouin social etiquette was still a bit lacking, as Andy did not realize that he was expected to remove his shoes before sitting down on the carpets – but this was soon sorted out.

The coffee maker was summoned, and we soon realized that coffee making was a fine art in this part of the world. The beans were carefully ground with a pestle and mortar, and then mixed with some unknown spices and water in a wooden calabash with a spout. This was slowly boiled over a small fire, while tiny cups were washed and placed on a wooden board; then two teaspoons of sugar were added to each cup. When the coffee was ready – very black and strong – it was poured into the cups and the visitors were each handed one. After finishing the tasty brew, we placed our cups back on the board, where they were immediately refilled.

This was repeated four times and each time we placed the cups back on the board. After the fifth cup Andy was starting to look doubtful and was obviously wondering just how many he had to drink, but he did not want to refuse in case he caused further offence. By this time the coffee maker was preparing his third brew and regarding us with interest. Only after the sixth cup did Tim notice that Yousef was out of the race, and realized what the form was: he placed his cup upside down – but Andy downed a total of seven before he got the message.

Over the coffee Tim tried to negotiate buying a small sheep from Ali. One of the boys was summoned, and soon came back with a smelly, bleating black bundle, which he handed over for inspection. Four hundred Egyptian pounds was the asking price, which amazed Tim, because that would buy a much bigger animal from the Bedouin sheep market in Aswan. When it was pointed out, Ali considered the question and said: 'You are right, but if I keep this small sheep until it is big I will sell it in Aswan for EL400, so why should I sell it for less now?' How could one argue with that logic? These people had so little need for money – the nearest shop was probably over 100 miles away!

Later the Bedouin, who were exceptionally friendly and hospitable, invited us to a barbecue, though we didn't think the method would go down well in an English back garden. Take one medium-size sheep and cut its throat; then split it in half from neck to sternum, opening it out flat with the skin still on. Remove most of the intestines and put them aside for other use. Place the whole sheep on a bed of coals (skin down to protect the meat from burning), and prod from time to time.

When almost ready, turn the whole thing over (a bit difficult without burning the fingers, though a couple of stout sticks will help). Cook the top half for a short while, and then flip it back over and dust off the excess ash from the meat. When ready, carve off chunks with a dagger, and then offer to diners who then remove the black bits with their daggers and cut off suitable sized bits for eating. As neither Andy nor Tim had daggers, they had to resort to tearing off chunks with their teeth – not very good Bedouin eating manners.

Ali then asked us a favour: would we take him in the boat to inspect one of his camel herds on the other side of the water? This would save him a day and a half's camel ride around the edge of the lake. We were pleased to agree, and told him that on the way we would take him fishing, which he thought was a grand idea.

We went over to a hotspot we had recently discovered and taught him how to use a trolling rod. Then sure enough he was into a fish. Ali handled the rod very well and had great fun landing a 30lb Nile perch, which Tim has no doubt is the desert Bedouin's world record fish caught on rod and line.

Otherwise, most of the safari was dedicated to shore fishing or casting from the stealth boat while it drifted. We did not have to use the engine to adjust the drifts – just a few strokes of the oars put us back on course again.

For the record, Andy's best fish from the shore was 91lb, and Tim's was 86lb. The Bedouins' hospitality was a wonderful surprise bonus and an unforgettable experience.

13 GIANT CATFISH AND OTHER SPECIES

A giant vundu catfish nears the boat...just hooked.

To understand more about the species of fish that now live in Lake Nasser you must take into account that for millions of years before this modern lake was formed, the fish were living in a river, and not a huge man-made reservoir. Also, from mid-July the Nile would start its annual flooding, and by August or mid-September the floodwater would have spread out across the flood plains throughout the Nile valley, inundating the land. The flat flooded farming plains of the Nile Valley provided a very rich, seasonal habitat for fish, which in the shallow floodwaters was easily accessible to fishermen. The annual flooding would last approximately four months, and was the time of abundance,

when it came, to both fishing and farming. The fish that lived in this ancient annual flooding cycle were adapted by nature to live and spawn within these prevailing conditions. Now, with the building of the huge dams at Aswan, the original habitat has changed dramatically.

The fish species from the original Nile's annual flooding system have had to adapt to a new reservoir environment. Also, the fish living in the Nile river north of the dams now live in a 'clean water' river that is no longer subject to annual flooding. We say 'clean water' because all the rich silt that once helped to create abundant food cycles is now trapped in the man-made lake and is of little use for anything.

Many smaller species have not survived, but several of the more resilient species from the original river have adapted well to the changes that man has imposed on them. Aside from the Nile perch, which are thriving in this reservoir, of most interest to us are the tilapia, tigerfish and *Alestes*, all of which are favourite prey of the Nile perch; and there are also two species of catfish, which are a formidable challenge to the angler.

Tilapias

Tilapias, which are members of the family Cichlidae, are the most important species in Lake Nasser because they are a staple diet fish, and as a result are an important addition to the fishing industry in Egypt. Seventy species of *Tilapia* have been identified in North Africa and the Middle East, but only three – *Tilapia niloticus*, *T. galilaea* and *T. zilli* – are found with any frequency in Lake Nasser.

    Tilapia niloticus is the most common member of this family present in the lake, and it is predominantly a weed eater. Tilapias inhabit inshore waters, especially sheltered bays with shallow water and an abundance of vegetation. Given enough time to develop, mature tilapia

can grow to 6lb. These bigger fish tend to spend the daylight hours in deeper water, and are most active at night when they come into shallower water to feed – which is the reason you will find that the local fishermen on Lake Nasser do most of their serious fishing during the night. (*See also* Chapter 14, on fly fishing.)

ABOVE: Two youngsters admire each other: vundu catfish on the right and Attila Portrat on the left.

BELOW: Tilapia – beautiful fish, that fall to tiny spinners, small baits and, with difficulty, to flies and nymphs.

Tilapia are often referred to as 'bream' and are excellent sport on light spinning tackle or a fly rod, but because the predominant species on the lake are weed eaters, so we have done little to investigate the potential of targeting these fish – a point we need to address in the near future.

ABOVE: Puffer fish…and friend!

BELOW: It has good reason to smirk. Could you eat this?

ABOVE RIGHT: OK, unhook me then!

RIGHT: Good tigerfish.

Tigerfish

Tigerfish abound in the lake, the most common being *Hydrocynus forskalii*, which can grow to 16lb. Tigerfish are said by some to be related to the South American piranha, and just one look at their vicious teeth leaves you in no doubt that they are savage predators that can feed on fish up to 40 per cent of their own length. The adult tigers feed mostly on fish, while the youngsters, which live next to weedbeds and bushes close to the bank, feed on insect larvae, tiny freshwater shrimp and fish fry.

For sheer sport on light tackle, tigers take a lot of beating. Not only is it a beautiful fish, but its ferocious elegance will excite any angler's

Tigerfish mouthparts – always use pliers to remove hooks.

adrenalin. Size for size, fewer fish will give the angler such a fierce fight.

Fly fishing for tiger, especially the bigger ones, is spectacular sport. Small tiger, up to about ½lb, live in great abundance close to the bank next to bushes and weedbeds. These smaller tigers make ideal deadbait, and are easily caught using a small fly replicating a flashy minnow, or by using light spinning tackle with the smallest Mepps spinners and spoons.

The adult tiger actively prowl open water in small shoals seeking prey. From time to time anglers will encounter a shoal of feeding tiger, and then all hell breaks loose, and fish after fish will be caught for about half an hour – after which the survivors suddenly melt away, and all is again quiet. They seem to be attracted by the disturbance of fighting fish, probably mistaking this action for a feeding frenzy.

The best time of the year for tigers on Lake Nasser is during the annual flooding of the lake, which takes place approximately from July until August.

Catfish

There are eighteen species of catfish in the lake, of which two are of the most interest to the angler: vundu and bagrus. Vundu (*Heterobranchus longifilis*) is a large tropical catfish that favours deep water in large rivers and impoundments, moving into the shallows at night. Vundu are well respected sport fish in southern Africa, where they are the largest freshwater species. They can grow as big as 130lb (60kg), but the more common bigger cats grow to about 55lb (25kg). The vundu is a powerful predator that attacks virtually any small prey, especially fishes, young birds and baby crocodiles. They are also opportunist scavengers.

Bagrus (*Bagrus bayad*) can be easily distinguished from other catfish by its long adipose fin, deeply forked tail plus dorsal and pectoral fin spines; also a head that is much more depressed. Their habits and feeding patterns are very similar to the vundu, although they are not as common in Lake Nasser. The biggest bagrus

Tilapia patrolling the margins. When you see this, then big Nile perch will be close by.

we have seen on the lake was a fish of over 80lb, which would have been an all-tackle world record, had we realized it at the time of capture.

Catfish on Lake Nasser, predominantly vundu, can be caught whilst trolling or bank fishing, but you have a better chance ledgering for them at night with deadbait. Catfish are definitely worth targeting – if you do hook a big 'cat' it will give you an unforgettable fight. Heavy tackle is required to handle these monsters, which are very powerful swimmers.

Catfish forage along the shoreline looking for food that has been washed up, so cast the bait 2 to 3yd from the bank. Don't cast far out into deep water where your bait will only be lost in deep weeds.

We recommend anglers bring some tins of luncheon meat to use as bait. Fish fillets are all

A hefty bagrus catfish on board.

'Here's looking at you, baby,' says a bottle-nosed bream.

right, but luncheon meat is oily and gives off a good scent trail. Prepare the luncheon meat by taking it out of the tin and cutting it into bait-size squares, which are then dried in the sun. The reason we do this is to firm up the squares of meat so they will stay on the hook better – meat fresh out of the can is too soft and can easily fall off the hook: the bait must be hair-rigged to the large hook.

Another useful item for your vundu arsenal is commercial catfish scent – a few drops of this in the water will provide a good scent trail, and will work the same way as chumming.

When ledgering for vundu at night, sometimes your bait might be taken by an electric cat-fish, a strange, ugly-looking fish with a bloated cylindrical body and a soft scale-less skin. This fish can give a strong electric shock (350 to 450 volts) from electric organs situated all round the body. The electric organs are used for naviga-tion, to locate and stun prey and in defence. The electric shock is harmless, but can give quite a heavy jolt to anyone who tries to handle this fish; there have been many times when we have had a good laugh at the expense of an angler who has found one attached to his vundu hook.

Alestes

There are three species of *Alestes* in the Nile system; the most common on the lake is *Alestes baremose*. The *Alestes* are similar to tigerfish in general form and appearance, but are smaller and feed predominantly on insects rather than fish. They do not grow to a large size: an adult *Alestes baremose* is between 12 to 16in in length, which makes them ideal for rigging as deadbait with two treble hooks, and then casting and wobbling from the bank or a drifting boat. This method is especially useful for fishing areas where the Nile perch have become shy to the lure.

Alestes frequently travel in small shoals near the surface of the water, and often jump, espe-cially in the evening. Next to tilapia, *Alestes* are important commercial fish, which are targeted by the local fishermen, together with tigerfish, using long fine mesh nets in the open lake. These nets are left in the lake overnight and are an obstacle course for our fishing boats, espe-cially when they are returning to camp in the late evening when there is not enough light to see the net floats on the top of the water.

14 FLY FISHING

Charles Jardine with a good bank fish caught on fly.

Whilst most visitors to Lake Nasser use lures to catch Nile perch, there has always been a hard-core of fly-fishing enthusiasts who exploit both bank and boat to pursue their art. It is true that most of the very largest Nile perch have fallen to lures rather than flies, but in all probability, lure anglers outnumber fly anglers by at least ten to one – and fly fishing can certainly be very pro-ductive. This was brought home to us, particu-larly in 2006, when a team of Nathan Robert-son, Geoff Currier and Chris Bailey from the USA caught far more fish on fly in a week than did six lure anglers in the same week – and they had some good fish, too.

One of the themes of this book is the manner in which Nile perch wise up to the lures. In fact, with many thousands of Nile perch caught on them, and even more lures thrown at them by hundreds of anglers, we probably have the most convincing database to prove that a big predator *will* wise up to lures. In other spheres – such as pike fishing in Europe – the matter is still debated (though not

Chris Bailey, producer of Reel Outdoors television, USA, with a 38lb fish caught on fly.

on Lake Nasser in 2007). Now consider the fly fisherman: he offers them something they have not seen before, in a manner not used before. It could be that now is the time for more fly fishing.

Barrie's best fish from the bank on fly weighed 15lb or thereabouts. However, many others who put in a bit more time perhaps, as well as skill, have had numbers of thirty- to forty-pounders, and a few bigger ones: the record now stands at 56lb. This does raise problem number one: big Nile perch are caught very close to the bank, and before too long someone will hook and land on fly a fish in excess of 100lb. That *is* a bit of a challenge!

Choosing your Tackle

Obviously you cannot use a number 5 brook rod, so you do have to go heavy. We are not aware of anyone using big salmon fly rods and appropriate lines, but perhaps it wouldn't be a

bad idea. The Australian Rod Harrison uses a big, double-handed fly rod, and flies up to 6in long. In the meantime, geared-up anglers are using ten- to twelve-weight rods and the correct lines to go with them. Barrie uses a 3m, ten-rated, Shakespeare XtraPower Special, together with a simple salmon fly reel, a Condex in the largest size. Others use ten- to eleven-weight tarpon fly rods and tarpon reels. The reels come with a spare spool so it is possible to take the two lines Barrie uses, namely a fast sink and a floater. These lines are attached, usually on shooting heads, to about 200yd of backing, which is usually braid, but sometimes monofil. In all probability, monofil is better because if a big fish goes on a long run, and the line goes around boulders, then you are in with a much better chance with mono. The breaking strain could be 30lb or so. A real fly-fishing fanatic, doing no lure fishing at all, would probably take two extra lines, namely a medium sink and a sink tip. We will return later to the use of the latter.

At the business end of the fly line you need a leader or trace. Considering what we said earlier in the book, it is best if this is in the 50–60lb mono range. The leader doesn't have to be long, say a couple of yards, so the heavy weight of the leader does not cause undue casting problems.

You can, of course, tie the fly directly to the leader, but with such thick mono this isn't the easiest of exercises (but if you do it, use a three-turn, half blood knot and Superglue it). What Barrie does is to use one of those Ad Sweir steel traces described earlier in the book (*see* Chapter 6): these are only about 5 or 6in long, and can be left permanently on the end of the leader. It is a simple matter to put the fly on and off quickly. Such a trace also gets around the perennial Lake Nasser 'problem', namely tigerfish.

You'll catch quite a few tigerfish whilst fly fishing, but many do shy away at the last minute, often at your feet as you are about to lift the fly from the water. Tigerfish are very, *very* fast, and they simply streak up to the fly at a speed far in excess of your retrieve speed, so much so that they may well miss the fly and overrun by yards. Then they see you, or sneer at the fly and clear

Even a big fly looks small against the head of a Nile perch.

off; but if they do take, you stand a good chance of hooking them on single hooks – and then the aerobatics start. And tigerfish grow up to 16lb in the lake! In general, tigerfish flies should be bright and flashy: Crazy Charlies, Small Deceivers, in hot orange, red, white and silver.

Rate of Retrieve

The matter of speed of retrieve is crucial in lure fishing, as we pointed out earlier on, and in general, a fast retrieve is needed. The exception here would be use of jigs and rubber wiggly baits, which the Nile perch seem to accept on relatively slow retrieves. And this also seems to be the case with fly fishing. Barrie had some discussions (and lessons) with the above-mentioned US fly fishers, and their retrieve rate was certainly much too slow for lures, but clearly worked well for flies. Many of the takes came as the fly came up from the depths, quite close to the bank: just as the fly was about to escape, it was snapped up.

Other takes, rather gentle ones in Nile perch terms, occur at depth. The Nile perch will also take a fast retrieved fly, as we have proved by trailing them behind a trolling boat. Tigerfish also increase their enthusiasm for flies when you do this. The fly is naturally very close to the surface, but that doesn't seem to matter.

Choice of Flies

We do not yet know enough about particular flies to be able to recommend varieties, but any resembling tilapia fry are good, and tarpon flies have also proved to work well, especially with size 3/0 and 4/0 hooks. The range of pike flies now available seems to work well, but it is worth noting that the fly does not need to be big. Pikers tend to use flies up to 6in long, and whilst these do work with Nile perch quite well, you seem to get just as many takes on flies half that length – and the latter are much easier to cast, of course. The better flies are those with a deep profile (in side view), and in general it is better if they are loaded to sink quickly.

Choice of Line

The depths you fish and hence the choice of line is dictated by the nature of the bank. If deeper water is only a few feet from the shore for some distance as, say, along a rocky promontory, then a floating line is called for. A steeply sloping rocky bank might more usually need a fast sink line. Casting distances do not have to be great because most fish are close in to cover, caves or drop-offs, and backcasts are rarely a problem on Lake Nasser – no grass and no shrubs where the Nile perch are. But some of the best Nile perch swims do have cliffs

A big Nile perch to fly. Nile perch are built to withstand rock surfaces like this, so no need to worry if care is taken.

behind them, and for these locations the stealth boats are the answer. From the boat, of course, casting can be minimal, and at the extreme you can simply feed out fast sink line from a drifting boat until the fly gets down to where the echo sounder tells you the fish are.

One final matter concerns the time of year to fish, and it does look as though the best period is from March to July, when perch tend to move into the shallower water.

Strike Technique

For any fly fisherman, a great variety of skills and situations can be exploited: in short, it is a bit of a fly fisher's paradise. However, there is more: in addition to tigerfish, the tilapia and *Sardinia* also take flies. And this is where the sink tip comes into its own. Lighter gear can be used than for Nile perch, as long as Nile perch are not expected. The bays where the boats moor up for lunch and supper are often quiet, sandy bays with good weed growth in the area, and here you often find shoals of tilapia and other fish. Tilapia take flies readily, especially small nymphs, but – and there is always a 'but' – they are the very devil to hit. When Barrie first tried this he used the standard UK nymph fisher's style of watching for a slight sliding of the

Another way of fly fishing demonstrated by Rudi Hager – with a posh float tube.

Fly fishing in comfort and solitude, although crocodiles might be a problem!

line, a straightening of any bends in the floating line, that sort of thing.

Well, he saw the bites well enough, but the strike was always too late! He partially solved it, hitting one in every two bites, by using a figure-of-eight retrieve tight to the fly – that is, no loops, curves or 'swing-tip' procedures. In all probability the tilapia like the look of the nymph, mouth it, realize it's artificial, and spit it out very quickly indeed. If you are tight up to the fly there is less chance of them doing this. When tilapia fly fishing you will also attract small tiger-

fish, and these will get out a set of razor blades and hack the fly into bits. Just in case you are thinking that tilapia and tigerfish do not impress like Nile perch, it is perhaps worth mentioning that both species can reach double figures. A proper match angler using match techniques would have a field day with big tilapia (or a field week might be a better way of putting it). More-over, some day, with the right gear and Lady Luck smiling, some angler is going to land on fly a Nile perch of well over 100lb. What a thought, what a challenge!

15 THE 200LB FISH

Note the huge head of the 200lb fish as it comes inboard, hauled by Willie Colquhoun, Will Wragg and guide.

The Nile perch is one of the biggest freshwater fish in the world, and is perhaps only exceeded by the arapaima in the Amazon, the Mekong catfish, and the sturgeon in various parts of the world.

The maximum Nile perch weight we can find referred to in scientific literature is around 200kg (well over 400lb), and several approaching 400lb have been landed. If Nile perch do not hold the distinction of being the biggest freshwater fish in

Wilma Macdairmid with her 200lb world record, ably assisted by Willie Colquhoun, with Will Wragg and guide.

the world, then they are certainly the biggest that are readily accessible to anglers, and they are also the most numerous. A huge Nile perch is a truly awesome sight, and even when you see one, you find yourself wondering how a fish can really grow to that size – it's just so huge and solid. Looking at photographs of world record trophy shots will give you some idea of the size they can reach, but seeing for yourself is a very different experience – and it can be sentimental, too: if a big fish dies it is a sad time, and one can brood about it for several days – those who have been through the experience will know what we mean. Fortunately, this is unusual.

When it comes to finding out exactly the weight of the biggest Nile perch ever reliably recorded you almost start to think in myths, especially when you consider that we are talking about a freshwater fish. The *Guinness Book of World Records* lists an incredible 232kg (510lb) Nile perch caught by local fishermen on Lake Victoria. The most reliable record from Lake Nasser is a perch of 176kg (392lb): this fish was found, only just alive, floating on the surface by local fishermen; the weight was recorded by the Egyptian fisheries department.

Record Safari Fish

The largest Nile perch caught on our safaris in Lake Nasser was 6ft 2in (1.9m) long and had a girth of 4ft 11in (1.4m). Gerald Eastmure, a 78-year-old tea planter from India, landed this huge perch in 1997 during the early days on Lake Nasser. The only scales that were available measured weights to 220lb, but this perch took the scales right off the scale chart. Calculating using a formula that included the fish's body measurements, Barrie came up with an estimated weight of approximately 275lb.

The International Game Fishing Association has ratified three world records that have been captured on Lake Nasser. The largest freshwater fish officially weighed in accordance with IGFA (International Game Fishing Association) requirements was caught by an American angler Bill Toth, whose 230lb Nile perch is, to date, still the all-tackle world record. The IGFA allowed 230lb, but in fact this fish was bigger because the limit of the only available scales was 230lb, and the needle went right off the chart.

The second largest freshwater fish that has been ratified by the IGFA was caught by an

English angler, Adrian Brayshaw, with a 213lb Nile perch: for a time this was the original all-tackle world record. This is now the current IGFA 30lb line world record. English angler Darren Lord still holds the 50lb line class IGFA world record with a Nile perch of 210lb. Darren has to be the all-time champion of the 'Golden Bollocks' award. The safari he was on was free of charge, because he won it having entered a fishing magazine competition. Not only that, in addition to his world record perch, he caught a second perch on the same day weighing 140lb. This was in June 1998, which is in the height of the summer and not a popular month because of the heat. His guide was Mohamed Elephantine, who is also John Wilson's favourite guide.

The third largest fish caught on Lake Nasser, but not registered with the IGFA, was a 211lb

World record of 213lb caught by Adrian Brayshaw, assisted here by Nubian guides.

Nile perch caught by a German Angler Franz Retzinger using 25lb breaking strain line.

Research shows that Nile perch have a better chance of reaching record sizes in lakes rather than in river systems, and there is every indication that there are some very large perch still living in Lake Nasser. Several incredibly big fish have been sighted by anglers, and when they recall their experience, the angler can get quite moved by the memory. John Wilson, who has spent a lifetime's fishing and filming across the world, recalls his sighting in his excellent book *John Wilson's Greatest Fishing Adventures*:

> I can vividly remember a particular afternoon when working an orange Rapala CD14 plug (my favourite shore lure) up from the lake bed thirty feet down from the sheer-sided wall at Khor Maria, along Nasser's eastern shoreline, when I took a perch of around 15lb that simply went berserk. It even jumped completely clear of the surface by several feet. Then as it neared the rocky shore I could see why. A couple of feet below, looking up at its next meal, was a monstrous Nile perch, fully 6ft long, 2ft deep and around 20in thick. I had been trolling for marlin off Madeira that same year and caught a 220lb big-eyed tuna, so I knew what a two hundred pounder looked like. This perch dwarfed it. It was truly awesome. Part of my brain hoped it didn't take the hooked perch, because on an 18lb reel line, small multiplier and 11ft stepped-up carp rod (standard shore gear), frankly I was out of my depth; but something inside also reminded me that one of the trebles on the small plug in the hooked perch was dangling free. Then the giant slowly sank down again and despite my continuing just about every lure in my armoury through the same area for the following hour I never saw that monster again – and haven't since.

The story of Wilma Macdairmid's 200lb fish was recorded in Chapter 12, so we will not go into it further, but since then the 200lb barrier has been broken several times. Wilma's fish was Lake Nasser's first 'unofficial world record'. We have to say 'unofficial' because Wilma's application to

the IGFA (International Game Fishing Association) in America was rejected because her leader (trace) was considered to be 6in too long. It makes official records look a little silly when this sort of distinction is made.

Adrian Brayshaw's Record Fish, December 1997

Lake Nasser produced its first IGFA ratified all-tackle world record with a magnificent 213lb Nile perch caught by Adrian Brayshaw on 18 December 1997.

Steve Dunbar, who was on his sixth Lake Nasser safari, witnessed the fight and helped with weighing the fish; his long experience with handling big fish helped to ensure that this splendid Nile perch was returned to the lake safe and sound. The expedition was nearing its end as Adrian and Steve set out, with Mohamed Elephantine skippering the fishing boat for the final evening's trolling. They had been moving north, heading back towards Aswan, and were due to spend the night near to West Kalabsha, some four hours' run to Aswan. The water was fairly choppy as they started to troll their lures near to the 'Beacon'.

Steve was the first to make contact with a large fish, which proceeded to run and snapped his 20lb line like cotton. Troy, the third angler on the safari, was the next to connect with a large perch, which took him straight through some large boulders on the lake bottom – his line was also broken off. They were obviously into a 'pod' of very big Nile perch. Adrian was the last to get a strike, and luckily his perch did not hit a snag. It started on a long run away from him, which very nearly emptied the spool of his Abu Ambassador multiplier, despite the fact that it was set on a tight drag. Adrian also applied thumb pressure to try and slow the fish down, but it kept going and to his dismay he saw only a few yards left on the reel. Luckily Mohammed had turned the boat in time and started to chase the fish, which gave Adrian a chance to recover much needed line back on to his reel.

The perch stayed deep, going on shorter, but unstoppable runs. On several occasions during the fight, Adrian had to scramble along the boat's outer deck with his rod tip sunk under the boat to prevent a break, as the fish continually changed direction. The perch eventually went to the bottom where it 'sulked' for a minute or two, before sustained pressure from the fully bent rod began to takes it toll. The fish then went on another run, but this time came up from the bottom: when it hit the surface, its huge body heaved above the water with violent head shakes and gills flaring, which left them with little doubt that attached to Adrian's lure was a record-breaking Nile perch.

After a few more short runs, the fish was eventually brought alongside the boat. The leader was held, and the fish was lip-gaffed. However, the gaff straightened due to the weight of the fish, and it took a second attempt before the fish was secured and stringered. It was then slowly towed to a nearby island for weighing and measuring. The huge fish weighed 213lb, after the weight of the sling had been deducted, and nearly took the Salter scales to their limit. It was 6ft 2in (1.9m) long, with a girth of 4ft 3in (1.3m), a new IGFA all-tackle world record.

The fight took twenty-five minutes, and the perch was caught on a perch-patterned Depth Raider. This magnificent fish was allowed to recover on the stringer in deeper water before being returned alive, to grow to even larger proportions.

Bill Toth's Record Fish, December 2000

The second IGFA-approved all-tackle world record, which beat the 213lb Nile perch caught by Adrian Brayshaw on 18 December 1997, was captured by Bill Toth, an American angler, on 20 December 2000. It is interesting to note that this second record perch was also caught in

A giant Nile perch picture sent in from a fish factory on Lake Victoria.

December, but not in the same part of the lake – in fact it was almost at the opposite end, because Bill and his wife were on a safari that started from Abu Simbel, more than 124 miles (200km) from where Adrian caught his record perch.

When Bill started the safari he told Yousef Mohammed, his fishing guide, that he would be really satisfied if he could catch a fifty-pounder. This was achieved on the first day, and Bill was to do much, much better. They spent three days shore fishing, catching a succession of reasonable fish, enjoying the safari atmosphere and having a good time. Then in the late afternoon of the fourth day while they were trolling the Kasr Ibrim area, Yousef spotted several big fish on his finder at about 20 to 25ft, lying on some structure between two islands. Yousef suggested to Bill, who was fishing a Depth Raider at the time, that he should change to a CD18 fire tiger because Yousef was concerned the Depth Raider might get snagged on the bottom.

They then trolled back over the area where the big perch had been seen, and within a few minutes Bill hooked into a huge fish that took off on several unstoppable runs. After a while the fish jumped, about 100yd from the boat, almost clear of the water and shaking its massive head with red gills flaring. They found it hard to comprehend the size of the fish, which, to say the least, was a real knee-shaker. Bill had to be very careful because he was using 20lb breaking strain line, which feels like flimsy thread when you have such a monster attached. It took him thirty to forty-five minutes to bring the perch alongside the boat, where it was secured by a tough stringer and then towed slowly to the shore for weighing and trophy shots. When they weighed the perch it took the scale's needle right past the scale's maximum of 230lb. The IGFA allowed 230lb, and at the time of writing this

Nile perch is still the all-tackle world-record freshwater fish.

Bernard Bru's Record Fish, Summer 1998

In the summer of 1998, French angler Bernard Bru caught Lake Nasser's bank-casting record Nile perch, weighing 179lb. The fish was part of an extraordinary sixty-fish haul landed during a five-hour period by Bernard and English angler Paul Ciaputa, whose catch included a second large fish of 104lb. The rest of the fish caught weighed between 15 and 45lb, giving a total weight of over 1,400lb.

Bernard's 179lb perch took a green mackerel Rapala CD18 fished on 60lb braid; he was using a Daiwa Emblem 5000 reel, and a Conoflex 3lb TC carbon Kevlar rod.

Lake Nasser's Top Twenty Fish

The list below records the top twenty biggest fish correctly weighed on Lake Nasser; we have not included Gerald Estumre's 275lb perch because the weight was estimated. The records marked with IGFA on the chart are the three largest freshwater fish in the world caught on rod and line that have been ratified by the IGFA (International Game Fishing Association) as sport fishing world records. Bigger fish might well have been caught on rod and line, but have not been officially recorded as such.

Lake Nasser's Top Twenty Fish

Line class	Angler	Country	Weight	Record
20lb	Bill Toth	USA	230lb	IGFA
30lb	Adrian Brayshaw	England	213lb	IGFA
25lb	Franz Retzinger	Germany	211lb	
50lb	Darren Lord	England	210lb	IGFA
30lb	Peter Bond	England	205lb	
50lb	Darren Lord	England	202lb	
50lb	Wilma Macdairmid	Scotland	200lb	
20lb	Larry Dhalberg	USA	200lb	
25lb	Dietmar Rittscher	Germany	200lb	
30lb	Robert Fry	England	200lb	
30lb	Colin Campbell	England	195lb	
40lb	Olivier Portrat	Germany	192lb	
40lb	John Bogle	England	192lb	
30lb	Paul Burnside	England	190lb	
30lb	Rory Collins	England	190lb	
30lb	Roger Durham	England	186lb	
50lb	Tim Baily	England	186lb	
25lb	Olivier Portrat	Germany	185lb	
50lb	David MacIntyre	England	184lb	
30lb	Werner Gritsch	Germany	182lb	
40lb	Hans Emmenegger	Switzerland	180lb	
40lb	Barrie Sayers	England	180lb	

16 NEW CHALLENGES

Lake Nasser dawn, with rare, silvered clouds.

You will have noticed that throughout this book we have been careful to show how times change: how, for example, the Nile perch wise up to certain lures so the angler has to be constantly on the lookout for new lures and new techniques. Such a range of lures has been used on Lake Nasser since the early days there, that one could expect some of the earlier lures to come back into their own as new populations of Nile perch grow through. To some extent this may have been happening with the Rapala Super Shad Rap. This was always a good bait, but the decline in the effectiveness of the original floating divers seemed to be halted when a greater range of colours became available, and when the scale-finish 'hologram' versions came in. Later, a sinking Rapala SSR was introduced (Rapala refused our earlier request for them to do this, but eventually relented), and this increases the versatility of this lure.

Three giant Nile perch over 100lb each and three happy anglers. The result of two hours' fishing after sunset.

Ring the Changes

We use this example of the RSSR to suggest that at some point in the future Nile perch anglers will have to learn to keep more on their toes. It will not be enough simply to troll what is thought to be the going lure of the moment. Ring the changes: try completely new styles of lures; and re-try some of the old ones. It is likely, for example, that the Russelures, hardly used for a few years, would be worth a try. Similarly, some of the traditional colours and sizes of the Rapala floating minnow and count-down series might be worth trying again at intervals because they are not much used today, despite being exceptionally successful in the past. It is even possible that as the repertoire of the lure angler increases, the Nile perch itself may become less fussy.

As we write this, jigs and various rubber lures are working well, and being used almost exclusively by some anglers. In time they will become less effective, and anglers will revert to these being a standby bait. With lure fishing very slowly becoming slightly less effective, the angler will need to be versatile. It's worth asking whether jerkbaits have been given a thorough trial. There is no point in using them when the fish have gone 'off' in a hotspot – that is no test at all. They need to be tried in new spots, or when the fish are known to be feeding. Another lure perhaps seriously worth trying is big surface poppers. We have seen these used very effectively for a similar fish, the trevally, in Australia. These lures are up to 10in long, and are retrieved fast and savagely across the surface. Jerkbait rods are needed. A limited trial in 2007 produced no results, but we do know that Nile perch will take lures off the top.

Fern Lyne with a big perch, assisted by Hani.

BELOW: *Barrie with a big fish – almost a golden form (see Appendix I, page 164).*

Keeping One Step Ahead

The Nile perch has become aware of the association between the standard trolling boats and anglers and their lures. This was spotted by Tim several years ago, and there is really no doubt about it now. So the stealth boats were introduced as an adjunct to the main craft. These smaller, quieter boats allow the boat angler to approach hotspots much more carefully, whether trolling or casting on the drift or at anchor. This kind of approach will help to keep one fin ahead of the Nile perch. Alternatively, we can increase the frequency of beaching the trolling boat, and the anglers proceed on foot back to the taking zone. This can be a highly productive approach, with fish after fish being taken on occasions.

One of the ways forward, then, for fishing techniques on Lake Nasser, is to use the stealth boats more often, as they provide anglers with an alternative fishing platform to fish areas more quietly and efficiently. The main fishing boats have to be big enough to live in, and whilst they are also excellent fishing platforms, a stealth boat has an advantage in that it is much quieter and less alarming than the bigger boats. The stealth boat can be quietly drifted or rowed over underwater promontories or past rocky drop-offs, allowing anglers to cast lures or wobble deadbait without the commotion caused by a bigger boat.

Casting from a small drifting boat to drop-offs that can't be reached from the shore is a very effective method and one that is difficult to achieve when using the larger, less manoeuvrable fishing boats. The stealth boat approach is ideal because the boat itself is light, can be anchored easily, and has oars that make drift adjustments quiet and easy.

The sun goes down on Lake Nasser: is the night fishing unexplored?

Bait fishing with natural dead- or livebaits, either trolled or static, is another area that needs much more attention now. In the past, when lures continued to produce fish all the time, baits were neglected: it is, after all, a slower way of fishing, as a general rule, in that it takes longer to set, hook, and unhook the fish. You could probably land three fish on lures in the same time as it takes to land one on bait – provided, of course, that they'll take the lures! If other predatory fish are considered – pike, for example – it is unlikely that the Nile perch will wise up to natural baits. They may ignore them for a while, but they do have to feed eventually, and a natural bait is just that: natural.

Consider New Waters

Then there is the little matter of new water, or waters, to consider. Many anglers are reluctant to try anything new, preferring those that have succeeded in the past, whether lure or fishing spot. What may be needed when times are hard is to seek out new hotspots. We have run a number of exploration safaris on Lake Nasser, when the objective was to try out new places and not to worry too much about catches. This was quite successful. Whether one can expect an angler out for his once-a-year holiday, for one week, to adopt such an approach is perhaps doubtful, but when we have done this ourselves, it has been immensely pleasurable and quite successful. The old lures may work in a new spot, after all. Lake Nasser is extremely large, and one simply cannot argue that it has all been covered.

What about other waters? Appendix II (*see* page 177) gives some idea of the distribution of Nile perch, and it is surely down to the enterprising angler to sort out some of these places, as did John Wilson (Murchison Falls) and Andy Orme (Lake Victoria), or Linda and Jim Tyree or the Deterdings (*see* John Bailey's book in the Bibliography).

The part of Lake Nasser that lies within the Sudan looks interesting, but the only inadvertent efforts made so far resulted in temporary arrest!

Then there is Lake Tana and other lakes, again in Ethiopia, but high in the mountains and on the River Nile. These lakes are known to hold big Nile perch, but are not yet fished much by rod and line. Will Wragg made an adventurous and brave trip to two such lakes a few years ago, and this is what he reported:

Both lakes are reputed to hold big Nile perch, but for six days we had to sit on a hotel veranda, looking at both lakes spread invitingly below us, but unable to fish them because of lack of permission from the authorities. Finally by paying an outrageous amount of US dollars, we managed an illicit day on Lake Chamo, the southern and smaller of the two lakes.

We saw no Nile perch, although they are definitely in there. What we did see were crocodiles... lots of crocodiles, more than fifty during the day! Our 'guides', local fishermen, would not let us within five meters of the water's edge. This made shore fishing somewhat awkward. We caught a lot of small Barbus (up to 5lb) on bread – landing and returning these fish was somewhat fraught, with crocodile heads popping up suddenly in front of us. As well as crocodiles we saw hippos and a wealth of bird life – so the lack of big fish did not really matter.

There were undoubtedly large Nile perch in Lake Chamo, and there may well still be. However, there is quite an effective black market fishery on the lake. The fishermen concentrate on the Nile perch, ignoring the huge tilapia; consequently bigger fish may be few in number. Nevertheless we spoke to a Russian scientist who had recorded a 78kg (173lb) Nile perch in 1994.

Lake Abaya, which is twice as big as Chamo, is reputed to hold huge perch, but is a very foreboding place. It's windswept, wild, heavily coloured, and the crocodiles have an evil reputation.

APPENDIX I
THE BIOLOGY AND ECOLOGY
OF NILE PERCH

The scientific name of the Nile perch is *Lates niloticus* (Linnaeus 1758). When the scientific name is written like this it tells you several things very clearly. First, that the celebrated Swedish scientist Carl Linné, father of the modern binomial (two names) system of scientific naming, first described the Nile perch under the species name *niloticus* (after the River Nile) in his classic work of 1758. But because his name is enclosed in brackets, it also tells you that Linné did not use the generic name *Lates* but rather chose *Labrus*. The name *Perca* used by some workers immediately gives us the hint that the Nile perch is of the perch family, *sensu lato*. In fact most modern workers have a family Latidae or Centropomidae (*lates perches*: the *idae* ending indicates a (scientific) family) and this family is grouped with other, similar ones in the (scientific) order Perciformes (perch-like fish). The scientific generic name *Lates* was conferred by Cuivier in 1828. Subsequently other researchers grouped the Nile perch with some similar species and placed them in the genus *Lates*. We'll mention the similar, related species in a short while.

Note that we refer to *Lates niloticus* as the scientific name. We do not refer to it as the Latin name, which is wrong. Scientific names may well have – indeed, often do have – a Latin root, but they may also have a Greek root or an Anglo-Saxon root – any dead language root, in fact. So Linné's binomial names are scientific names. The name *Lates* does derive from the Latin *latere* (to be hidden). Notice also that the species name *niloticus* is written with a small, or lower case n, despite the fact that the River Nile

Golden Nile perch caught by Susheel and Nanda. (John Wilson)

is a proper name. All specific names have a lower case first letter to distinguish them from the larger grouping or generic name, in this case *Lates*. You will often see *L. niloticus* written as *L. Niloticus* even in scientific papers. It is wrong, and it has no meaning whatsoever under the rules of scientific nomenclature.

A number of other species are placed in the genus *Lates* along with *L. niloticus*, the Nile perch. It will come as no surprise to experienced anglers to learn that one close species is the Australian barramundi. This freshwater to brackish water species not only looks like the Nile perch, it tastes like it, too! The scientific name for the barramundi is *Lates calcarifer*.

ABOVE: Youseff Mohammed displays a small Nile perch to show its main features of dorsal spines, pelvic fin spines, pectoral fin spines, topside eyes and big tail.

RIGHT: A well-shaped Nile perch of medium size.

What is interesting is that research is being carried out on stocks of Nile perch in Australia, as Tim relates elsewhere in the book (Chapter 7, Appendix II). If the genetics of the barramundi were 'contaminated' with *L. niloticus*, the results could be interesting, to say the least. After all, the Lake Victoria fish are not pure *L. niloticus*, as pointed out below, and what happened after that introduction was the extinction of about 200 native (endemic) species of cichlids, a tragedy of enormous proportions (because the evolution of those cichlids was one of the most rapid known and had been widely studied before the tragic event – done, of course, with the best of intentions).

Other species included in *Lates* with the Nile perch include *L. angustifrons* (in the Lake

Tanganyika region); *L. japonicus* (in Japan); *L. longispinus* in the Lake Rudolf region); *L. macrophthalmus* (in the Lake Albert lakes, and which we have already mentioned as a 'contaminant' in Lake Victoria); *L. mariae* (known by the common name of 'bigeye lates'); *L. microlepis* (known by the common name of 'fork-tail lates'); and *L. stoppersii* (known by the common name of 'sleek lates'). The genus *Lates* is native to the Indian and western Pacific oceans and in lakes and rivers in Africa, including the Rift Valley system.

Some species and subspecies are considered synonymous with the Nile perch *L. niloticus*, and were described subsequently as new forms of *Lates*; but later workers rejected the science, and placed them as junior synonyms. So if you come across the following forms in the literature, you will know that they are just Nile perch: *L. nobilis* (described by Cuvier in 1828); *Perca latus* (Saint-Hilaire in 1827*); L. niloticus macrolepido-ta* (a subspecies described by Pellegrin in 1922);

L. albertianus (described from Lake Albert by Worthington in 1929); and *L. niloticus rudolfi-anus* (a subspecies described from Lake Rudolf by Worthington in 1932).

The common name for *L. niloticus*, and the one we are familiar with, is Nile perch. Other common names are really related to different regions of Africa and to different languages; thus: nijlbaars (Dutch); nilabborre (Swedish); Nilbarasch (German); Peche du nil (French); persico del nilo (Italian); perca di nilo (Spanish) (all of which are fairly obvious); as well as Mkombozii sangola sangara (Kiswahili), chen-gu (Kijitta); mbuta (Koluo); victoriabaars capi-taine and Victoria barsch; samos (Arabic).

Physical Appearance and Structure

The Nile perch varies in both colour and shape, and those anglers fishing Lake Nasser will have seen the majority as silver or bluish silver, and occasional very dark, almost black fish. Bars and spots only seem to occur on very young, small fish, such as those under 1lb weight. Several features are very apparent when you have one on the bank, namely that some fish are very short and deep, whilst others are more streamlined and slim: one fish of 95lb caught by Barrie was 5ft 8in (1.7m) long, and had an almost circular cross-section! Most fish are, however, on the deep side of fusiform ('centropomid' is the correct term).

Dorsal fin spines are what next strike, sometimes quite literally. The dorsal fin is in two parts (most anglers would say two fins), the first being seriously spiny with seven or eight big spines, the third spine being the longest and most robust after two relatively rudimentary ones. There are other spines on the gill covers and on the anal fin (as in some other perch species), so handling of Nile perch must be done with care, not only for the fish's sake. However, there are no teeth to worry about, the large mouth having hard, rough plates near the front – though the grip of a Nile perch jaw is considerable. Whilst smaller prey are simply engulfed (as with anglers' lures quite

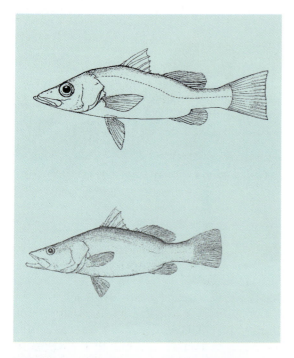

Lates mariae *(big-eye* Lates*) (above) and* Lates angustifrons, *species from Lake Tanganyika (see text).*

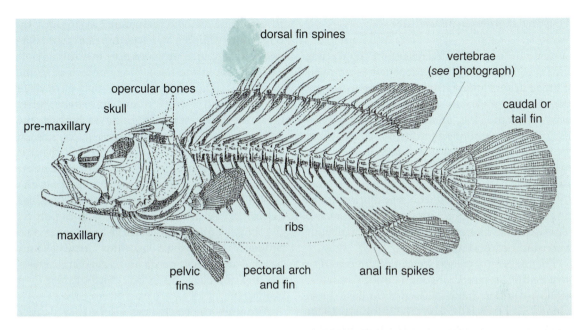

Skeleton of Nile perch (see *text*).

often), large prey, if gripped in these jaws, will be easily incapacitated.

Perhaps the tail is one of the most impressive features of this fish – it is certainly clear where the acceleratory power comes from. The lateral line is conspicuous, and whilst it is midway dorsoventrally at the tail end, it rises to a slightly more dorsal position at the anterior end of the fish.

The illustration of the skeletal parts of the Nile perch is modified from *A History of Fishes* (Ernest Benn, 1931). The original illustration was by Lt Col W. P. C. Tenison, and the book's author was J. R. Norman. Notice that he gives nine spiny rays in the first part of the dorsal fin, whereas most modern accounts give seven or eight. We haven't checked this on Lake Nasser, but will do so in the future. What descriptions of the Nile perch do not do is give a clear idea of the bones themselves. If you look at the photograph you will see that the bones are not massive and heavy, which perhaps you might expect for such a big fish, but are porous and almost spongy in texture. These are illustrations Barrie

Nile perch vertebra, and upper jaw from 100lb-plus fish (see *text*).

made from a freshly dead carcass of a 100lb Nile perch that Tim found high up a cliff (taken there by jackals) on his first ever trip to Lake Nasser. Bones like this would confer lightness, coupled with considerable strength, and may go part way to explaining the extraordinary acceleration and acrobatic agility of the fish. Not many fish go completely airborne at a weight of 100lb plus when they are on the end of the angler's line.

Feeding Habits and Habitat

When you look at the literature on the feeding habits of Nile perch, there does not seem to be a great deal of interest to the angler! After all, they eat fish of various species except when very tiny, when they eat small items of plankton – they soon become piscivorous, however. What we really want to know is whether they feed extensively at night, and do they scavenge dead fish off the bottom? We'll have to find out ourselves. They are cannibalistic, but that comes as no real surprise, because most big predators are. They also eat crustaceans, given the chance, as well as insects and molluscs.

The maximum weight we can find referred to in scientific literature is around 200kg (well over 400lb), and on Lake Nasser they have been caught commercially up to 375lb, so 400lb seems like a reasonable upper limit, which is about twice the size of the Murray cod maximum and maybe four times the barramundi maximum. A weight of 400lb is enough to whet the appetites of many an adventurous angler, we feel.

Scientific accounts of the habitats of Nile perch do not help the angler a great deal. One might even consider that they do not like rocks, which will certainly raise the eyebrows of anyone who has fished Lake Nasser, where they seem actually to seek out any form of rocks, be it giant boulder or cliff face. Sandy or muddy bays seem to be disliked, and anywhere where the oxygen level may drop seems to be avoided, such as swamps and the leeward shallows of island. Tiny Nile perch may like weed as cover, but once the fish become big they seem to avoid weedbeds.

Observing Nile Perch

Tim has spent many, many hours just watching Nile perch in their natural habitat, not fishing, just watching from vantage points overlooking swims. It's an incredible experience to sit quietly and watch these huge fish gliding around in the water below, and these observations are perhaps more valuable and accurate than those currently available in any scientific literature.

Perch are in the habit of coming close to the shoreline along rocky margins that have deep drop-offs and escape routes into deep water close by. They seem to enjoy basking in the warm shallow water and getting some sun on their backs. The best time to observe them is from about 10am until about 3pm in the afternoon, depending on how much sun the swim gets. This is a habit more common with the bigger perch, which seem to have the monopoly on the best sunbathing areas. The smaller fish probably don't dare use the same swims, because the bigger perch are in the habit of eating any other fish up to one-third of their own bodyweight.

Although they will take a lure they do not seem to be actively feeding but rather resting up for the night hunt – on Lake Nasser we believe the perch feed mainly at night. An unusual event sometimes takes place: we have observed Nile perch and tilapia mixing in the same swim, not too close, but well in sight of each other. This does not happen very often, and reminds us of lion in the African bush when they casually walk close to a herd of zebra or antelope, and none of the prey animals seem overly concerned about the close proximity of a predator – the signal seems to be 'it's safe, they have had their meal'.

Only having the chance to observe Nile perch during daylight hours means we only have the chance to see a very small part of the perch's daily life. But all the same, some lessons are learnt, and also these great fish leave the observer with a special feeling of wonderment to see them undisturbed and going about their daily life. All too often the only memories that an angler has of these magnificent fish is when they are fighting for their lives, or as a picture of one lying in the arms of an angler.

If you remain completely still, perch will think you are just part of the shoreline structure; but just one small movement, and the fish will immediately be alerted to potential danger and then disappear in a blink of an eye. There have been many times that Tim has been standing on a rock, right on the edge of a deep drop-off, when a 100lb-plus fish has swum past just a few yards away from his feet, which, to say the least, gets the adrenalin pumping. Perch not noticing an angler standing on the bank is rather a strange phenomenon; so why is it that these fish do not recognize a shape as being dangerous?

One particular example always brings a smile to Tim's face as he recalls the experience. He was casting quietly from a big rock on the edge of a particularly good swim and had just retrieved his lure; then, just as he was about to cast again, out of the corner of his eye he noticed a movement in the water to his left. Tim froze as a big perch of about 70–80lb swam up to the edge of the rock he was standing on. The perch had a good look around the rock, and must have decided that it would be a good ambush point; and so it settled down, tucking itself into a big crevice immediately below Tim's feet.

Tim stood there absolutely immobile, holding the rod out in front of him straight above the crevice, from which the perch's nose was now sticking out slightly. There was no way Tim could cast the lure without the fish seeing the movement; but then he realized the lure was dangling from the tip of the rod almost straight above the perch. The only option was to release the clutch and then very gently lower the lure – a floating Rapala SSR – into the water in front of the perch's nose. The lure gently hit the water, very slowly, without a ripple, about 3ft from the perch's nose, and floated there bobbing gently.

The perch visibly tensed up, and for two or three seconds lay motionless gazing at the lure – then suddenly lunged forwards … but no… it was spooked, and disappeared into the depths. It had taken a second or two for it to work out that something was seriously wrong: food just should not appear suddenly from the sky.

Depth of Habitat
What depths Nile perch live at is a particularly important question for anglers because they need to have accurate information to target the size of fish they want to catch. We will tell you about what we have observed on Lake Nasser – although this information might not necessarily apply to perch inhabiting other venues, for example Lake Victoria, which is quite a shallow lake, or Lake Tanganyika, which is remarkably deep. We are told that species of Nile perch live at great depths in Lake Tanganyika. Then when Nile perch are living in a river system, there will be another set of rules about depth.

Keep in mind that much of what we say about the target depths for Nile perch on Lake Nasser is not a proven fact, but more of a 'gut feeling' brought about by observation over the past fifteen years. This sense of the unknown – 'do we really know the answer?' – makes fishing an interesting pastime. First of all, on a day-to-day basis, a good fish finder is the most important tool to determine the depth at which Nile perch are living. It seems there are several factors that determine this: for example, weather fronts (barometric pressure), the season (winter or summer), and different sizes of fish live at different depths.

Life Cycle of the Nile Perch

From the time Nile perch hatch from their eggs, as tiny fingerlings, they will hide among the rocks and weeds in the shallow margins, which is naturally the safest place for them to hide when there are predators around. As the fingerlings grow they will gradually move into deeper water and feed on the layer of smaller fish living just above them. As this process continues and the perch grow, they will gradually be moving into deeper water; and when they get to sizes in excess of, say, 100 to 150lb we believe these huge fish might well live most of their life in deep water 50 to 100ft down. Food for these big fish also lives in deeper water, and we think these 'big boys' feed on the bigger tilapia that favour deeper water during daylight hours, and then they probably follow them into shallower water at night. Fishermen are always telling us that the

Juvenile Nile perch.

big Nile perch can be found at night, especially when there is a full moon. The full moon probably helps the fishermen to observe better what is going on around them. Another source of food for the big perch are the layers of other Nile perch living just above them: yes, Nile perch are very cannibalistic.

Whenever we are looking for the bigger Nile perch, within target range of our lures, we nearly always find them in shallower areas that are close to deep water. We feel these perch like to have the security of deep water close by so they can disappear into the depths when danger threatens them.

During the summer months, when the lake is at its shallowest, from approximately mid-March through to the end of July, Nile perch are more often found in shallower water. This is because tilapia, the Nile perch's principal prey, are spawning. The breeding tilapia come into shallow water to build their nests and then spawn. Some weeks after spawning, a huge population of tilapia fry start to grow up in the shallows, encouraging the presence of the smaller predators such as tigerfish and juvenile perch, which are both a favourite food of the bigger Nile perch. All this action takes place in water from the margins down to about 10ft deep.

The exception we have found during the summer months is when there are sudden strong changes in the prevailing weather patterns; this will drive the Nile perch into deeper water, especially when the barometric pressure rises or falls rapidly. From late September until the end of January, when the lake is at its highest level, Nile perch are more often found in deeper water. Year after year we capture bigger fish during the winter season, and almost all these fish are caught while trolling over underwater promontories and sunken islands at some depth. The winter months are not the best time for shore fishing, and fly-fishing is also difficult because it is harder to get down to the fish lying in deeper water.

As we have argued earlier, it is our current opinion that Nile perch will not scavenge dead fish off the bottom, and what biological information there is supports this opinion.

Reproduction of Nile perch does seem extremely flexible, and could help explain the success of the species. It can occur at any month of the year, but has peaks in the rainy season where a rainy season occurs (not Lake Nasser, where Barrie has only seen a few raindrops twice in fifteen visits). The fish prefer shallow, sheltered areas, and, unlike tilapia which build nests, the Nile perch scatters the eggs freely. Up

RIGHT: Nile perch scale. Note the annual growth rings. Reading scales suggests fish of 200lb may only be fourteen to fifteen years old, but the method may not be accurate. (Olivier Portrat)

BELOW: Nile perch are cannibals and eat fish, or attempt to eat fish, that are too large for them.

A very greedy Nile perch. This aspect of their behaviour is discussed in the text on page 173.

to sixteen million eggs may be deposited per breeding cycle. Male fish mature at two years, and females at two to four years; mortality in males is higher; females may grow larger. The lifespan is supposed to be up to sixteen years. Some of the 200lb fish (*see* Chapter 16) seemed to be around twelve to fourteen years old on Lake Nasser, if the scale readings by Barrie are accurate (which is by no means certain). It would be better to estimate the age of fish using sections of the operculae over the gills, but this can only be done at present on dead fish, and most Lake Nasser fish are returned alive to the water.

Most research on Nile perch has been carried out on Lake Victoria. This could be atypical in several respects: for example, the peak productivity in the 1970s and 1980s is now in decline, as is the weight achieved by individual fish; and the genetics are 'contaminated' by cross breeding with another species of *Lates*.

From our observations we feel the bigger Nile perch feed up to get ready for spawning, which usually seems to start to take place sometime in February. Nature is logical and we feel that, in the scheme of things, the best time for Nile perch to spawn would be some months before their prey spawns. From late January into March we have observed many male Nile perch 'milking' just after they have been captured. By 'milking' we mean they exude sperm, which would otherwise be spread over the eggs laid by females.

Having said that Nile perch provide no parental care, many of the local fishermen on Lake Nasser tell us that Nile perch will stay close to where they have spawned. The eggs, when hatched, turn into literally millions of tiny fry, and these are very vulnerable to predatory juvenile tigerfish. They say these perch guard their young from these tigerfish.

In Lake Victoria, male size at sexual maturity is 20 to 22in when they are about two years, and females 26 to 33in, at two to four years. Maturity sizes have strongly decreased in recent years.

The most common cause of natural death of Nile perch that we have observed on Lake Nasser is due to suffocation as a result of the perch trying to swallow a tilapia that is much too big to pass down its throat. Whenever we find a dead perch floating in the lake we stop to inspect it and try to find out how it was killed. Over the years there have been quite a lot of occasions when we have found a dead perch floating in the lake with a large tilapia firmly trapped in its throat.

It seems that in a feeding frenzy a perch will grab and swallow a large tilapia, which gets trapped in its mouth. The perch's gullet is too narrow to swallow the prey into its stomach. In every case we have observed the tilapia has been swallowed head first and can not be rejected because the tilapia's dorsal fin spines have risen and got firmly trapped in the roof of the perch's mouth. If the perch could breathe it would die a slow death due to starvation and the tilapia would be rotten. In all cases we have found the tilapia has always been quite fresh, hence our conclusion about death by suffocation as opposed to starvation.

Commercial Uses

The Nile perch has commercial uses. They took decades to become evident in Lake Victoria and then burst into a huge biomass in the late 1980s and 1990s, and the subsequent harvest for export. It rose to become the main fishery species in the lake in the late 1990s, and the basis of a huge export industry. This raised the price of Nile perch to something beyond the reach of many lakeside communities. All of this was documented in the first two phases of an IUCN-World Conservation Union's Nile perch project, which culminated in the making of the film *Big Fish, Small Fry*. The project has moved on to conflict resolution and capacity building using 'beach units' to give more responsibility and management involvement to local people. This work is supported by the three riparian government fisheries departments, through the Lake Victoria Fisheries Organisation (LVFO), and is currently being reviewed.

In recent years the Nile perch population has begun to stabilize, and the availability of large fish has declined, as has the catch, which is now way below the capacity of the factories that process and export the fish to the USA, Europe, Australia

Australian barramundi. Note that it is a stockier form compared with the Egyptian form, and it has more dorsal spines.

and New Zealand. The view of the three riparian governments is that Nile perch is an essential export earner, and they have attempted to brand it as 'organic', as it is wild and without artificial additives (although cage-rearing has begun). This same export has brought some benefits to the local people (income from fishing and jobs in factories), and some drawbacks from the availability of fish for food, and economic and social upheaval (Howard, G., personal comment, August 2005).

Environmental Impacts

Nile perch were introduced to Lake Victoria and several other lakes in Africa where they have caused severe devastation, leading to the loss of many native species. The introduction of Nile perch into Australia was considered after a reduction in Queensland barramundi stocks, but this was decided against due to the devastation they caused in several African lakes.

Darwin's Nightmare is a 2004 film written and directed by Hubert Sauper. It was nominated for Best Documentary Film at the 78th Academy Awards. The film starts with a Soviet-made cargo plane landing in an airfield in Tanzania, near Lake Victoria. The plane came from Europe, and had come to ship processed fillets of Nile perch back to Europe. Through interviews with the Russian and Ukrainian plane crew, local factory owners, guards, prostitutes, fishermen and other villagers, the film discusses the effects of the introduction of Nile perch to Lake Victoria, and how it has affected the ecosystem and economy of the region. The film also dwells at length on the dichotomy between the huge amounts of European aid that is being funnelled into Africa, and yet at the same time the flow of munitions and weapons from European arms dealers that also flows unendingly into the continent, often on the same planes that transport the Nile perch fillets to European consumers. As Dima, the radio engineer of the plane crew, says later on in the film, 'The children of Europe receive grapes for

Christmas, the children of Angola receive guns.' The appalling living and working conditions of the indigenous people, in which basic sanitation is completely absent and many children turn to drugs and prostitution, is covered in great depth; because the Nile perch fish is farmed commercially, all the prime fillets are sold to European supermarkets, leaving the local people to survive on the carcasses of the gutted fish.

General Impacts

Nile perch stocks are now going down, and production is lower than ever, according to the August 2006 Globefish report on the Nile perch market. As a result, raw material prices shot up by 60 per cent in early 2006. Transport costs are rising, and there is tough competition on the EU market from other freshwater species such as *Pangasius* and *Tilapia* (overall, the quantity of Nile perch imported into the EU from the three Lake Victoria countries declined from 56,000 tonnes in 2004 to 52,800 tonnes in 2005). The situation in the EU market does not allow for a price increase in the processed product, so there is not much room for profit for the Nile perch processing industry, which is struggling to survive.

The Nile perch *Lates niloticus* was initially introduced into Lake Victoria in 1954. This introduction, together with that of four exotic *Tilapia* species, was made in response to the collapse of the original Lake Victoria fishery due to overfishing of two native tilapias (*Oreochromis esculentus* and *O. variabilis*). The idea was that the large, predatory Nile perch would feed on the lakes *Haplochromis* species, and in turn become a food fish for the locals.

For reasons that remain a mystery, the numbers of Nile perch remained relatively low until the mid-1980s, when it underwent a population explosion. Within the space of a few years, the Nile perch simply ate its way through the cichlids of Lake Victoria. Because the Victorian cichlids had not been completely catalogued at the time, we can never know precisely how many cichlid species perished in what may be the largest vertebrate extinction in tens of millions of years. A widely accepted estimate is that 300 of some possible 500 haplochromines native to the lake have become extinct since 1980.

As appalling as this figure may be, closer examination of the pattern of these extinctions reveals an even grimmer reality. Lake Victorian cichlids, like those of lakes Malawi and Tanganyika, are an outstanding example of the phenomenon of adaptive radiation. Simply put, if there was a way for a fish to make a living in Lake Victoria, a haplochromine cichlid evolved to take advantage of it. These *Haplochromis* managed to invent a lifestyle quite without parallel elsewhere! Fish ecologists recognize ten to fourteen distinct trophic guilds – assemblages of species with a common feeding pattern. However, not all were equally impacted by *Lates*.

The duration of the Nile perch's impact on the Lake Victoria ecosystem is open to question. It may have done its worst. Those haplochromines still in existence have demonstrated that they have the ability to coexist with this formidable predator.

Since at least the 1920s, Lake Victoria has been undergoing a progressive shift from a nutrient-poor to a nutrient-rich state. This process has been driven by the progressive deforestation of its watershed, which accelerates the movement of such plant nutrients as nitrates and phosphates from the soil into the lake. Increased nutrient levels have resulted in increased planktonic algae.

Prior to the introduction of the Nile perch, these algal blooms supported a diverse community of planktonic crustaceans, as well as a substantial assemblage of phytoplankton-feeding *Haplochromis* species. These small, open-water cichlids were among the first casualties of the Nile perch's voracious appetite. With their removal from the food web, vast quantities of phytoplankton remain unconsumed, die and fall to the bottom. Here their decomposition has had the effect of turning the formerly well-oxygenated deep waters of Lake Victoria into an oxygen-deficient environment – killing or forcing into shallower water the distinctive *Haplochromis* species of this zone. Eighteen metres (60ft) now marks the lower distributional limit for oxygen-consuming organisms in Lake Victoria.

Note that eliminating *Lates* from the picture at this point would not reverse this trend. The phytoplankton-feeding *Haplohromis* species are gone forever. For hundreds of years the population living around Lake Victoria in East Africa has been able to draw its sustenance from the lake's rich fishing grounds. Until twenty years ago the catch of fish from the lake went primarily to the population around the lake and to the surrounding areas. About 100,000 tons of fish were caught in Lake Victoria every year up until 1980. For the poor people who could not afford to buy meat, fish was the most important source of animal protein. The production and processing of fish, as well as the trade associated with this, took place in the local communities around Lake Victoria. Several hundred thousand men and women were employed in and earned income from fishing-related activities at Lake Victoria.

The local population adapted quickly to the explosion in the catch size. Tens of thousands of unemployed and underemployed women and men made their way down to the beaches along Lake Victoria and found work as fishermen or in fish processing and trading. After a rather slow start, the demand for Nile perch grew rapidly throughout East Africa. Most people liked Nile perch, and they could afford to buy it.

However, the Nile perch also had potential outside the local market. An international market for the fish developed quickly. In the early 1980s the first processing factories, financed with foreign capital, were established along the shores of Lake Victoria. This is where the Nile perch was filleted. The fish fillets were exported to Europe, the Middle East, the USA and Japan, where Nile perch became quite popular. Large grocery store chains in the industrialized countries began to seek out the fish from Lake Victoria. Since the catch of fish in the northern hemisphere is declining, the market for Nile perch in the North now appears to be unlimited.

APPENDIX II
DISTRIBUTION OF NILE PERCH

When Carl Linné chose the scientific species name *L. niloticus* for Nile perch, he was recording the association of the fish with the River Nile in Egypt; and I think if you asked the man in the street about the Nile perch (and he may well have eaten it from Waitrose!) he would probably say that it came from the Nile. The known natural range of the Nile perch is, however, much greater than that, and what is more, it is spreading rapidly as a result of human introductions and scientific research, not to mention fish farming.

Nile perch are generally present in lakes and rivers in the Ethiopian geographical region of Africa, including, obviously, Egypt, the Nubian Desert (Lake Nasser), the Sudan, Ethiopia, Uganda and so on. It is present in the river basins of the Nile, Chad (for example Chari), Niger, Senegal, Volta and Zaire, and in terms of giant lakes it is present in lakes Albert (Lake Mobutu Sese Seko), Kyoga, Rudolf, Nabugabo, Nyanza (Victoria), Turkana and Tana. (For comment on the last of these, *see* Chapter 16.)

For the most part the Nile perch is associated with freshwater, but it has also adapted to living in brackish water, for example in Lake Mariout situated in the Nile delta, near Alexandria (although reports seem to indicate that it has been heavily fished and as a result is now relatively rare in this lake). Nile perch can also be found in relative abundance in Lake Turkana, a big, isolated brackish lake in northern Kenya on the border with Ethiopia.

Being able to adapt to thrive in brackish water is interesting because the very similar species, the barramundi (*L. calcarifer*) in Australia, occurs in both freshwater and brackish water. In fact, in order to explain the global distribution of the genus *Lates* to which the Nile perch belongs, one must postulate not only a tolerance of salt, but also an adaptation, at times, to the fully marine environment.

Nile perch have also been introduced quite widely, and this process is far from over yet, as we shall explain. Perhaps the most famous – or infamous – introduction of Nile perch was into Lake Victoria. Whilst done with the best of intentions, namely to produce a major food source and industry for the countries surrounding the lake, a consequence was the extinction of several hundred species of cichlid fish that had been involved in one of the most spectacular evolutionary records known to man – a tragedy of gigantic proportions. What is more, the Nile perch of Lake Victoria is a genetically 'contaminated' form (*see* Appendix I), unlike most of the other introductions elsewhere.

The Nile perch was introduced to Cuba from Ethiopia and to Morocco from Mali in west central Africa. In central USA, notably Texas, Nile perch were transported from eastern Africa (the exact source is not known to us) but may not have established themselves as wild populations. We do not know the current status of Nile perch in Cuba; given reasonable waters they should be able to thrive there.

There is no Nile perch aquaculture farming in Australia. The Queensland government researched the potential of farming Nile perch in Australia on an experimental basis because at that time they were exploring all opportunities for developing a fish-farming industry in

Worldwide Distribution of Nile Perch

Country	Status	Location
Benin	Native	Ouèmé river
Cameroon	Native	Sanaga, Congo river (=Zaire river), Benue river, Lake Chad, and in the coastal rivers of the west
Chad	Native	Lake Chad
Congo Rep.	Introduced	Inland water. Introduced from the Sudan in 1997
Côte d'Ivoire	Native	Comoé, Bandama and Sassandra basins
Cuba	Introduced	Introduced from Ethiopia in 1982. Not established in the wild. Aquaculture assisted or artificial reproduction. Also introduced for angling/sport. Present status unknown
Egypt	Native	Lake Nasser. Largely fished out in the Nile and most inland lakes. However, occurs in Lake Mariout
Ethiopia	Native	Blue Nile and most rivers and lakes
Ghana	Native	Widely distributed in the Volta basin. Important to aquaculture and fisheries
Guinea	Native	Kogon, Fatala, Kokouré and Great Scarcies rivers
Guinea Bissau	Native	Géba and Corubal rivers
Kenya	Native	Lake Turkana. Introduced to Lake Victoria in the late 1950s and early 1960s from the shallow waters of Lake Albert and Lake Turkana. An unpublished introduction in Lake Naivasha in the early 1970s and since the early 1980s several perch have been caught. Present status not known. Apparently the species has not established in the Tana river after it escaped from Sagana Fish Culture Farm into the middle Tana river after exceptional floods at the end of 1961
Liberia	Native	St Paul and St John rivers
Mali	Native	Minor commercial
Mauritania	Native	Commercial
Morocco	Introduced	Introduced from Mali in 1954. Species disappeared possibly because of poor state of founder stocks
Niger	Native	
Nigeria	Native	Ogun and Niger rivers. Exploited commercially in Kainji lake. Also recorded from Benue, Chad and Upper Niger
Senegal	Native	Senegal river
Sierra Leone	Native	Little Scarcies, Rokel, Jong, Sewa and Moa rivers
Sudan	Native	White and Blue Nile. Probably one of the last 'outposts' of truly wild Nile perch
Tanzania	Introduced	Introduction to Lake Victoria virtually eliminated numerous unique cichlids in the area and has been the subject of many debates. Highly commercial
Tanzania	Native	Lake Tanganyika (*Lates mariae*)
Togo	Native	Mono river
Uganda	Native	Introduction to Lake Victoria virtually eliminated numerous unique cichlids in the area and has been the subject of many debates. Highly commercial

Australia. The Australians were concerned about the practicality of being able to successfully breed barramundi fingerlings in brackish water and then transfer them to freshwater ponds to grow. They have always been very wary about Nile perch, with the concern about the ecological impact of introducing Nile perch to Australian freshwater habitat. In the end they abandoned the project because they found efficient methods of breeding barramundi fingerlings in freshwater. Barramundi farming is now a thriving industry in Australia.

We are investigating the research in the UK as we write this, but we think that research is taking place in the New Forest, and it may be that some of the small Nile perch you see occasionally in Waitrose actually come from here, or at least from a UK farm. It would be highly improbable that a wild breeding population could survive in the UK, given that tropical temperatures are necessary.

Finally, the Nile perch is known to be established at Banque in the Central African Republic, which puts it in the Congo basin (in the River Oubanquhi). As far as we know the Nile perch does not occur any further south in western Africa, nor further south in eastern Africa than outlined above. If it has been introduced to South Africa we are unaware of it. Interestingly, Fox-Strangways in *Wandering Fisherman* (1955), at a time when the geographical distribution of Nile perch was not fully known, refers to fishing in the Orashi river in Nigeria and in Lake Nyasa (Lake Malawi). The Murchison (Kabalega) Falls are on the Victoria Nile in Uganda near Lake Albert (Lake Mobutu Sese Seko).

LEFT: *Barrie in 2007 with Youseff and Meso, Nubian guides.*

BELOW: *Youseff Mohammed, master guide and brilliant boatman.*

APPENDIX III
WHERE TO FISH AND HOW
TO GET THERE

The Lake Nasser story forms the core of this book because it can truly be said to have transformed Nile perch fishing and made it available – in safety and yet in wilderness – to any anglers who care to go. So to go on the Lake Nasser safaris all you need do is contact African Angler by e-mail at enquiries@african-angler.net or through their website at www.african-angler.co.uk. Alternatively you can contact Christine Taylor at Tailor Made Holidays or christine@tailormadeholidays.co.uk. She is very experienced at organizing trips to Lake Nasser, and can also deal with trips to Lake Victoria and the Murchison Falls.

Lake Victoria and the Murchison Falls

When it comes to Lake Victoria in Uganda, and the Murchison Falls, one man to contact is Paul Goldering of Wild Frontiers at Entebbe. He is the man who organizes trips for John Wilson, including trips to the Murchison Falls (*see* Chapter 2 for details of John's exciting adventures there, or watch the DVD). In order to give a fuller idea of Lake Victoria Nile perch fishing, we asked Paul Goldering for some thoughts in response to some of our questions.

One question was why was it that there were no Nile perch in Lake Victoria before man stocked the water with them (this was done, by the way, by Major Bruce Kinlock). Paul pointed out that the lake dried out between 12,000 and 18,000 years ago, and only reflooded after the end of the last Ice Age. Only a few cichlid species survived the dry period (in small water bodies presumably), and of course in the post-Ice Age period they evolved dramatically, but natural barriers existed to the natural reintroduction of Nile perch.

Paul also pointed out that on Lake Victoria there are no noticeable seasons, being on the equator. Sometimes in July/August there is a strong southerly wind, which makes boat fishing uncomfortable. He goes on to say:

We troll with four rods out at varying lengths to avoid foul-ups. Generally the deeper you get the lure, the more strikes you get. The best depth range is between 4.5 and 7.5m (15 and 25ft), although we have had some large fish in shallower waters, around 2 to 3m (6 to 10ft). On the lake 99 per cent of all fish are caught by trolling. In the past ten years the perch in Lake Victoria have been heavily over-fished for the export market, causing a massive decline in their numbers: as a result the angling is not so good. Casting from the bank in the mid-1990s produced many fish; at the time of writing, casting from the shore produces fish no bigger than a few kilograms. We used to sell trips for two nights in Sesse: if there were four anglers, all would land a 15kg fish, and one lucky chap would get a 30kg+ – and sometimes that 30+ would hit the 80/90kg mark. The largest fish caught on our boats is 99kg, but unfortunately no picture exists.

These days all serious anglers are pushed towards the falls, with no more than a day on the lake. We have spots on the lake called the 'supermarket' and 'under 100', the theory being that you couldn't count to a hundred before getting a strike. Sadly those days are over, and now we weave between nets and their buoys. Up at the falls, however, the fishing can be beyond description! The changing world weather patterns and river levels means that every year conditions are a little bit different, which just adds to the challenge. The most popular season is January/February and March. The rainy seasons are avoided, but we have some good fishing at the back end of the season. The biggest problem is the run-off from rain, which colours the water. Having said that, in water the colour of coffee in late August two years ago I had a run, but the client hit the free spool; when the reel finally jammed it snapped one of John Wilson's Uptide voyager rods clean in half. I managed to grab the rod. The fish came to the surface belly up: from 150m it looked like some one had chucked in a deep freeze. Needless to say on its second run we parted company, with the air turning an unfamiliar shade of blue. I'd give my left digit to know what size that fish was.

At the falls the gorge has produced the best fishing, but that's because everyone goes there. More recently, large fish are being caught downstream nearer to Paraa Lodge. At different times of the year the fish react in different ways. The majority of anglers swear that livebait is the best route. The bait size around 20–30cm (8–12in) gets the most hits. I have had baits swimming perfectly well for hours around a pool. First cast with a Shad Rap and a 30kg fish landed; at other times you can flog the water with every lure in the box with no results. Chuck in livebait, and seconds later the reel is screaming! Preferred lures for the falls are Rapala Super Shad Rap, floating Depth Raider and jointed Lil Ernies.

For livebait we use two species of *Alestes* and whatever tilapia we can get, and a barbus or yellow fish (the largest fish in February this year was caught on a fish head). These can either be freelined with a single hook in the nose, or on a float with a weight to keep the fish down, or with a running weight off the bottom (different areas of the river require different methods). The single hook vs. a treble, or a combination of the two, has anglers embroiled in endless hours of debate. In fact, a 6/0 circle hook through the nostril has produced the highest number of hook-ups, and this may be much better for the well-being of the fish.

We then asked Paul: when you catch perch from deep water do you have problems with them 'gassing up'? And if so, what do you do about it? Because of the nature of Lake Victoria maybe you are not very concerned about 'catch and release', and as a result might automatically kill fish that are gassed up?

We try and return all fish to the lake or river, but this is not always that easy on the river. The odd one does head for the pot, but the majority are returned. When they come from deep we have tried putting a rock in their mouths to get them back down. Most of the time we put them back in the water and push them down with a long stick pressing on the bottom lip. Sometimes after holding in the water a good slap on the lateral line by the tail gets them going.

At the falls we leave them in the water for at least ten minutes before removing them for photos and weighing, and this dramatically increases the success rate of returning large fish. Large fish are extremely difficult to weigh on the bank, even with slings and four people to help. Some of the claims therefore from some anglers at the falls have got jackanory written all over them, as most don't own scales.

A friend, Steve Dunbar, has been working on a method of measuring the length and the circumference of the fish just in front of the dorsal fin, and will soon be able to reasonably judge the weight from those measurements. He is able, he says, to get the gas out by holding the head higher than the tail and rubbing /squeezing the belly of the fish, and apparently it burps. Hopefully more fish will return alive due to damage being avoided by eliminating weighing. (Note this is also a method used in the past by pike anglers.)

I once kept a 35kg fish on a string for five hours to weigh in at a competition. It survived and won the competition. We did nothing more than leave it tied up, and every five minutes turned it upright and held it for a few minutes until it could stay upright by itself.

We then asked him if he had any opinions about fishing for Nile perch during daylight hours when there is a full moon at night:

On the lake a full moon is a disaster. The theory is that the perch then feed longer because they have better visibility, and so are less likely to hit a lure as they are already full. At the falls at the last fishing competition the last day was a full moon, and the largest fish – 84kg – was caught at 3pm. The fish seem suddenly to come on the feed. Sometimes upriver and downriver fish are caught at the same time. Over the years there has been a number of occasions when it has started to rain, and for some reason woke the fish up and resulted in some good fish being caught simultaneously.

The more obvious contribution to not-so-good-fishing, especially at the falls, is angler pressure. We are trying with national parks to limit numbers to keep the standard of fishing at peak times. I have tried fishing at night on the lake covering all the hotspots, with no results. An interesting observation is that there are no fish on the finder at these hotspots once the sun is down. Sometimes trolling with a lure in the engine wake has produced results right at sunset.

Finally we asked Paul whether he had ever heard about the rare 'Golden' Nile perch being caught on Lake Victoria:

No. We have very dark perch sometimes (usually the smaller ones) and silver coloured: some folk put that down to a deep water species and a shallow water species that came from Lake Albert (as was described in an old East African book for anglers from the 1930s). They all look remarkably similar to me in shape, so colour is probably due to what's available to feed on at the time, and local conditions, water temperature, oxygen levels and so on.

As you can now see, some of the Lake Victoria and Murchison Falls angling experiences are a little different from those on Lake Nasser, so go prepared mentally for this.

Lake Turkana

Lake Turkana, formerly known as Lake Rudolf, is a lake in the Great Rift Valley in Kenya, with its far northern end crossing into Ethiopia. It is the world's largest permanent desert lake and the world's largest alkaline lake. The water is potable but not palatable. The climate is hot and very dry, and the surrounding area is predominantly volcanic. The central island on the lake is an active volcano, emitting vapours. Onshore and off-shore winds can be extremely strong, as the lake warms and cools more slowly than the land. Sudden, violent storms are frequent. Three rivers – the Omo, Turkwel and Kerio – flow into the lake, but lacking outflow its only water loss is by evaporation. Due to temperature, aridity and geographic inaccessibility, the lake retains its wild character.

Kenya's north is desert country – hot, parched and broken by volcanic activity, where ancient blackened lava flows and endless thorn trees stretch from horizon to horizon. Life here is limited to the hardiest species of wildlife, and the seldom seen human culture follows well-worn paths beaten by the tracks of nomadic camel trains. Fossil evidence found in the earth around Turkana suggests that humans have survived these conditions for a very long time – and that Turkana may be the true 'Cradle of Mankind'. Paul Goldering can advise on how to get to Lake Turkana.

One of the first anglers to get on Lake Turkana was the famous pike angler from Norwich, John Watson, who, by booking a three-day expedition to 'the cradle of mankind', was able to fish successfully for Nile perch in 1987 (*see* 'Monsters of the Jade Sea', The *Coarse Fishing Handbook*, 1988). After a two-hour final plane journey, plus several hours in a 25ft aluminium boat, John and Kath, together with a cook, a tent, a boat's captain and an interpreter, managed to fish Alia Bay, catching fish to 60lb (losing several other big ones on 18lb bs line).

Lake Tanganyika

Lake Tanganyika is another lake in the Rift Valley, and Bert Fourie, who runs a fishing lodge, Nkamba Bay Lodge in the Nsumbu National Park, provides the following information:

Lake Tanganyika is part of the Great Rift Valley and extends for some 680km (422.5 miles) from Burundi in the north to Zambia in the south. It was formed as a consequence of faulting and tectonic processes in the earth's surface, probably around 7–10 million years ago, which makes it the second oldest lake in the world. The lake reaches down to depths below 1,400m (4,700ft) at its deepest point, but the main depth is 'only' about 570m (1,870ft); it is the second deepest lake on the planet, after Lake Baikal in Russia.

Lake Tanganyika has existed for a very long time in relative isolation and as result, an abundance of endemic species have developed. More than 250 of the fish species in Lake Tanganyika cannot be found anywhere else in the world, and it is expected that even more endemic species will be found as the lake is explored further.

Cichlids have developed to fit very diverse environments and ecological niches, and we know of more than 150 different cichlid species from over fifty different genera. Approximately 98 per cent of these cichlids are endemic to Lake Tanganyika.

The largest amount of fish biomass is found in the pelagic zone. This zone is dominated by six fish species. Four of them are *Lates* species, predator fish closely related to the well known Nile perch. Nile perch of over 80kg (180lb) have been caught; the main method of fishing in the lake is trolling with lures. Species of particular note include the Giant Nile perch (*Lates angustifrons*) and Small Nile perch (*Luciolates stappersii*), which are important commercial and sports fishing (that is, angling) species, and goliath tiger (*Hydrocynus goliath*).

The names for the perch species present here are *Lates mariae* (what we call silver perch is the deep water perch), *Lates augustifrons*, and *Lates microlepis*.

The fishing is generally good throughout the year. As the lake is so big a lot of the water does not get affected by rain, and stays quite clean. After big wind storms the water can turn a funny pea soup colour, and it is believed that it affects the fishing, but I have still had fish in the green waters. The main methods for targeting the perch are bottom fishing, lure fishing, 'mulenga' fishing and, of course, fly fishing is in its infancy.

Lure fishing: there are so many different colours and shapes that have caught fish here that it is almost impossible for me to tell you what the best is. The ones that work well, though, are Shad Raps, Fat Raps, and Rattlin' Raps, all in medium to big sizes. For the deep water we use deep divers such as Mann +20 and +30. Downriggers or diving plates are also used for deep channels. It is, however, recommended that smaller sizes are also brought along for the yellow bellies. They are in their own right a worthy opponent on light tackle.

The silver perch is generally the deep water perch. However, it is not uncommon to find them in the shallow waters as well. They seem to prefer sandy areas when they do come into the shallows. There is no life in water deeper than about 200m (650ft). The other perch species are usually found within 4–20m (13 to 65ft) of water. With bottom fishing, the deep perch tend to gas up as most anglers crank the daylight out of the reels. But the ones that are caught on lures tend not to gas up and can be released.

Finally it should be said that Lake Tanganyika is host to some of the most spectacular freshwater sport fishing in the world. Some of the better catches are the large Nile perch, Goliath tigerfish, vundu catfish, lake salmon and the tasty yellow belly or 'nkupi'. Occasionally the much sought-after golden perch is caught. The Zambian National Fishing Competition takes place here every February or March, and attracts up to eighty local and international tournament fishermen each year. Several world records have been set.

So there are some challenges for all you adventurous Nile perch fanatics!

APPENDIX IV
COOKING NILE PERCH

Baked Nile perch as served up on one of Barrie's safaris.

One of the great pleasures of the Lake Nasser safaris is that once in your week the cooks will prepare a Nile perch for supper, and as a rule this will be baked whole and presented fully garnished on a large plate. It should come as no surprise to well travelled anglers that the Nile perch is excellent eating. After all, it is of the perch family, and almost without exception all perch are good eating, even the humble (and smaller) British one! A very close species to the Nile perch (*Lates niloticus*) is the Australian barramundi (*Lates calcarifer*), and it really is one of the prized dishes in Australia. Cook a barramundi and you can cook a Nile perch. Both are now occasionally available in UK supermarkets such as Waitrose, although the fish there do tend to be on the small side, which means that the only option is to cook them as whole fish. Much better is when you have a sizeable fish, of say 10lb, when all the options of steaking, filleting or whole baking are available to you. Note that the Nile perch is not an excessively long fish – and no myriads of tiny bones – which once again makes things easier.

The flesh of the Nile perch is thick and white, like all perch species, and breaks into large white flakes, not unlike the manner in which cooked cod behaves. The taste is certainly superior to most fish, and we would rate it above trout, for example. It is not necessary to soak Nile perch in salty water, simply descale it, clean it and wash it, and then prepare it for whole cooking, steaks or fillets. You will not find recipes in cookbooks for Nile perch (we did a scan of a large kitchen library of cookery books and fish cookery books and found not a single reference to them; although Mrs Beeton does deal well with fried, stewed or boiled perch, which you could easily adapt).

However, an easier adaptation would be to use recipes for bass. Any way of cooking bass (whether sea or freshwater) works perfectly well for Nile perch, because they are very similar fish. The following recipe is adapted from Chantal Dunbar's recipe for pan-seared barramundi in *Australia's Natural Treasure with Recipes from Paradise*.

This suggests using baby barramundi, which equates well with taking some Waitrose or Tesco small Nile perch instead. It doesn't tell you how to prepare the fish, but we suggest you proceed as above, and if the fish is big enough, remove the head and tail and bones – roughly filleting it, in fact. The pan needs olive oil heated to above a moderate temperature. The fish can at this stage be sprinkled or rubbed with a little sea salt, and then placed in the pan, skin side down. It needs turning after a few minutes, and thus both sides receive a few minutes' cooking. The flesh turns from translucent to a nice opaque white colour, and it is then ready. You can char grill the fish just as successfully, and it is worth noting that a Nile perch tends to have very slightly oily flesh, which helps when you grill them.

The recipe we saw suggested serving the perch on a layer of ratatouille, which works well; we'll not tell you how to do that because you no doubt prefer your own recipes. They also suggest a tapenade (coarsely processed) sauce to top off the fish. This is also a good idea. As a matter of interest we can strongly recommend Chantal Dunbar's book, dealing as it does with splendid Australian fish cooking on the Great Barrier Reef, where both of us have been.

If you prefer to modify a bass or snapper recipe, try Rick Stein's recent *Sea Food* (BBC Books). He deals with char-grilled snapper and baked bass (which he unfortunately calls 'sea bass'). These work well because we have had similar dishes, differing only in the ingredients with which you bake the fish, or add to the char-grilled fish. Being Nile perch it is the fish that matters, and after trials you may well decide that not much needs adding!

If you use the internet you'll find a couple of Nile perch recipes on the website uktv.co.uk/food/. Both are by Mike Robinson of Safari Chefs, and are of smoked Nile perch and curried Nile perch. What the article does not tell you is how to smoke your Nile perch, and certainly you cannot buy it in this state at the moment. So you need to invest in a smoker (from most big tackle firms, such as Shakespeare), or take the fish to a local smokery (there are a scattering of these around most big towns). Then all he does is prepare fillets (as we have described above), and make a sauce using olive oil, three garlic cloves, 3cm of ginger root, some honey, soy sauce and chopped red chillies. The sauce is brushed over the fish, which is then 'smoked for 30 minutes on a trivet.' Get a smoker.

For the curried Nile perch he cuts the fillets into 4cm cubes. Olive oil is medium heated, and onion and garlic fried until soft. Lemon grass, ginger and chopped chillies are added. The 200cc of fish stock is stirred in with lime juice, coconut milk, coriander, parsley and half a papaya coarsely chopped.

The actual proportions of all these ingredients will be to personal taste and practice; and with both methods of cooking the risk is that of destroying the flavour of a nice fish!

Returning very briefly to Mrs Beeton, we suggest that you don't boil or stew Nile perch. If you do, then it is unlikely that you'll need quite as much salt as Mrs B. suggests. Or you could try the following:

Mustard-topped Nile Perch

Servings: 4
Preparation time: 30min
Cooking time: 20min

Ingredients

2 tbsp mayonnaise
2 tsp Dijon mustard
2 tsp mustard seeds
4 (6–8oz) Nile perch fillets
1 tsp dried dill weed

Method

Combine the first three ingredients; mix well. Arrange fillets in a lightly greased baking sheet. Spread mustard mixture over each fillet. Sprinkle with dill weed. Bake at 350°F for 20min or until the fish flakes easily when tested with a fork. Garnish with fresh dill weed. Serve immediately.

Capitaine and Pili-Pili in Palm Oil

This is a recipe from central Africa where the Nile perch is often referred to as 'Capitaine' and is a popular eating fish throughout this region of Africa. This recipe combines Nile perch with two essential elements of native cooking: hot pili-pili peppers and palm oil.

Servings: 4–5
Preparation time: 15min
Cooking time: 10min

Ingredients

1 cup palm oil
1 onion, finely chopped
1 hot chilli pepper, cleaned and chopped (or left whole)
2lb of filleted Nile perch
salt, black pepper

Method

Heat the oil in a large skillet. Cook the onions and chilli pepper for a few minutes. Use chopped chilli peppers for a hot spicy dish, or use whole chilli peppers and remove them after cooking for a milder taste. Cook the fish in the oil for a few minutes, and then turn it (once) to cook the other side. Adjust seasonings to taste.

Variations: Add tomatoes, okra, green pepper or garlic with the onions and chilli pepper. As is often the case, this recipe can also be applied to other fish.

Nile Perch Moroccan

Servings: 4–6
Preparation time: 20min
Cooking time: 2hr

Ingredients

2lb Nile perch fillets marinated in the juice of 2 or 3 small limes for at least 20min; preferably leave overnight in the refrigerator
Enough olive or vegetable oil to cover the bottom of a large skillet
1 whole head of garlic separated in cloves, peeled and finely minced
2 carrots, peeled and sliced into thin strips
1 large (don't skimp, it is important to the dish) bunch cilantro, chopped coarsely
4 medium-large tomatoes, sliced
1 14oz can tomatoes, with the juice
2 tiny red peppers, dried or fresh, or ⅛ teaspoon hot pepper flakes
¼ teaspoon turmeric
Salt, pepper and paprika

Method

Heat the oil and add half of the minced garlic, half of the hot peppers, tomato slices and canned tomatoes and juice also, half of the carrots and cilantro. Place half of the fish fillets on top of the mixture and sprinkle with turmeric, salt, pepper and paprika. Repeat another layer as above with the exception of the paprika, which is now mixed with a little oil and poured on top of the fish. Bring to the boil on a high heat, and immediately lower the heat and simmer for about 45min well covered. Uncover and continue cooking until the liquid is almost absorbed and the fish is well done, about another 1hr, over low heat. It will improve, and remain moist. At the end of the suggested time, try the fish. It should be perfect.

Rabey's Baked Whole Nile Perch

Exclusive to African Angler
Preparation time: 30min
Cooking time: 1hr

Ingredients
10lb whole Nile perch
1 tbsp ground coriander
6 tbsp coriander leaf, chopped
6 cloves of garlic
2 tbsp English mustard
2 tbsp distilled vinegar
2 tbsp lemon juice
1 tbsp lime juice
salt and black pepper to taste

Method
Gut and clean the fish. Descale. Cut two diagonal slashes ½in deep across the fish on each side. Mix the rest of the ingredients, and rub into the fish. Marinate for 2hr. Bake in a moderate oven 1hr.

Nubian Fish Tagine

Serves 4
Preparation time: 30min
Cooking time: 45min

Ingredients
8 fillets of Nile perch
1 tbsp ground coriander
1 tbsp coriander leaf chopped
3 onions chopped
6 cloves of garlic
3 large fresh tomatoes diced
salt
2 lemons and 1 lime sliced
3 green peppers sliced

Method
Fry the fish for a maximum of 1½min each side, and then set aside. Make up the tomato sauce by frying the onion, tomato and garlic, and adding the rest of the ingredients. In a tangine dish (or an ovenproof dish) layer the fish, then tomato sauce, then peppers, then lemons and lime. Cover with a lid. Bake in a moderate oven 45min.

Fried or Grilled Fish

Serves 4
Preparation time: 10min plus marinade 2hr
Cooking time: 4min

Ingredients
8 fillets of Nile perch
1 tbsp ground coriander
6 cloves of garlic
salt and black pepper
juice of 2 lemons and 1 lime
flour for coating

Method
Mix all ingredients together except flour to make marinade. Cover the fish and leave in cool place for 2hr. Remove from marinade and lightly coat in flour. Deep fry until golden, approximately 4min, or grill for a maximum of 5min, basting frequently with the marinade throughout.

Egyptian Rice for Fish (Sayyadiah)

Serves 4
Cooking time: 10min

Ingredients
125g brown rice
2 large onions
tbsp oil
½ tbsp salt

Method
Fry onion till dark brown. Add ½ltr of boiling water and the salt. Bring back to the boil. Stir in the rice. Simmer for 10min, or until tender.

BIBLIOGRAPHY

Papers and Books with Chapters on Nile Perch

Acere, T. 'Observations on the biology, age, growth, maturity and sexuality of Nile perch, *Lates niloticus* (Linne), and the growth of its fishery in the northern waters of Lake Victoria.' *FAO Fisheries Report,* **335**, 42–61, 1984.

Asila, A. and Ogari, J. 'Growth parameters and mortality rates of nile perch (*Lates niloticus*) estimates from length – frequency data in the Nyanza Gulf (Lake Victoria)'. *FAO Fisheries Report,* **389**, 272–287, 1988.

Bailey, J. *Casting Far & Wide: Great Angling Adventures of the World.* David & Charles, 1993.

Cuvier, G.A. and Valenciennes, M.A. *Histoire naturelle des poisons.* Levrault, Strasborg. Paris, 1828–1849.

Dadebo, E., Mengistou, S. and Gebre-Mariam, Z. 'Feeding habits of the Nile perch, *Lates niloticus* (L.) (Pisces: Centropomidae) in Lake Chamo, Ethiopia'. SINET; *Ethiopian Journal of Science,* **28**, 61–68, 2005.

Fox-Strangways, V. *Wandering Fisherman.* Arthur Barker, London, 1955.

Goudswaard, P. and Witte, F. 'Observation on Nile perch, *Lates niloticus* (L.), 1758, in the Tanzanian waters of Lake Victoria.' *FAO Fisheries Report,* **335**, 62–67, 1984.

Hopson, A. 'A study of the Nile perch (*Lates niloticus* (L.) Pisces Centropomidae) in Lake Chad.' Foreign and Commonwealth Office overseas development administration (Overseas Research Publication), **19**, 1–90, 1972.

Johnson, T.C. *et al.* 'Late Pleistocene Desiccation of Lake Victoria and Rapid Evolution of Cichlid Fishes.' *Science,* **273**, 1091–1093, 1996.

Kitchel, J. and Schindler, D. 'The Nile perch in Lake Victoria: Interactions between predation and fisheries.' *Ecological Applications,* **7**, 653–664, 1997.

Linné, C. 'Systema naturae per regna tria naturae, secundum classes, ordines, genera, species, cum characteribus, differentiis, synonymis, locis.' Laurentii Salvii, Holmiae, 8th edn. **1**, 1–824 [p.286 original description], 1758.

Moreau, J. *et al.* 'New functions for the analysis of two-phase growth of juvenile and adult fishes, with application to Nile Perch.' *American Fisheries Society,* **121**, 486–493, 1992.

Norman, J.R. *A History of Fishes.* Ernest Benn Ltd, 1931.

Ogari, J. 'Distribution, Food, and Feeding Habits of *Lates niloticus* in Nyanza Gulf of Lake Victoria (Kenya).' *FAO Fisheries Report,* **335**, 68–80, 1984.

Ogutu-Ohwayo, R. 'The effects of predation by Nile perch, *Lates niloticus* (Linne) introduced into Lake Kyoga (Uganda) in relation to the fisheries of Lake Kyoga and Lake Victoria.' *FAO Fisheries Report,* **335**, 18–41, 1984.

Orme, A. (*see* Bailey, J. above).

Pellegrin, J. 'Poissons de l'Oubanghi-chari recueillis par M. Baudon. Description d'un genre, de cinq espèces et d'une variété.' *Bulletin of the Zoological Society of France,* 1922.

Queensland Department of Primary Industries and Fisheries. Fish: Note, Nile Perch (*Lates niloticus*) Accessed Nov. 2002 at www.dpi.gld.gov.au/fishweb/2374.html

Saint-Hilaire, G. 'Poissons du Nile, de la mer rouge et de la Méditerranée.' *In:* Description de l'Egypte, ...Histoire Naturelle Paris 1809–30, 1827.

Schofield, P. 'Interactions between Nile perch (*Lates niloticus*) and other fishes in Lake Nabugabo, Uganda.' *Environmental Biology of Fishes,* **55**, 343–358, 1999.

Worthington, E.B. 'A Report on the fishing survey of Lakes Albert and Kioga'. Crown Agents, London, 1929.

Worthington, E.B. 'Scientific Results of the Cambridge Expedition to the East African Lakes 1930–1'; 'Fishes other than cichlidae.' *Journal of the Linnaeas of London Zoology,* **38**, 121–134, 1932.

Videos and DVDs

Bailey, Chris *Reel Outdoors* for American TV, includes a half-hour film on fly fishing for Nile perch. (Two programmes, 2006–7.)

Dale, L. *Expedition Nile Perch.* Hyperactive Films Ltd, 2000.

Meintjes, Malcolm *Fly fishing on Lake Nasser.* On South Africa's satellite channel and as a video, 1999.

Rickards, Barrie *In Search of Nile Perch.* Video Active, 2001.

Roberts, C. *Fishing for Wild Images.* 2002 Discovery Channel (available on DVD, enquiries@african-angler.net)

Wilson, J. *John Wilson's World of Fishing.* Pearson Publishing, 1995.

Wilson, J. *The Lake Nasser Safaris.* J. Wilson, 1998. (This is available in video or DVD from enquiries@african-angler.net)

In addition, Jakub Vägner made *Fishing with Jakub in Egypt* for the Czechoslovakian market, and two films, one for TV Osaha, one for TV Tokyo have been done by Hajime Muraka for the Japanese market; whilst Malcolm Meintjer produced *Fly fishing on Lake Nasser* for the South African media.

INDEX

Some people, such as John Wilson, some places, and some lures, such as the Rapala Super Shad Rap, are mentioned in so many places throughout the text that we have merely given a representative sample in our references or have only referenced especially important citations.